The Mature Laurel

THE MATURE LAUREL

Only through solitary wars
Are future readers won;
You will neither dwell in halls
In the Temple of your choice

Nor will own a private portal:
Others will unlock the grille,
And what in life were wings,
History may bring to heel! . . .

— Cyprian Kamil Norwid (1821-1883)

(tr. Adam Czerniawski)

THE MATURE LAUREL

Essays on Modern Polish Poetry

Edited by Adam Czerniawski

SEREN BOOKS

DUFOUR

SEREN BOOKS is the book imprint of
Poetry Wales Press Ltd
Andmar House, Tondu Road
Bridgend, Mid Glamorgan

'Noble Poet' by A. Alvarez first appeared in the *The New York Review of Books*

British Library Cataloguing in Publication Data
The Mature laurel : essays on modern Polish poetry.
1. Polish poetry
I. Czerniawski, Adam
891.8517
ISBN 1-85411-023-3

First published in the United States of America by Dufour Editions Inc, Chester Springs, Pennsylvania.
Library of Congress Cataloging-in-Publication Data
The Mature laurel : essays on modern Polish poetry / edited by Adam Czerniawski.
p. cm.
Includes bibliographical references (p.307) and index.
ISBN 0-8023-1292-6 (hardback) : $35.00
1. Polish poetry—20th century—History and criticism.
I. Czerniawski, Adam, 1934-.
PG7070.M375 1991
891.8'51709—dc20 90-24814
CIP

Cover illustration: a detail of 'In the Dust Cloud' by Jacek Malczewski
By kind permission of the National Museum, Poznań

The publisher acknowledges the financial support of the Welsh Arts Council

Typeset in 10½ point Plantin by Megaron, Cardiff
Printed by Billings & Sons Ltd, Worcester

CONTENTS

Foreword

In his recent documentary film *Nekropolis*, Tomasz Pobóg-Malinowski invites his audience to visit two dead cultures, two extinct forms of official art. At the old Zamoyski country house of Kalinówka there is an upstairs and a downstairs. The upstairs consists mostly of 18th and 19th-century paintings collected and commissioned by the Zamoyski dynasty to advertise its own virtue and power. The dark downstairs is a cellar, a place of confinement and shame in which the official sculpture of the Communist period serves an indefinite sentence.

Above, vacuous faces smile under wigs. Below, Lenin, Bierut, Stalin and Paul Robeson scowl in the half-light. Why is it so painful to see this place, these two sepulchres of style? None can dispute that their contexts, the bits of history in which this painting and that sculpture flourished, are perfectly dead. But Kalinówka goes further, saying that art itself can die. It can die peacefully of old age or catch a foreign virus and cough its heart out. But it can also be nailed up in a sunlit place to die of thirst, or mutilated and left in a bunker to starve, or even herded up against a wall and machine-gunned to pieces. Kalinówka says that art can also be executed.

Every instinct tells me that this is not true; the artistic act is irreversible. To pretend otherwise is totalitarian, and though Arno Breker was an abject booby whose marble morons served Hitler, the post-war German bureaucrats of culture who hid his statues and affected not to have heard his name were as guilty as he. Sculpture brings out the worst cultural sadism, and there was something pretty nasty about the Warsaw *Volksfest* which developed last year when a crowd knocked down Dzierżyński's effigy. Painting is given less severe punishment; it is many years now since that exhibition of "PRL painting" at Zachęta which included Kobzdej's 'Pass a Brick' — a work which had been released after over 20 years' internment for Stalinism. And poetry? There is no cemetery of dead poems. A poem is scarcely even torturable.

Here is the attraction of this book. Polish poets have been committing irrevocable acts for several centuries, although *The Mature Laurel* is only concerned with the last one: Norwid to Zagajewski, approximately. To say that the poets in this book have related to their changing times is a good joke. Between them, they have experienced four national insurrections, two world wars, seven or eight different flags, two hyper-inflations, five frontier wars, four ideologies, two invasions and two (successful) military coups. Some of them, at times, have modified their work to suit the régime of the day, either through conviction or because they could not stand being published at all. Some of them, at times, have come close to condemning one another for literary failings which could easily have been inflated, given the climate of post-war Poland, into evidence of political thought-crime by Communists or anti-Communists. Poets have been shot, mostly in the 1944 Rising. But there is no question — never has been — of taking poems out and shooting them.

In a country where little has resisted smashing or effacing, one of the virtues of poetry is that it is indelible. Poets have been throwing ink at Polish circumstances for generations: the circumstances have crumbled away but the stains remain. Zbigniew Herbert's 'Elegy of Fortinbras' is famous in the Western world which has long forgotten what little it knew about semi-freedom in Poland after 1956, and I can even imagine a time — our grandchildrens' time — when Auschwitz will be a reference they have to look up to understand the poetry of Różewicz.

Most of the poets discussed and appreciated here are non- or anti-romantic. In that, as Edward Rogerson remarks, they stand at a distance from the lush taste of the Polish verse-reading public. And Rogerson even suggests here that Herbert's "little god of irony" (which the barbarians so much enjoyed crushing under their heel and adding to their dishes) is a Western import rather than a native salt. Bolesław Leśmian (1878–1937) was a neo-romantic of sorts; an unpolitical metaphysician who argued for a poetry of shamanism — the poet as mediator of a tone, a rhythm, a wordless song of reality which came from outside the self. The early work of Czesław Miłosz was "Leśmianic" in that way, and he has continued to see the poetic force as "a thing . . . brought forth which we didn't think we had in us", a tiger which springs out from beyond the self and stands "lashing its tail". But shamans and oracles are set different problems at different times, and by the time that Miłosz was a young poet, the questions thrown into the darkness were not about how to dance or to acquire wordless song, but about how to remain a human being and how to tell good from evil.

This awareness of a duty is not far from any of these post-Leśmian poets, though there is a great distance between the direct preachiness of some of Miłosz and the "semantic flirtation" and "Mozartian joy" of Wisława Szymborska at the other extreme. In the first years after the war, this awareness created the danger that a poet might begin as seer and prophet and slither towards mere "commitment" or propaganda. A chapter here by Donald Pirie on verse during the "Socialist Realism" period reveals some depressing stuff by Iwaszkiewicz and even Słonimski, as well as the usual pimply doggerel about tractors. And yet these disasters did not lead to the sort of schism which developed in the visual arts in the West after 1945, where figurative work of any kind seemed tainted and personal freedom came to be associated with abstraction. The Polish poets learned from their mistakes and remained vatic.

The war and the Nazi occupation, rather than the postwar Communist experience, dominated imaginations. In this book, many critics and poets bring up Adorno's old remark about the impossibility of poetry after Auschwitz and test its absorption into Polish literature. Tadeusz Różewicz took it most to heart but, as John Osborne writes here, he did not so much strip poetry down as build it up again from nothing, syllable by syllable, as in his poem about creating life after the end of the world: "this is a man/ this is a tree this is bread". In Germany, at the same time, poets were also washing language down to monosyllabic, concrete nouns. Others, like Herbert, while eschewing "the artificial fires of poetry", were less reductive and were still able to draw imagery from the immediate past. Paul Coates remarks that the war left behind for Herbert "a Pompeii full of frozen, once-human forms", but for Różewicz it "submerged the old world's surface under level ash".

The vigilance of Polish poets against any "softening" of poetry into mere stylishness, aestheticism or allegory, is astonishing. The "New Wave", now some 15 years old, was a fresh attack of "directness", a declaration of war on linguistic decay. "A language failure has occurred nationwide./ Since the small hours language engineers/ have tried to hold back floods of words./ Drowned meanings have sunk to the bottom" writes Ewa Lipska. Yet Aleksander Fiut could be right in hinting, in a chapter on "martial law poetry", that yet another attack is due. Much verse written, and published underground, after December 1981 showed evidence that an old orthodoxy, that of the national-romantic myth of Poland as the bastion of Western values, had reasserted itself, and Fiut even reproaches Zbigniew Herbert's wonderful 'Report from the Besieged City' for merely dressing up that myth "in a more dignified costume". How, Fiut asks, "can one salvage the nation's sense of identity if the images which constitute its very essence have been overladen with obsolete meanings?"

In conclusion, this volume is also some kind of monument to those who have translated contemporary Polish verse into English. John Osborne guesses that "certain translations, such as Adam Czerniawski's Englishing of *Conversation with the Prince and Other Poems* (1982) by Tadeusz Różewicz, might constitute an intervention in British poetry as momentous as Chapman's Homer". I believe this to be true, and to Czerniawski's other translations — Norwid, Szymborska, Staff and others — we should add the work of Bogdana and John Carpenter on Herbert, of Czesław Miłosz on his own poetry and (with P. D. Scott) on Herbert's, of Bogdan Czaykowski and many others. All this labour has released a fresh wind of poetic energy to blow across the British Isles, where the stimulus of American verse had long subsided. This book will, I think, help poets here to distinguish more clearly the voices carried by that new "wind from the sea."

Neal Ascherson

Editor's Preface

Even a few years ago the appearance of a collection such as this would have been unthinkable. Serious and sustained Western interest in Polish poetry is a very recent phenomenon. Its origins can be traced precisely to Al Alvarez's vigorous championing of East European poetry, and especially of Zbigniew Herbert's, from 1965 onwards. Herbert's star rose because of a conjunction of circumstances: the cold war was at its height and the author of the universally admired elegy on the death of Hamlet displayed just the right literary qualities to be noticed by those able to appreciate his assured handling of a variety of themes that included the relationship of the individual to the state, to power, to God and to existential and moral issues at large.

The publication of this book coincides with the collapse of Communist order in Poland and the rest of Central and Eastern Europe. How will Herbert's poetry survive the change? Its fortunes in the post-communist world will be carefully and anxiously scrutinised, especially by those of us who mistrust the manipulation of culture by aparatchiks, be they of the communist or any other variety. This poetry undoubtedly deserves to survive on its merits in the face of even the most radical political and ideological upheavals, as against a great many more recent works by younger authors too closely concerned with the machinations of Communist power. One thing seems certain: Herbert's poetry will from now on be read and interpreted differently, perhaps by a somewhat different readership.

The poetry of Miłosz and Różewicz has also found favour in recent years; Miłosz's more than Różewicz's though Różewicz's is the more remarkable craftsman and in the vanguard of late twentieth century sensibility. Again, it will be instructive to observe how these two poets will fare in the radically changed political climate.

But one hopes that all three have established a secure enough base for appreciation and understanding which will not now be eroded; which will rather serve as a point of departure for the discovery of other poets, eventually resulting in the formation of a sizeable map of Polish poetry that will include at least Kochanowski, Mickiewicz and Norwid from past centuries, as well as some twentieth century poets now barely known or even totally unknown to the English-language reader.

My aim in editing *The Mature Laurel* was to compile a collection that would encompass modern Polish poetry from its roots in the work of Norwid to its most recent developments. To this end I sought contributions from four categories of writers in order to provide the survey with a wide variety of perspectives: (i) critics working in Poland, (ii) Polish scholars and critics working abroad, (iii) British specialists in Polish literature, and (iv) English-language writers who, while not claiming any expertise in Polish literature, have demonstrated their interest in Polish poetry on the evidence of available translations.

In housing such disparate groups of commentators under one roof my further aim has been to present a collection that would appeal at various levels: to the general reader, the student and the scholar.

A.Cz.
London, February, 1990

Acknowledgements

Barbara Plebanek and Iain Higgins have prepared translations of poems specifically for this volume; Edward Rogerson has translated Krzysztof Karasek's essay on Wisława Szymborska and Bogdan Czaykowski has compiled the bibliography of critical material. My grateful thanks to them.

I am also grateful to Bogdan Czaykowski, Krzysztof Karasek and Jacek Łukasiewicz for providing at short notice alternative material (on Norwid, Czaykowski, Czerniawski and Wojaczek) when prospective authors of a number of contracted essays had failed to deliver.

I have translated the other essay by Karasek, as well as the essays by Jacek Łukasiewicz and Zbigniew Bieńkowski.

A.Cz.

Publishers Acknowledgements

The publisher gratefully makes the following acknowledgements:

To Bloodaxe Books for Adam Czerniawski's translation of Cyprian Kamil Norwid's 'Yesterday-and-I', first published in *The Burning Forest* 1988.
To Anvil Press Poetry for Adam Czerniawski's translations of Tadeusz Różewicz's 'Pigtail' and 'A Tale of Old Women', first published in *Conversation with the Prince* (1982).
To Princeton University Press for Krynski and Maguire's translation of Tadeusz Różewicz's 'Following the Guide', first published in *Surivor and other poems* (1976).
To Book Club Associates and Douglas Lee for Czesław Miłosz's translation of Zbigniew Herbert's 'Elegy of Fortinbras', first published in *Encounter*, August 1961.
To Oxford University Press and The Ecco Press for John and Bogdana Carpenter's translation of Zbigniew Herbert's 'Mr Cogito and the Imagination' from *The Besieged City and other poems* first published in America in 1985, in the U.K. in 1987.

The publisher would also like to thank the Central & East European Publishing Project for its grant for translation costs.

I

Bogdan Czaykowski

The Author of *Vade-Mecum* in the Context of Nineteenth Century European Poetry and His Relevance to Modernism

The Author of *Vade-Mecum* in the Context of Nineteenth Century European Poetry and His Relevance to Modernism

Born in 1821 in the so-called Congress Kingdom, that is, in the Russian part of Poland, Cyprian Norwid grew up and was educated in Warsaw, where he frequented literary salons, but where he also witnessed harsh repressive measures directed by Tsarist authorities after the insurrection of 1830-31 against groups of youthful enthusiasts, who organised conspiratorial circles and wrote revolutionary poems. The extent of Norwid's personal involvement in the activities of these groups remains unclear, but it is certain that he was not indifferent to the fate of his contemporaries, 'the orphaned generation', as he was later to call it. His poetry of the time, though personal and vaguely Romantic, also contains unmistakable allusions to the patriotic and social ideals of these young men, some of whom were his acquaintances and friends. The fate of one of them was particularly tragic: Karol Levittoux preferred committing suicide in prison to risking the possibility of giving away any of his co-conspirators, and since he had no other means of taking his life, he set himself on fire in the prison cell and burnt to death.

Though Norwid wrote poetry, his ambition was to become an artist. In 1842 he left Warsaw for the West, ostensibly "to perfect himself in the art of sculpture". He stayed in the West far longer than he had intended, for the rest of his life in fact.[1]

The first few years of Norwid's stay in the West were extremely active; he travelled in Germany, Italy, Belgium and France, visited galleries, made friends. Most of the accounts we have of him from before roughly 1850, are full of praise for his intelligence, charm, good manners, talent and knowledge. But then things began to go wrong, so wrong that in 1852, in despair, Norwid sailed to New York to seek a new life. He was back in England in 1854, and then settled in Paris, where he stayed until his death in 1883. He died in Ivry in an old peoples' home run by the Sisters of Charity. Most of the references to him after 1850, and until the recognition of his work around the year 1900, are negative, sarcastic, condescending — bewildered at best. There emerges from them a picture of an insufferably principled man, half-deaf, destitute, proud and extremely touchy, a quixotic crank, eccentric in his manners and thought, and unredeemingly obscure in his writings.[2]

But there is one late and fairly extensive account of Norwid, written by a journalist, which attempts to convey a positive picture and is worth quoting at length:

> There has lived in Paris for some years now a writer little known in Poland, an artist even less known, a queer poet, a hieroglyph-stylist, whose every poem has to be read syllable by syllable ten times over, if one wants to get something out of it . . . a childishly noble man, a naive and unhappy enthusiast [egzagerant] . . . His ideas, despite his profound learning and detailed acquaintance with the achievements of contemporary knowledge, go in a diametrically opposite direction to that of the modern philosophical current. Even his name, when you transpose its letters, will give you the name of the nightmare that haunts him: Darwin . . . .
>
> Norwid's views differed radically from any others you might think of. Where people thronged lifting their heads in amazement, he would walk away bent double, indicating with his hand close to the earth, that the wonder of wonders wasn't even two inches tall . . . .
>
> Perhaps his paintings — if any are still left, for he reworked them with such labour, as if he wanted to put seven centuries of paint on each of them — would reveal more readily to an archeologist what was at the bottom of his mind, than his writings, which are even more condensed. This psychic ruin assumed under the brush at least a contour, a certain composition . . . but if you looked into his script you had to do it by means of hypotheses.
>
> But he was not a dilettante, less so a visionary, a mystic, or a lunatic . . . He knew how to uncover in every thing such relation of it to other things that it would become so original as to appear almost unrecognisable and quite different from the well-known and the familiar . . . .

> He carried his soul around as if it were some kind of a numismatic rarity, unknown to anyone, unwanted, of no use. Of less than middle height, lean, though shapely, with intelligent eyes . . . he had in his manner the assurance and suavity of someone who had been in good society, and in his thoughts and words the roughness of ore burning with an inner fire. He resembled a stone salvaged from some marvellous edifice, which somewhere, sometime had burnt down completely.[3]

Such, indeed, was Norwid in the early 1870s, refracted in the medium of literary journalism. But isn't this also an image of a poet, perhaps even a Romantic poet, depicted in a post-Romantic age? "A stone salvaged from some marvellous edifice, which had burnt down completely"! Although, to be sure, not a dilettante, a visionary, a mystic or a lunatic! Yet whatever the stylisation, and whatever the assumptions and distortions, this portrait is essentially a portrait of Norwid: those "seven centuries of paint", a certain nobility and a certain naïveté, anachronistic ideas, a sense of almost archaic uniqueness, suavity of manner and forcefulness of thought, concern appearing as exaggeration . . . Most valuable, however, is the stress on Norwid's tendency to take a strongly independent, idiosyncratic view of things, to look at things in perspective and from an unusual angle. A critic has described this characteristic of Norwid as his capacity for "autonomous thought".[4] I should like to call it Norwid's 'originality'.

II

Norwid's life was not what most people would call 'romantic'. It does not have the kind of tragic quality that characterised Pushkin's brilliant progress toward a paltry end. It lacks the dramatic character of Mickiewicz's struggle to fulfil his own prophecies: Sisyphean rather than Promethean, it is not the life of a national bard, a prophet-like ruler of souls. If it is Promethean at all, then it is in the sense in which Pierre-Simon Ballanche characterised the Greek mythological hero: "Someone who creates himself through the energy of his thought", the giver of consciousness and meaningful speech, a toiler and a craftsman, who in Norwid's *Promethidion* appears with a hammer; definitely not a rebel against God.[5] For the mature Norwid, who was not only, or not merely, a devout Catholic, but a follower of Christ, such a rebellion was no more than a Romantic gesture, although there was a moment in his life when he cried out, not just in his soul, but in a poem: "Oh, God, you who alone are, I too exist".[6]

Norwid did not allow himself to slide into mysticism, as happened to Mickiewicz and Słowacki. When, in the 1850s, he came close to it, he purged his soul of its potential for unorthodoxy, and even, as he admitted, for heresy, by going to confession.[7]

The lofty idealism of Schiller, or its rapturous counterpart in Shelley, and the no less lofty optimism of Victor Hugo, were foreign to Norwid, who insisted that "irony was being's inseparable shadow", that "the stigma of this globe was want",[8] and who based these views on personal experience, Christian belief and a non-utopian concept of history.

In contrast to Słowacki or Wordsworth, Norwid fought rather than sought solitude. For Norwid — an exile from his country, from the émigré community, from his epoch — loneliness, isolation were a curse, not a boon; Alpine peaks, soaring flights and bowery retreats carried few of their Romantic values and connotations. "For [he wrote] there on high — the grave of human ideas, while here below — of man's body."[9] Norwid's life, as well as his penchant for "autonomous thought", compelled him to revalue many Romantic notions. Since he lacked independent means, his entire mature life was a search for an audience that would enable him to make a living as an artist and a writer. Nor did he believe that the poetic word, however inspired, derived its power from the author alone, that it could be effective without the cooperation of the listener or the reader. To him being a poet meant engaging in a dialogue with one's contemporaries, and as that proved impossible, he placed his faith in "the eternal revisor", the future, in the "late grandson's" interest and understanding.[10] If that was unsatisfactory, as it clearly was, then it was not necessarily worse than the illusion of efficacy indulged in by such poets as Mickiewicz.

Although Norwid frequented literary salons and appreciated the value of "an exquisitely knotted tie",[11] and although he had, in his younger years, a streak of the dandy in him, he was not Byronic in the popular sense of the term, and anyway Byron was for him "the Socrates of poets".[12] After his quite Wertherian love for Maria Kalergis (whose salons were frequented by Liszt, Wagner, Heine, de Musset and Gautier, and who took piano lessons from Chopin), Norwid "exiled himself from love",[13] in which he sought a partnership, rather than a miraculous meeting of souls: the Platonic ideal was there, but it became modified. While Norwid has many bitterly ironic statements about women, and, more precisely, about women of noble birth, there is also evidence of his ability to look at marriage from a woman's point of view.[14] One of his last writings was devoted to the question of the emancipation of women, which he defined in his own, peculiar way.[15] Norwid wrote few 'confessional' (or conventional) love poems; the theme of love is, however, quite prominent in his plays (and it is from the plays that some of his celebrated love lyrics come) and in his longer poems, one of which was written with the specific purpose of filling what Norwid considered a gap in the Polish poetic tradition.[16]

Unlike de Quincey, Coleridge, Słowacki or Krasiński (who tried sniffing ether), Norwid did not taste any of the available forms of the "milk of paradise", with the exception of wine, which he may have drunk to excess, although the available evidence is far from conclusive.[17]

Compared to Lermontov's glorious military exploits, Norwid's three or four attempts to become a soldier add no heroic halo to his life. At any rate, he believed that "heroism is not to be sought in battles but in all aspects of life, and continually. In fact, battles occur only because heroism is not practised in all fields of life."[18]

If the wretchedness of Norwid's life resembles in a very real sense the predicament of the *poètes maudits* — for, like Verlaine, he could have easily asked the question: "Isn't it true that now and forever the sincere poet sees, feels, knows himself accursed by whatever system of self-interest is in power . . . ?"[19] — Norwid did not allow himself to draw extreme conclusions, whether in action, thought, or poetry, from this situation, which he tried to view from a Christian and a Stoic perspective.[20] One could not tell from Norwid's writings, however strongly some of his imagery evokes Blake's Land of Ulro or Eliot's *The Waste Land*, that he was born in the same year as Baudelaire or Dostoyevsky. He treated with extreme reticence those aspects of his life which could have provided him with the opportunity of laying bare "whole shrouded areas of human suffering, perversity and aspiration." Was he free of the torments of the flesh, was he lacking a psychological self, was he not himself his hell? Answering these, and similar questions, would require the writing of a searching biography. One can only indicate here the direction such an inquiry would have to take by quoting Norwid's 'Riddle':

Are steel, rope, or gold
The shackles deepest soaked in
Tears and blood?
No, the unseen! . . . [21]

And even then it would have to be a fairly speculative attempt, a psychoanalytical study, perhaps, if one believes in that kind of thing.

III

The belated recognition of Norwid's work, which began around the year 1900 with the enthusiastic discovery of his writings by Zenon Przesmycki, passed through a number of phases. Each of these highlighted a particular aspect of Norwid's thought or style, and each, in the end, failed to do him justice. By and large, it was Norwid's thought, expressed in his eminently quotable gnomic and paradoxical way, that received the most attention, while the style itself continued to evoke negative feelings and comments, even as it also found its imitators. Since he was discovered by a leading representative of a Neo-Romantic movement, which had some Symbolist and Parnassian streaks, Norwid became, in a lateral rather than direct way, a patron of the Romantic revival in Polish letters. It took some time, and the work of a number of scholars and critics, to disengage Norwid from the Romantic and Neo-Romantic context. Nevertheless, even as late as 1968 there was little consensus as to Norwid's place in Polish and European literary tradition. In an article entitled 'Norwid's Romanticism' Zofia Stefanowska argued that "Norwid was a Romantic, but a Romantic with a difference, if we compare him with his great predecessors. If he does not fit our model of Romanticism this is not because he is a deficient Romantic, but because our model of Romanticism is deficient . . . . We must seek for Norwid such a literary context in which he will cease to be a solitary phenomenon, and will become a carrier of more general tendencies. We find such a context for Norwid in the second generation of Polish Romantics."[22] In the same year as the appearance of Stefanowska's article, Czesław Miłosz, in his *The History of Polish Literature* put forward quite a different view: namely, that "both Norwid's philosophy and his literary technique went beyond the Romantic trend."[23] A third point of view was represented briefly by Kazimierz Wyka; in his view Norwid's position was anachronistically pre-Romantic. Later, Wyka abandoned this view, preferring to call Norwid an a-Romantic writer.[24]

The problem with Stefanowska's thesis is that strictly speaking there was no second generation of Polish Romantics. Thus Norwid had to do duty for his entire 'orphaned', suppressed and lost generation. Wyka's view concerning Norwid's anachronistic position has considerable validity in some respects, yet it ignores the fact that Norwid himself repeatedly stressed his opposition to various aspects of Polish Romanticism, developing his own standpoints and his own poetics in a fruitfully polemical way. It is enough to read one of the crucial texts of Norwid's self-definition, the poem 'Hands swollen from applause . . . ',[25] to realise that this assertion of independence from the great Romantic predecessors was written from a post-Romantic rather than a pre-Romantic point of view.[26]

The fullest scholarly discussion of Norwid as a post-Romantic writer is contained in Jacek Trznadel's book *Czytanie Norwida* (Reading Norwid). The author's thesis is that, although Norwid grew out of Polish Romanticism, he went beyond it, either abandoning or substantially modifying its main tendencies and notions. The book, while admirable in many ways, is not as comprehensive as one would have wished, and it will be necessary to enlarge the scope of Trznadel's discussion.

Trznadel's book deals mainly with Norwid's philosophy, with his ideas rather than his poetics. It takes a number of crucial notions of Polish Romanticism and shows the transformations they undergo at Norwid's hand. The question is, are these notions as transformed by Norwid still within the context of a broadly conceived Romanticism, one that would embrace not only Polish, but European developments?

In arguing for the inclusion of Norwid in a broadened definition of Romanticism, Stefanowska put great stress on his religiousness. "Norwid was religious in a different way [from some Polish 'positivist' writers]; he was religious in a Romantic way. Romantic religiousness could not be limited to the private sphere; it was expansive and aggressive . . . . This kind of religiousness aiming at a totally theistic vision of the world is perhaps the most Romantic feature of Norwid . . . ."[27] One could point out (and Trznadel does point this out) that expansive, all-embracing religiousness existed in many forms before Romanticism, and has reappeared in various guises in the post-Romantic period. But it is also obvious that Norwid's religiousness was not expansive or aggressive in the same way as the religiousness of Mickiewicz, or of Słowacki in his mystical period. Norwid did not rebel against the Church; he did not pit the poet, even momentarily, against God; he did not claim to have received personal revelation, or to have had mystical visions, or to have visited the other world; he had no use for reincarnation, or for marrying evolutionism or Hegelianism with Christianity. In the name of Catholic universalism and Catholic orthodoxy he strongly objected to Mickiewicz's Messianism (with its notion of Poland as the Christ of nations), and to Mickiewicz's "Vengeance, vengeance against the enemy, with or despite God", he objected equally strongly in the name of Christian morality. The two highest values for Norwid were goodness and poetry. It is a most telling combination, considering that both Mickiewicz and Słowacki had doubts about the value of poetry, and of art, during their mystical phases (Towiański, who exerted considerable influence on Mickiewicz, and more briefly on Słowacki, actually prohibited members of his sect from writing poetry). At the same time Norwid did believe that at least some poets were the continuators of the Prophets in changed historical circumstances, that it was the duty of the poet to utter not just words, but the Word, that is, the truth as revealed by Christ and as it could be attained by an attentive and humble reader of signs provided by God in his creation, in human history, and in individual lives. Norwid went even so far as to see an analogy between Christ and the poet, especially the rejected, unheeded, 'sincere' poet, whose words carried the stigma of the Cross.[28] And defending himself against the critique of his ironic mode of writing, he allowed the analogy to work both ways:

> Read what your Saviour said to the Pharisees . . . and you will see that you will not find a more colossal irony anywhere, either in the past or now. Even the form, questioning rather than asserting, is purely ironic!
>
> Yes, my dear, I am not ashamed of irony, for it is enough for a servant to be like his Master, and for the disciple to be like his Teacher. I won't correct the Saviour, that I won't.[29]

Finally, since this topic cannot be treated exhaustively here, let us recall Norwid's synthesis of elements that will not be found so readily in the Romantic period within a single stanza:

For light is not meant to stand under a bushel,
Nor is the salt of the earth for seasoning dishes;
For beauty tempts people into work,
And work — to earn salvation.[30]

Religion permeated every aspect of Norwid's thought and work, but it was neither bigoted nor fanatical. It enabled him to put everything in perspective, in its proper place: evil, death, sickness, irony, beauty, prayer, and originality, which he defined as "being incrementally faithful to one's sources."[31]

Romanticism does not seem to be a sufficient context for Norwid's religiously inspired thought, which derives from older traditions, from St. Augustine and the Church Fathers, Dante, pre-Christian myths and philosophers, and anticipates post-Romantic thought, including Teilhard de Chardin (as Trznadel suggests).[32] It requires further study and comparison with such Romantic poets as Wordsworth, and, in the Polish context, Zygmunt Krasiński, as well as with Hopkins and T.S. Eliot.

It would not be difficult to show that there is a similar blending of pre-Romantic notions and post-Romantic reflection in Norwid's thoughts on history, revolution, folklore, nationality, civilization, women, language, imagination, irony, and a number of other leading questions of Norwid's epoch; a fusion of Romantic and non-Romantic elements and, in some cases, not only a significant modification, but a rejection, or even absence, of a Romantic component. Such is the case with Norwid's relative lack of interest in the natural world,[33] his inability, as it were, to write landscape poetry, the far from central position in his aesthetics of the concept of the imagination, or of inspiration, and the exclusion from his writings of the Gothic, frenetic, Satanic and irrational aspects of Romanticism.[34] Such is, above all else, the case with the poetics of his *Vade-mecum*, a volume of one hundred lyrical poems for which Norwid could not find a publisher — to his deep chagrin, as it was designed to effect a necessary 'turn' in the evolution of Polish poetry.

IV

The *Vade-mecum* opens with a preface 'To the Reader', which itself is prefaced by a motto drawn from various statements by Byron, critical of contemporary English poetry, of the mistaken direction it had taken (Byron includes himself in this statement) and the bad effect it was having on public taste. Norwid's own text is relatively short, barely two pages. The brevity is emblematic: Norwid points out that, while a single lyric had sometimes changed an age-long course of poetry, the long prefaces to poetic volumes which had become the fashion during his time were usually crowned by a lack of effect.

He characterises Polish poetry as being in a critical phase, and defines his position with regard to his "great and famous predecessors", that is, the Polish Romantic poets, as follows:

> This School, which was marked by explanations and pronouncements [or: prophecies] relating to broad historical situations or the *rights of the Nation*, did not apparently have sufficient time to allow in its works for a greater concentration on *responsibilities*, i.e. the *moral side* . . . . Altogether, in our literature the moralists are few in number, which derives from the fact that the situation of the Nation encourages those voices which call for its rights . . . .[35]

Norwid notes that the power of Polish Romantic poetry was enhanced to the extent to which it was a substitute for such activities as journalism and painting (hence: descriptive, landscape poetry), and embraced folk elements, but that in gaining thus in power, Polish poetry declined in art. Since journalism and painting were not developing fast enough, the stimulus for change in Polish poetry remained weak; it was already sufficient, however, to undermine its prevailing character.

Norwid's manifesto is reticent; the poems are, in fact, more outspoken; moreover, they fully exemplify a new direction in lyric poetry. But a new direction only in Polish lyric poetry or more generally?

In a recent article, based on a German translation of Norwid's *Vade-mecum*, entitled 'Norwid and Baudelaire as Contemporaries: A Notable Case of Overdue Concretisation', Hans Robert Jauss attempts to define the place of Norwid's poetry in a broader context. His conclusion is as follows:

> I suspect Norwid's work became effective so late because of the paradox that it was, to a great extent, in touch with the times, but in a way that was out of joint with the times. If this expectation has been confirmed, then further effort to place him within questionable movements or styles such as the Parnassians, symbolism or

> hermeticism should become superfluous. This should also be true of efforts to explain his accomplishment primarily as that of a forerunner of later themes and programs of modern lyric. Measured against the hermeneutics of poets schooled on Mallarmé or against the linguistic deformations and *montages* of the surrealists and dadaists, Norwid's obscurity, eccentricity, and stylistic admixture would seem modest. Hindsight adds little to the actual profile of his lyrics, which in their time provocatively expanded the boundaries of what could be expressed poetically. But Norwid's work can cast new light on the direction of modern poetry, which since the publication of H. Friedrich's *Die Struktur der modernen Lyric* (1956), we have been accustomed to see following Baudelaire, Rimbaud, and Mallarmé on the path of progressive dissolution of mimetic and subjective poetry. Norwid's *Vade-mecum*, which did not follow this path, allows us to recognise more clearly the high price of modernity which rejected the relation between poetry and the world for an ideal language as the last refuge of pure meaning . . . . As far as the present is concerned, one may suppose that Norwid's *Vade-mecum* will not only accompany and legitimise the development of Polish lyrical poetry in the post-Stalin era, but perhaps, as a recently discovered classic of repressed modernity, it may also be able to serve the German lyric in the establishment of a new canon.[36]

My own conclusion would be somewhat different. Norwid's poetry, whether or not it was meant to be an alternative to Baudelaire specifically (and the question remains open),[37] did provide an alternative model for poetic modernity, not just because Norwid avoided the path of the "dissolution of mimetic and subjective poetry" in the name of an ideal language and poetic purity, but because his poetry represented a conscious attempt to create a new structure of the modern lyric and a new style, one of whose significant elements was verse "moulded on the rhythm of common speech",[38] precisely for the purpose of giving *poetic* expression to intellectual content and moral commitment. Furthermore, Norwid attempted these innovations being acutely aware of the function of reading as a constitutive term of the poetic equation, and, in a broader sense, of the existence and importance of what today would be termed the semiotic space of communication and culture (an awareness which Norwid put also to excellent use in some of his plays).[39]

The new structure of Norwid's lyric poetry consists, on the one hand, in the tightening of form, by means of the internalisation of rhetorical and discursive devices, and, on the other hand, in the loosening up of certain poetic conventions (generic, tonal), a departure from outward perfection, smoothness, facile unity achieved by means of melodiousness, tone, mood or uniformity of style.

It is true that Norwid's lyric poetry, while enlarging the scope of what could be expressed, and while constituting a new departure, achieved its novelty by a revival and re-application of pre-Romantic, and actually quite ancient ways of making speech maximally meaningful, such as the parabola, the gnomic sentence, the riddle, the paradox, the oracular formula. In this connection one should also mention Norwid's use of the Platonic dialogue, in a more extended as well as in a compressed form, and of the various means of increasing the dialogic and phatic functions of poetic language, including the device of putting the reader, as it were, in the poem.[40]

These strategies and techniques were made structurally functional by what may be called the semanticisation of form, by allowing for a juxtaposition and interplay of its various elements, some of which could, and did, serve as the basis of an entire poetics. Norwid's novelty in this respect consisted in his retaining rather than neutralising the achieved play of formal difference. As he himself put it: "Perfect lyric poetry should be like a plaster cast: those rough edges where forms cross each other and leave cracks should be left intact and not smoothed over with a knife."[41]

One way of claiming such perfection for those of Norwid's poems in which he has obviously succeeded is to say that they compete in the complexity of structure, economy of means, and even purity of poetic effect with the best poems in the tradition of Baudelaire, Rimbaud and Mallarmé, as an alternative solution to meeting the predicament of poetry in its critical phase, and that they do so without the loss of the mimetic and subjective aspects.

In his desire to make words serve the Word, and in his belief that poetry could stand alongside goodness in the hierarchy of true values, Norwid created out of ancient and new elements of poetic form and expression a synthesis which has been gradually, though belatedly, achieving an increasingly fruitful 'concretisation' among readers, poets and scholars alike.

Notes

1. For Norwid's life, see 'Kalendarz Biograficzny Cypriana Norwida', in Cyprian Norwid, *Pisma wszystkie*, vol. XI (Warsaw, 1976), edited by J.W. Gomulicki.
2. *Ibid.*, and C.Norwid, *Pisma wybrane*, vol.I (Warsaw, 1968), edited by J.W. Gomulicki, as well as other sources, such as the correspondence of Z. Krasiński and J.I. Kraszewski.
3. C. Norwid, *Pisma wszystkie*, vol.XI, pp.489-494.
4. See G. Gömöri, *Cyprian Norwid* (New York, 1974), p.25.
5. *Ibid.*, p.30. Gömöri's suggestion that "the key to Norwid's general and in some ways un-Romantic concept of *Promethidion* lies" in Ballanche's *Palingénésie*, requires further research, as Gömöri himself admits. The concept of Prometheus in the Romantic movement varied so much from writer to writer, and sometimes within the work of a single writer, that it is difficult to be definitive on this point. Cp.Louis Awad, *The Theme of Prometheus in English and French Literature* (Cairo, 1963), and Raymond Trousson, *Le Thème de Promethée dans la Litterature Européenne* (Geneva, 1964), vol. II.
6. C. Norwid, *Pisma wybrane*, vol.I, p.178.
7. Cp. Norwid's letters to Fathers A. Jełowicki and P. Semenenko, *Pisma wszystkie*, vol. VIII, pp.217-220, and to Father Semenenko, pp.229-230.
8. See Norwid's 'Fortepian Chopina' (Chopin's Piano), *Pisma wybrane*, vol.I, p. 312.
9. C. Norwid, 'Idee i prawda' (Ideas and Truth), *Ibid.*, p.397.
10. C. Norwid, 'Klaskaniem mając obrzękłe prawice' (Hands Swollen from Applause), *Ibid.*, p.192.
11. C. Norwid, 'Marionetki' (Marionettes), *Ibid.*, p.389. For an English version by Adam Czerniawski, see Cyprian Kamil Norwid, *Poems* (Kraków, 1986), pp.27-29.
12. C. Norwid, 'O Juliuszu Słowackim' (Lectures on J. Słowacki), *Pisma wybrane*, vol. IV, p.205.
13. Jan Błoński, 'Norwid wśród prawnuków' (Norwid among his Great-grandchildren), *Twórczość*, 1967: V, p.70.
14. C. Norwid, 'Archeologia' (Archeology), *Pisma wszystkie*, vol. VI, pp.71-76.
15. C. Norwid, 'Emancypacja kobiet' (The Emancipation of Women), *Ibid.*, pp.652-655 (for a translation of two excerpts, see C.K. Norwid, *Poems*, p.111).
16. Cp. Norwid's remarks in a brief preface to the poem in question (entitled 'Assunta'): "It has been rightly observed that in Polish literature only a few long poems can be described as love poems, as if this noble and so multi-radiant feeling cast a glance upon itself only a couple of times . . . Only [Mickiewicz's] *Dziady* [Forefathers' Eve], part one, and Słowacki's *W Szwajcarii* [In Switzerland] belong to the genre — two only in the

entire Polish literature!" Among Norwid's plays dealing with the theme perhaps the most deserving to be more widely known is the very fine "white tragedy" (as Norwid called it), *Pierścień wielkiej damy* (Her Ladyship's Ring). It may be added that these, and some other of Norwid's works, amount to a standpoint that could very well be described as Christian feminism.

17. See Jacek Trznadel, *Czytanie Norwida* (Warsaw, 1978), p.256.
18. Translation by Adam Czerniawski, *Oficyna Poetów*, 1973: 2, p.14.
19. Paul Verlaine, *Les poètes maudits*, 1884.
20. See J. Trznadel, *op. cit.*, pp.121-123.
21. C. Norwid, *Pisma wybrane*, vol.I, p.422. Translation by Adam Czerniawski in C.K. Norwid, *Poems*, p.53.
22. Zofia Stefanowska, 'Norwidowski Romantyzm', *Pamiętnik Literacki*, 1968: 4. p.15.
23. Czesław Miłosz, *The History of Polish Literature* (London, 1969), p.268.
24. See J. Trznadel, *op. cit.*, pp.324-325.
25. C. Norwid, *Pisma wybrane*, vol.I, pp.191-193.
26. See J. Trznadel's discussion of the poem, *op. cit.*, pp.12-58.
27. Z. Stefanowska, *op. cit.*, p.14.
28. See J. Trznadel, *op. cit.*, pp.154-163 and *passim.*
29. C. Norwid, *Pisma wszystkie*, vol. VIII, p.186, letter to Jan Koźmian.
30. C. Norwid, *Promethidion*, *op. cit.*, vol.III, pp.439-440.
31. C. Norwid, 'O Juliuszu Słowackim', *Pisma wybrane*, vol. IV, p.215.,
32. J. Trznadel, *op. cit.*, pp.161-163.
33. See Wacław Borowy, *O Norwidzie* (Warsaw 1960).
34. See J. Trznadel, *op. cit.*, pp.241-244.
35. C. Norwid, *op. cit.*, vol. IV, pp.266-267.
36. Hans Robert Jauss, 'Norwid and Baudelaire as Contemporaries: A Notable Case of Overdue Concretisation', in P. Steiner *et. al.*, *The Structure of Literary Process* (Amsterdam, 1982), pp.293-294.
37. See J. Trznadel, *op. cit.*, p.241.
38. See Adam Czerniawski, 'A "Flawed" Master', *Oficyna Poetów*, 1973: 2; J. Pietrkiewicz, 'Cyprian Norwid's *Vade-mecum*: An Experiment in Didactic Verse', *Slavonic and East European Review*, 1966: 102; W. Borowy, *op. cit.*, *passim.*
39. See especially Z. Łapiński, *Norwid* (Kraków, 1971).
40. See Z. Łapiński, *op. cit.*; M. Staszewska, 'Paradoksy w liryce Norwida', in J.W. Gomulicki, ed., *Nowe studia o Norwidzie* (Warsaw, 1961); Z. Bieńkowski, M. Głowiński, Z. Łapiński on three of Norwid's poems in Jan Prokop, ed., *Liryka polska: Interpretacje* (Krakow, 1971); A. Czerniawski, *op. cit.*, and introduction to *The Burning Forest* (Newcastle, 1988); M. Kridl, 'O lirykach Norwida', in *W różnych przekrojach* (Warsaw, 1939); M. Jastrun, *Gwiaździsty diament* (Warsaw, 1971).
41. See Z. Łapiński, *op. cit.* Norwid's use of genres would deserve a separate discussion. On Norwid's plays, see the works of Irena Sławińska,

especially *O komediach Norwida* (Lublin, 1953) and *Reżyserska ręka Norwida* (Krakow, 1971). On Norwid's irony, see S. Kołaczkowski, 'Ironia Norwida', in *Pisma wybrane* (Warsaw, 1968), vol. I., and comments on this study in Jacek Trznadel, *op. cit.*, and Z. Łapiński, *op. cit.* On Norwid's versification, see A. Okopień-Sławińska, *Wiersz nieregularny i wolny Mickiewicza, Słowackiego i Norwida* (Wrocław, 1964). Cp. also the various issues of the periodical *Studia Norwidiana* (1983-).

BOGDAN CZAYKOWSKI

From Rhythm and Metaphysics to Intonation, Experience and Gnosis: The Poetry of Bolesław Leśmian, Aleksander Wat and Czesław Miłosz

From Rhythm and Metaphysics to Intonation, Experience and Gnosis: The Poetry of Bolesław Leśmian, Aleksander Wat and Czesław Miłosz

1. Texts of Songs without Music

Not much will remain Richard really not much
of the poetry of this insane age undoubtedly Rilke Eliot
a few other distinguished shamans who knew the secret
of bewitching words into a form that can withstand
the action of time without which
no phrase is worth remembering and speech is like sand

The above lines of Zbigniew Herbert, written close to a hundred years after the birth of Bolesław Leśmian (1878), to whose concept of poetry they indirectly allude, come from a poem (addressed to a younger poet, Ryszard Krynicki) which laments the situation of those postwar Polish poets who felt compelled by their social conscience to take upon "their thin shoulders public affairs the struggle with tyranny with lies," lowering "holy speech" to the level of "the babble of rostrums of the black froth of newspapers," accepting too readily the conclusion that "beauty doesn't save," with the result that

none of us knew how to awaken the dryad in the poplar
to read the writing of clouds
and so no unicorn will retrace our steps
we will not bring to life a ship in the bay a peacock a rose
to us nakedness was left and so we stand naked
on the better the right-hand side of the triptych
called the Last Judgment.[1]

As is typical of Herbert, both the words of praise and the words of deprecation in the poem are tinged with irony. Yet despite the relativisation of the values juxtaposed, the contrast is meant to be taken seriously, and it obviously has descriptive power. For although poets like Herbert or Tadeusz Różewicz have produced excellent poetry within the limits of the poetics they developed, their verse is not on the whole memorable in the way in which the verse of Leśmian, Rilke, Eliot, Dylan Thomas, or Pasternak undoubtedly often is. In that sense their poems may be called, as Herbert does call them in the poem quoted, "texts of songs without music."

It was, of course, Różewicz who initiated in postwar Poland what came to be known as "naked poetry," and who occasionally protested against tendencies which, in his view, led to the "shedding of the burden":

> He comes to you
> and says
>
> you are not responsible
> either for the world or the end of the world
> the load has been lifted off your shoulders
> you are like children and birds
> go, play
>
> and they play
>
> they forget
> that contemporary poetry
> means struggle for breath[2]

What underlay the moral astringency of Różewicz's radical programme of poetic austerity was, as is well known to his readers, the horror of the war. The question "how to create poetry after Auschwitz" became fused in Różewicz's mind with a contemptuous attitude not only towards aestheticism, but towards the pursuit of the poetic principle in general. To be sure, he retained considerable admiration for poets such as Leopold Staff, who embodied for him the idea of the poetic as a realm with its own *raison d'être*. Nevertheless, that ideal had, in Różewicz's mind, not only to be rejected in the practice of his own writings, but occasionally aroused a more general hostility. It was, after all, with considerable passion that he announced that "poetry is dead," that he was not a poet, and that his aim as a writer was the creation not of "poems but facts." If the opposite of the Arcadian myth were true, then attempts to inhabit "the paradise of language" were not only immoral, or a-moral, but poetically suspect: poetry which could not withstand the test of reality was for that very reason flawed as poetry, and those poets who tried to revive its magic were both irresponsible and laughable. Instead of lamenting his predicament as a poet, Różewicz found himself compelled by the force of his outraged sensibility to ridicule anyone who would want to emulate the "distinguished shamans" of poetry unmindful of the exigencies inhering in the "task of how to create poetry after Auschwitz":

> The season in the *Paradis du Langage*
> has ended long ago
> I spoke of this for twenty years
> to our wordspinners
> wordmongers wordmagicians
>
> only now do the real difficulties
> begin
> of how to write verses . . .
>
> you will have to lay
> the egg the poem
> not into the chaff of words half-words quarter-words
> but directly
> into a void into a precipice
> here is a problem worthy of a poet:
> how not to write verses
> how not to write
> just another poem[3]

The force of Różewicz's formulations is undeniable, but there is an equally compelling power, which it would not be wrong to describe as attractive, in Herbert's evocation of a poetry whose character has not been shaped primarily by a sense of direct responsibility "for the world or the end of the world," but by a concept of the poetic which embodies its own justification.

Such a concept of poetry informs and permeates especially the work of Bolesław Leśmian, and the radical nature of its self-sufficiency is well conveyed by the mockingly grave way in which a voice asks in one of his later poems "how to ground economic being in nothingness,"[4] a question which scandalised Marxist critics during the relatively brief period of the ascendancy of socialist realism in postwar Poland.

2. Words to a Song without Words

Leśmian's joke about the hollow metaphysical status of economic activity should not be taken as indicating a lack of awareness of the importance of the economic and social dimension of human reality, or insensitivity to suffering other than the "pain of existence": he himself experienced extreme poverty and near starvation during his stay in Paris in the years 1903-1906, and intermittently acute financial problems during the rest of his life (he died in 1937); he was subjected to anti-semitic taunts in the right-wing press in independent Poland; and he certainly did not receive the recognition he deserved as a poet, which added to his sense of humiliation. His life spanned the revolution of 1905-6, the First World War and the subsequent revolutionary upheavals as well as the years of the Great Depression, which in Poland caused acute misery and widespread turmoil. In fact, his poems testify to his awareness of, and great sensitivity to, human suffering of every kind. Nor was Leśmian incapable of thinking in political terms. Writing around 1912 to the novelist Stefan Żeromski (the custodian of the ideological conscience of the Polish intelligentsia at the time) in connection with his project to translate into Polish the works of the Russian satirical writer Saltykov-Shchedrin, Leśmian justified his proposal by stressing Shchedrin's "penetrating exposure of the very core of the techniques of administrative repressiveness and his unmasking of that dark region from which spring directly the automatism and mechanism of inborn and habitual baseness, one that is almost gratuitous . . . and of the entire structure of inanity and subjection, which affects us also."[5]

Yet despite his awareness of the social and political dimensions and determinants of individual fate, Leśmian's concept of the function of poetry was entirely a-political, one could even say a-social, at least in the usual senses of these terms. Influenced by the neo-Romantic and modernist reaction to positivism, including the Russian version of the Symbolist movement, inspired by the philosophy of Bergson, whose lectures he attended briefly in Paris, and by Nietzsche's concept of individualism, Leśmian held a view of poetry that was uncompromisingly metaphysical.

At the core of Leśmian's beliefs about poetry lay the idea that the poet was a natural metaphysician, or at least that such a "myth" came close to defining the mystery of poetic creation. Leśmian would not have objected to having his central belief concerning poetry described as a "myth." In his view all systems of human thought, whether philosophical, religious or scientific, rested on unproven assumptions or myths which linked the human mind with the "a-logical sphere of existence, with this precipitous shore of mystery, whose visage is very much unlike the human face."[6] At the basis of all systematic thought about, or knowledge of this non-human world (the mythical "thing in itself") there lay direct, unmediated cognition or intuitive grasping of some aspect of its reality. The capability of such direct cognition had characterised the primitive man especially, and it characterised the poet who, in this respect, was *like* a primitive man (which was not at all the same as being "primitive"). Grasping reality in this direct fashion, however, did not mean for Leśmian the mere uncovering of some finished "thingness"; for Leśmian reality was not only complex, relative and hence multifaceted, but also dynamic. The philosophical myth that he found most compelling was the one which divided reality into *natura naturata* and *natura naturans*. This duality applied, in Leśmian's view, both to the "thing in itself," that is whatever stretched beyond the sphere of the human mind, separated from it by the "precipitous shore of mystery," and to the human world. Neither the non-human universe nor humanity was completed and whole, both were evolving, a fact which could and did find its expression in language. But for this to occur, speech had to be responsive to a "tone" which came as if from outside the self and demanded to be put into words; it had, as it were, to allow itself to become an embodiment of the creative force, revelatory both of the mystery of the non-human world and of the human potential for self-creation.

Only rarely was human speech of this kind. Leśmian believed (and expressed the idea with some brilliance in an address prepared shortly before his death for a meeting of the Polish Academy of Literature) that most of human speech belonged to the realm of *natura naturata*, i.e. to the kind of language which was either societal and practical in its intent or merely elaborated the myths or leaps of intuitive cognition already achieved by others. Carefully stressing in his address (which appeared in 1939 under the title

'From Meditations on Poetry') that "whatever one said about poetry would always be untrue," Leśmian nevertheless deplored the tendency to ideologise poetic speech, to make it serve social causes, to deprive it of "magic" and to substitute for the shaping power of rhythm the organising principle of syntax, which by its very nature imposed on poetic expression the constraints of "songless reality," of received ideas, logic, pragmatic and conventional communication, and ideological content. He was particularly distressed by the contemporary trend to depersonalise literature, to deprive it of individuality. Such attempts brought to his mind the image of the King-Rat, a monstrosity resulting from too many rats crowding in a small space and becoming so entangled with their tails that they eventually become ingrown and serve as conduits for the circulation of their collective blood.[7]

Poets were always seers, looking into the future, yearning to leave behind them old forms and received notions, and what made them capable of liberating the word from such constraints and move beyond *natura naturata* was their readiness to listen to and be carried away by rhythm, the immaterial "song without words" of reality. "Rhythm enables us to capture in a poem that which evolves in words and beyond them, what either stands for the essence of time, or is time itself. This quality flows in the manner of a repeatable melody, one which can be sung again and again from beginning to end with the complete assurance that it will repeat itself as before, retaining, every time it ends, undiminished rhythmical power to become resurrected. We recognise a poem not only by its words and their meaning, but also by this wordless melody which becomes fixed in our memory independently of words and their content. This melody, this ungraspable streaming of words represents the time saved in a given poem, the time which is indispensable for its unfolding, for its very meaning . . . Creation is, as a matter of fact, a recording of this process. If a flower could record on a leaf in words that are both adequate and right the rhythm of its gradual unfolding from the moment it felt the desire to become a flower until it had actually become one, this seemingly insignificant jotting would indeed be a most wonderful poem."[8] Poems that originate in rhythm not only add new meaning but make it memorable (and poems "like to dwell in memory rather than in books"). Moreover, without the music and radiance that poetry brings into the world's darkness, "life becomes a burden which it is impossible to bear."[9]

3. From Sound Poetry to a "More Spacious Form"

The worship of rhythm reached its apogee at the turn of the century, and although individual poets, including several major ones, continued to subscribe to the idea of its being the *differentia specifica* of poetic discourse, the poetics which unified for a time, even if superficially, various national poetic traditions by stressing the paramountcy of rhythm began to undergo in the decade preceding the First World War considerable fragmentation, resulting in the rise of a number of poetic currents. Each of these currents privileged a different feature of poetic discourse as the basis of true poetry: some poets wanted to liberate the word from all systemic constraints, whether it was versification, syntax, logic or lexicality, going in some instances as far as poetry of pure sound; others stressed the self-sufficiency of the image; still others identified poetic discourse with metaphorisation; while a reaction to what was common to most of these currents, viz. the pursuit of the sharpest possible differentiation of poetic language from all other kinds of speech, had also made itself forcefully heard in the form of socially and ideologically committed poetry.

One of those who set out to overturn all traditional poetics was Aleksander Wat. He participated in the expressionist-futurist-dadaist movement in Poland in the years immediately following the war, and at the age of nineteen (he was born in 1900) published a slim volume of Rimbaudian-dadaist poetic prose entitled characteristically 'I on the One Side and I on the Other Side of my Pug-Dog Iron Stove', which was a mixture of fantasy (sexual and exotic), absurdity, ego-mania, violence, metaphysics, lyricism and verbiage. He also experimented with sound poetry, and one does not have to translate the original to show the nature of the experiment, though it should be added that Wat used actual words and morphemes to achieve the double effect of sound orchestration and estrangement of words:

> Ptachorenki rozchorongwił roz i grajoncy na pstrych charmonikach w pachnurach chromawy charun chrapał w chmurach i wbarwistach. A chmurawie munrawy ogroi i grujce rozgrai na grajkatych guranach. W ranach gorun garbi ogury gromach i gromadach pagur. Na pagurach chrabonszczy lew o chrabonczyna o chrabonczyki rozchrabonczyn i lew chrabonszczony onże chrabonszcz. [10]

Wat's experiments with sound poems were more successful than his proto-surrealist poetic prose, but the scope of such poetry was obviously rather limited. Altogether, the futurist-dadaist experiment quickly ran out of steam in Poland, and its participants moved to what appeared greener pastures. In the case of Wat that meant the complete abandonment of poetry, trying his hand at dystopian prose, and becoming an intellectual fellow-traveller of the Polish Communist Party, whose above-ground literary monthly Wat edited in the years 1929-1932. That identification also proved abortive. After his brief imprisonment for pro-communist activities in 1932 (when he shared the prison cell with the revolutionary poet of interwar Poland, Władysław Broniewski), Wat withdrew both from politics and from literature, and it was not until 1939 under the Soviet occupation in former Eastern Poland that he tried again (mainly out of fear) to play a literary role, only to be arrested on the grounds of being a renegade and a Trotskyite (he was later accused of being both a Zionist and an agent of the Vatican), and deported to the Soviet Union, where he had to stay until 1946 on account of his refusal to adopt Soviet citizenship and his, by then, fiercely anti-communist views. It was not until the early 1950s that Wat again took up poetry, but by that time he had found himself in the grip of a mysterious illness, which made his life painful and miserable, and which he sometimes regarded as a punishment for what he considered the greatest sin of his life: serving communism.[11]

Wat's poetry of the postwar period (he died in 1967) is not entirely devoid of links with his youthful experimental phase, but it is primarily, in the words of Miłosz, "a poetry of experience and of bitter wisdom,"[12] and its formal range, although narrower than Miłosz's, is considerably greater than that of Różewicz's or Herbert's.[13]

Fate was kinder to Czesław Miłosz, although he also had enough resolve and acumen to prod it at some decisive moments in the desired direction. Born in 1911 in what was then Russia (and what in 1919 became an independent Lithuanian state), Miłosz went unscathed through the First World War and the Russian revolutions, and found in interwar Poland an enclave of relative opportunity: he studied law at Vilnius, a city with a rich mix of cultural traditions; found a few like-minded young poets to organise a poetic group (known as the *Żagary* group); and was able to travel to Paris on a government scholarship, which not only enabled him to observe French intellectual and literary life at close quarters, but to come in contact with his cousin, Oscar de Miłosz, a French symbolist poet and mystic, who exerted on the young writer a crucial and life-long influence.[14]

Miłosz spent the first year of the Second World War in Vilnius, which was incorporated in Lithuania, and managed to escape to Warsaw after that country's annexation by the Soviet Union in the summer of 1940. Critical of what he considered unnecessary sacrifice of life, Miłosz limited his underground activity under Nazi rule to literary affairs.[15] After the war he did not join the opposition to the new regime, and was sent as a cultural attaché to the United States. This gave him the opportunity to become acquainted with American poetry: he translated the works of a number of American poets into Polish and wrote critical essays about it.[16] The imposition of socialist realism on Polish literature and art in 1949 eventually confronted Miłosz with a dilemma: whether to remain in Poland at the cost of losing his literary independence, or choose the freedom of exile, at the cost of losing his readers and the opportunity to publish. At a dramatic moment, Miłosz decided to choose the latter, and turned his decision to good account by analysing in a book, *The Captive Mind*, the predicament of writers and intellectuals under Stalinist communism. Miłosz's stay in France between 1951 and 1961 was not free of hardships (the more so as the French Left regarded him as a reactionary and a renegade), but he was fortunate to find a devoted publisher in the editor of the Polish cultural émigré monthly *Kultura*. Miłosz's situation improved considerably when in 1961 he moved to Berkeley, California, where he became professor of Polish and Slavic literature and where he still lives. Although transformed into an academic, Miłosz was able to devote considerable time to writing, and has thus had an almost uninterrupted literary career of nearly sixty years, crowned by the Nobel Prize for Literature in 1980 and the attendant publications in many languages and countries, as well as in Poland, where his poetry was finally allowed to appear after a ban of thirty years.[17]

Miłosz's early poetry (published in two volumes in 1933 and 1936 respectively) exhibits to a large extent the quality that Leśmian thought poetry should have above everything else: rhythm. We also know that many of Miłosz's early poems originated in a mood which Leśmian described as "tone." Answering some questions (in 1978) on the early phase of his poetic development, Miłosz recalled that during that time he lived "under an incredibly strong lyrical pressure," in an aura of ecstasy, and that this lyrical pressure was especially strong during his first stay in Paris (1931), when he walked through the city "intense to the point of bursting . . . trying to find an incantation that would measure up to the inner pressure".[18] Of 'Hymn', one of the most striking poems of the second volume, Miłosz said that "it was almost a piece of *écriture automatique*, dictated by a daimonion."[19] The words that came to the "song without words," heard by young Miłosz, were of course influenced by various poets, from Adam Mickiewicz to Mayakovsky and Oscar de Miłosz, and thus their rhythmic shape could not be attributed solely to some metaphysical tone. At the same time, a number of the poems (including 'Hymn') have a clear stamp of Miłosz's poetic temperament and quite astonishing incantatory power (their lines do in fact stay and reverberate in memory). Having tasted "shamanic power," Miłosz could have concluded that poetry not only was but should be a dark, mysterious gift, to be accepted when it came, even if it brought a blush to one's cheeks, as something shamefully elemental. "In the very essence of poetry — he wrote years later — there is something indecent:

> a thing is brought forth which we didn't know we had in us,
> so we blink our eyes, as if a tiger had sprung out
> and stood in the light, lashing its tail."[20]

As it happened, Miłosz did not entirely reject rhythmic speech, nor did he, however, equate it with the essence of the poetic. Already in these early poems there is a feature that would later become the hallmark of Miłosz's poetry, viz. a distinct speaking voice, or rather, a whole gamut of voices. For not only does the speaking voice oscillate between a "we" of socially-committed poetry (which occurs mainly in the earliest poems) and an "I" pregnant with meaning, which as yet portends rather than signifies thought, but it is already multivocal. As Miłosz himself put it: "in that volume [i.e. the one from 1936] there are many openings, self-contained passages, which are autonomous . . . One could detach various lines from these poems and analyse them as instances of dramatic speech . . . It's as if I were carrying in me innumerable voices, which spoke dramatically."[21]

The blending of richly modulated yet often strikingly climactic rhythmic flow with near-dramatic speech, and the gradual emergence of a strongly felt poetic 'I', placed Miłosz's early verse somewhat apart from the various warring groups of contemporary

Polish poetry, dominated, as it was, by two major poetic schools, the *Skamander*, which was basically traditionalist and eclectic, and the *Awangarda*, which emphasised metaphor as the constitutive element of poetic language and wanted to distinguish the poetic construct as sharply as possible from all other types of discourse, defining a poem as an artefact rather than as a mode of speech.[22] For Miłosz both trends seemed too restrictive, and the realisation that neither of them suited his own poetic temperament led him to search for a form that would allow modern poetry to regain the scope it once had (he cited as his model the poetry of Mickiewicz). The nature of the search was described by Miłosz with consummate modulation in *Ars Poetica?*, written in 1968, whose first stanza states the underlying principle of his mature poetics:

> I have always aspired to a more spacious form
> that would be free from the claims of poetry or prose
> and would let us understand each other without exposing
> the author or reader to sublime agonies.[23]

Developing and fusing disparate voices in such a way that they would become integrated into a richly modulated yet distinctive *dramatis persona* of the poet's self that articulates and orchestrates its polyphonic potential — this is one important feature of what the pursuit of a more spacious form meant in Miłosz's case. There was to be no surrendering or depersonalisation of the "I" (and it has been a singularly expansive, searching and Eros-driven, but also, as far as poetry was concerned, a remarkably non-Freudian "I", at least till the late 1970s) [24], but rather its expansion, differentiation, and re-integration at higher levels of understanding and self-understanding (or if understanding was not possible, of meaningful wonder). Being a poet did not mean being a medium, a lyrical instrument, a craftsman, an artificer of verbal constructs, though it did involve all of these things; a poet was above all else a self (soul, *pneuma*), someone "born just once on earth," into a place, and a time, who faced the mystery of existence, the world's and his own, and had to try, confronted with the phenomenon of suffering and death, to make sense of reality. Nothing at all was as crucial as this "will to reality."[25]

Yet in pursuing this supreme quest the poet could no longer put his trust in moods, tones, inspirations, rhythmical transports, illuminations and revelations, as these too had to be comprehended. Moreover, in the absence of incontrovertible illumination, knowledge had to be earned the hard way, and language as the instrument of understanding had to have a formal scope capable of doing justice to everything that was, and that included not only the non-human reality, but the phenomenon of humanity, with its history of consciousness, i.e., among other things, a verbal record of repeated attempts at comprehension. The poet had also to be "a *thinking* creature."[26] Finally, and especially if he came from a background of Catholicism, and became "quite early . . . a gnostic, a Marcionite, a secret taster of Manichean poisons,"[27] he could not avoid linking understanding with the choice of the right path (which has led some critics to describe Miłosz's poetry as "tinged . . . with moralising"):

> Until you reach the crossroads. There will be two paths.
> One difficult and down, another easy and up.
> Take the difficult one, simple Johnny. Again two paths.
> One difficult and up, another easy and down.
> Go up . . .[28]

Thus the search for a more spacious form came gradually to mean, in Miłosz's case, that in fact few of the major strands in the Western (or, for that matter, Polish) poetic tradition were rejected outright: the poet remained a natural metaphysician and a seer; good and evil and the choice of the right path were of as much concern to him as formal excellence, while the predicaments of history and the dilemmas of social conscience retained their crucial importance, given the acute nature of the political and social conflicts of the age, and the claims made on the poet's allegiance, and on his very integrity, by various ideologies. Hence, whatever Miłosz's later view of the often quoted lines from his 1945 poem 'Dedication' (and he did not include the stanza in question in the volume published in London in 1967)[29]:

> What is poetry which does not save
> Nations or people?
> A connivance with official lies,
> A song of drunkards whose throats will soon be cut,
> Readings for sophomore girls.[30]

— a degree of social commitment, while noticeably diminishing, remained a significant feature of his verse.[31]

What was rejected was the modernist narrowing down of the scope of poetry. In Miłosz's own words (written in 1961):

> In the middle of the 19th century something happened to poetry (and to art in general). There appeared on the scene the lonely artist, a rebel, a martyr to his vision. He found precursors, patrons in such poets as Edgar Allan Poe or Hölderlin. Why did it happen that way? . . . Whatever the answer, the result was that, having entered this path, poetry from then on exhibits a considerable continuity in its autonomous development — autonomous — for its development seems to be governed by the laws of literary technique alone, and this happens in countries of vastly different structures . . . The characteristics of modern poetry are generally known: the poem shrinks in size, gains in conciseness and density, loses melody that is pleasing to the ear, and often the communicative potential of ordinary, everyday speech; it becomes an "object" by means of which the author suggests certain emotional states, which require of the reader special attention and effort . . . The end result is poetry as a song about poetry . . . [32]

There are in Miłosz's writings numerous other formulations of his sense of modern poetic developments. Perhaps the most interesting (as well as the most balanced) occurs in his Berkeley lecture (1980) 'On Ignorance, Learned and Literary':

> Two basic tendencies may be observed in the poetry of our century: first, a movement from a chaos of images attacking the mind, toward their distillation and such a selection, that they serve one aim only, purity of intonation. And second, an anxiety when form has already erected a barrier between the raw material of life and arrangements of words, thence immediately a reverse movement, to the point of passively receiving everything which flows in from outside. It is probably in those rare cases when these two tendencies clash within a poem and attain a sort of equilibrium, that durable works are written.[33]

"Equilibrium" here stands obviously for a poetry of selective integration, and the qualification of the last sentence ("probably") limits the negative implications of Miłosz's definition of "durable works", so that in the end *poésie pure* (or a Burnsian lyric), and the creation of verbal anti-worlds presumably need not be excluded from the realm of the perennially poetic, even if the writing of such poetry did not interest Miłosz personally. But even if the intent of the passage, and of similar passages in Miłosz's writings, is not only to justify his own poetics, but to effect a change in the development of poetry in general, this is not sufficient ground to draw normative conclusions, such, for instance, as Donald Davie seems to have drawn (however ambivalently) regarding the "insufficiency" of lyric.[34] What the history of literature teaches with incontrovertible force is that there are different kinds of poetry, and that excellence or meaning do not come automatically with any poetics, however authoritative some of its practitioners might be as proponents or models of poetic form.

4. The Poetic Art of Czesław Miłosz

Miłosz's poetry has received wide critical attention in the English-speaking world, especially since 1980. Yet much of that attention has been focused on Miłosz the East European intellectual, the author of the *The Captive Mind* (a book written in 1951 and published for the first time in English in 1953), "the conscience of Poland", "the conscience of modern man", or, at best, "a historical poet of bleak illumination",[35] rather than on Miłosz the poetic artist, and this despite the fact that a large body of Miłosz's poetry has been translated into English, with the author himself supervising the translating effort very carefully.[36] A paradoxical situation has developed: a poet who strove throughout his life to open poetic form to reality and ideas, has found himself in need of protesting that the attention he was receiving was not exactly doing justice to his achievements as a poet.[37]

Yet there is a further paradox that has to be addressed: although Miłosz's verse is uniformly excellent in its own way, one finds critics and discerning readers baffled by the apparent discrepancy between the claims made for him as a poet (e.g. Joseph Brodsky: "Miłosz is one of the greatest poets of our time, perhaps the greatest")[38] and the difficulty of identifying unquestionable masterpieces; and the problem is compounded when the inquirer has no knowledge of Polish, since many of Miłosz's best lyrical poems have either remained untranslated, or their translations have failed to pass the author's strict scrutiny when he made the selection for the 1988 edition of his *Collected Poems* (e.g. the extremely fine 'Today I Walked Through the Garden', whose English version was included in the 1975 Polish issue of *Modern Poetry in Translation*); furthermore, even those translations that have passed Miłosz's scrutiny do not always convey adequately the excellence of the original, as is the case with the translation of the undisputed masterpiece of Miłosz's earlier phase, the "neo-classical" cycle of poems written under Nazi occupation, 'The World' (the English version, despite its many qualities, fails to evoke the delight that comes from the recognition of the effortless mastery characteristic of the original, which is at least partly the effect of Miłosz's use of rhyme, on the whole absent in the translation).[39] Hence an American critic (an unfriendly one, to be sure) stated flatly: "I do not think Miłosz is a Great Artist and I would be very much surprised indeed were he to prove an enduring one". And complained, with understandable irritation: "The predominant pattern in Miłosz's commentators is the expenditure of disproportionate amounts of critical energy in explaining just why the reader *won't* be able to appreciate the poetic miracle before him but must believe it anyway".[40] (Compare also the following statement by D. J. Enright: "The difficulty with Miłosz lies less in understanding him than in establishing or recognising what one thinks or feels about him: not what the author says, but how the reader responds".[41] Donald Davie quotes several other examples in his *Czesław Miłosz and the Insufficiency of Lyric* (pp.9-10)) Yet what is an admirer to do when he cannot quote in the original language? It will be enough, to illustrate the problem, to juxtapose two English versions of a few of Miłosz's lines from a poem which is undoubtedly among his best ('Bobo's Metamorphosis'):

As life goes, quite a lot of these mornings.
My eyes closed, I was grown up and small.
I was wearing plumes, silks, ruffles and armor,
Women's dresses, I was licking rouge.
I was hovering at each flower from the beginning,
I knocked on the closed doors of the beaver's halls and the mole's
It's incredible that there were so many unrecorded voices
Between a toothpaste and a rusted blade,
Just over my table in Wilno, Warsaw, Brie, Montgeron, California.
It's incredible that I die before I attain.[42]

So many mornings for a single lifetime.
With my eyes shut, I was both great and small,
I wore plumes, silks, ruffles, armour,
Women's dresses, licked rouge.
From the beginning hovering over every flower,
Knocking on the closed doors of the halls of beaver and mole;

Unthinkable, so many voices left unrecorded
Between the tube of toothpaste and the rusted razor blade,
Bending over a table in Wilno, Warsaw, Brie, Montgeron,
California.
Unthinkable, that I should die without fulfilment.[43]

The reader can choose the version he or she prefers. The point is that the two versions are certainly very different in the way in which they attempt to recreate in English the effect of Miłosz's original lines.

Above everything else, Czesław Miłosz is a master of the full poetic line ("One recognizes good poetry by being able to detach from a poem one line and appreciate its fulness.").[44] One line may not sound like much form, at least in the case of some postwar poets, but most poems are made of lines, and a group of full lines would have a cumulative effect even if their only structural principle was juxtaposition. Secondly, Miłosz's lines are hardly ever very short, as is the case with Różewicz. Detaching a line from a poem by Różewicz gives us very little non-lexical structure, if any:

lies on his back

★

defenceless

★

his life[45]

Only as part of the poetic 'paragraph' (since one cannot use the term 'stanza') do the above lines become elements of form:

God fell

lies on his back
defenceless
his life
eternal
stands revealed

One could say that Różewicz's lines are often vertical, whereas Miłosz's are invariably horizontal. 'So Little', one of the few Miłosz poems written in short lines, is a good example of Miłosz's care to make even short lines as full as possible:

I said so little.
Days were short.

Short days.
Short nights.
Short years.

I said so little.
I couldn't keep up.

My heart grew weary
From joy,
Despair,
Ardour,
Hope.[46]

Even when the line becomes vertical, as in the last part of the fragment, the punctuation marks alert us to syntax. Lineation in Miłosz is seldom an exclusive line-forming device. Miłosz's lines are either complete syntactic units, or distinct parts of complete syntactic units, and their fulness is the result of his mastery over syntax and phrasing. It is the inner organisation of syntactic units that constitutes the basic pleasure of his use of language. But the care expanded on each line and each sentence is not purely aesthetic or formal: everything which goes into the making of a line or sentence affects its meaning.

A short prose obviously meant to serve as the poet's own epitaph gives the metaphysical, or perhaps religious, reason:

> To find my home in one sentence, concise, as if hammered in metal. Not to enchant anybody. Not to earn a lasting name in posterity. An unnamed need for order, for rhythm, for form, which three words are opposed to chaos and nothingness.[47]

It should be noted that this brief statement bears underneath the following information: "Berkeley-Paris-Cambridge, Massachusetts, 1981-1983", which is meant to underline the work that went into its "hammering". Furthermore, it is highly revealing that order, rhythm and form are invoked in connection with some ideal sentence, and not with any higher-level structure. And even more revealingly, the passage speaks of "one sentence" only as being perfectly sufficient for the poet's home, which clearly cannot be the desire of a poet *qua* poet and this interpretation of the passage is reinforced by the statements that neither poetic enchantment nor fame are the goal. That goal can only be some final truth, gnosis. Achieving *such* a sentence "as if hammered in metal" would, indeed, be tantamount to fulfilling the need for order, rhythm and form at a level deeper than what is left for smaller men (and Miłosz includes himself in this particular instance among them):

> A feast of brief hopes, a rally of the proud,
> A tournament of hunchbacks, literature.[48]

Examples of Miłosz's attention to syntactic structure could be given at will. Miłosz is the author of a number of single-line poems and distichs, which he simply calls "sentences", rather than "maxims" or "aphorisms", possibly because some of them have a lyrical quality, and while a few are, most are not didactic. These "sentences" invariably exhibit taut inner structure as well as a distinct intonational contour. A fair number of Miłosz's longer poems have substantial sections of unistichs of remarkable poetic beauty; other poems are composed of long versets that undoubtedly derive from the Bible (and especially the Psalms, which Miłosz has splendidly translated into modern Polish), Whitman and Oscar de Milosz (who thought that poetry would again one day become "freely flowing prose forged into versets"[49]); there are also numerous poems in which syntactic units are subordinated to over-arching structures of versification, argument or rhetorical effect, or become fluid and even loose under the impact of incantatory rhythm: yet in such instances, too, Miłosz's syntax retains a quality of its own.

I must resist the temptation to give examples of the verset-type lines, or of the treatment of syntax in poems with a clear overall structure, as there is not only a great variety of them, but a profusion of excellence. Some are dithyrambic, others gnomic or aphoristic, some are stylised as hieratic speech, others have a colloquial touch; there is poignant lyricism, philosophic reflection, pithy judgment, irony, wry humour, masterful description, vivid evocation, imagistic epiphany, prophetic ardour and gnostic oracularity, all enclosed in individually wrought syntactic structures that compel attention and modulate receptivity with their power, tautness, authority, limpidity, clarity, distinctive intonation and other characteristics that only a detailed discussion of examples in the original Polish would show, although much of their quality comes out remarkably well in the English translations, as is the case with the opening unistichs from the already mentioned 'Bobo's Metamorphosis':

> Sloping fields, and a trumpet.
>
> ★
>
> Twilight. A bird flies low, and waters flash.
>
> ★
>
> Daybreak unfurls the sails beyond the narrows.
>
> ★
>
> I was entering a lily along a bridge of gold brocade.
>
> ★
>
> Life was a gift but unattainable.
>
> ★
>
> From childhood till old age ecstasy at sunrise.[50]

One other feature of Miłosz's style on the level of micro-structure should be noted, as it goes to the heart of his poetics. Being, unlike English, an inflected language, Polish allows considerable flexibility in the order of words. Miłosz's use of this flexibility is characteristic: except for the early poems driven by rhythm, the sequencing of words in Miłosz poems not only avoids structural ambiguity (e.g. inversion) and is careful not to transgress against the rules of euphony (while eschewing the more blatant kinds of sound instrumentation), but is additionally governed by what may be called the principle of denotational, and more broadly, semantic space, whose aim is evocative mimesis and conceptual clarity. "A word", says Miłosz in 'From the Rising of the Sun', "should be contained in every single thing/ But it is not. So what then of my vocation?"[51] Elsewhere he says: "As for me, I have always, I don't know why, in a sort of impulsive way, taken the side of extreme realism . . . There is horseness, and there is a horse. The latter is a realization of the former. But I am not saying this too seriously."[52] In poetry, however, Miłosz behaves precisely as an "extreme realist, even as far as the realism of St. Thomas Aquinas", since to be a poet means "to approach the mystery of existence more directly than through mere concepts".[53] The world is, things are, individual beings exist:

> Shout, blow the trumpets, make thousand-strong marches, leap,
> rend your clothing, repeating only: *is*![54]

In this ecstasy over the actuality of being the primary level is ontological revelation, which manifests itself by repeated attempts "at naming the world". And so just as things are surrounded by space (however a particular thing is constituted as a separate entity), so the words that name them should be given a space of their own, in an unceasing epiphany of reality. Another way of making the same observation is to say that Miłosz consistently keeps his poetry close to the mode of referential speech in contradistinction to the category of linguistic construct or autonomous language. Not interested in creating poetic anti-worlds, and generally scornful of mere literariness, at times even capable of shuddering at the thought of "Odious rhythmic speech/ Which grooms itself and, of its own accord, moves on . . . "[55] Miłosz may be said to have in common with Różewicz, as well as with Herbert, the intense dislike of writing "just another poem", but he differs from them substantially not only in his readiness to use more fully the resources of natural language but also in his compulsion to "bring to life a ship in the bay a peacock a rose", although his way of doing this again places him closer to Różewicz (though less so to Herbert) in that he is very sparing of metaphor, preferring such more prosaic tropes as metonymy and synecdoche, as well as direct naming. If one were to translate the above observations into semiotic terms, one might say that Miłosz attempts to correct the deficiency whereby things do not have their signifiers in them by reducing as much as possible the undesirable consequences of the systemic (as distinct from the semantic) character of language: not only are signifiers given positional space in syntactic structure, but the metonymic nature of the imagery situates their signifieds, as it were, in their natural/ mimetic spatial environment with the effect that the signified loses its pure conceptuality and thus, if one may be permitted a paradox, has its absence both increased and attenuated. But while the technique of making things and their contiguities as existent as possible may vary, the general tendency is invariably not to foreground the sign itself but what it stands for:

> What is pronounced strengthens itself.
> What is not pronounced tends to nonexistence.[56]

It would be wrong to leave the impression that Miłosz's mastery over micro-structure and poetic diction is not matched by his command over larger units of form (poetic paragraph, stanza, short poem, long poem, cycle of poems). There are in his *opus* poems that are breath-taking in their rythmic development and climactic closure; there are superbly sustained verse compositions as well as brilliantly crafted poetic arguments; there are poems that sing (which Miłosz sometimes recited as songs) and poems that resound with deftly orchestrated trumpets and zithers; there are Miłoszian poetic treatises and his equivalents of haiku; in short, there is richness, variety and perfection at that level also. But Miłosz's insistence that poetry should not disregard the nature of its medium (neither pure sound, nor shape) has prevented him from pursuing formal perfection beyond a certain limit, and at the expense of his principally discursive and metonymic modes; hence what is sometimes called inner form is not a hallmark of Miłosz's poetry, except at the level of syntax. Moreover, in his later writings Miłosz chose quite consciously to loosen his compositional form: the long poem 'From the Rising of the Sun' contains highly heterogenous matter (prose commentary, extracts from documents, quotations in several languages, etc.), and the heterogeneity of the volume *The Seperate Notebooks* has led a critic in Poland (Ryszard Nycz) to classify the work as a "contemporary *silva*".[57] It could almost be said that Miłosz preferred poetry to be a reflection of beauty rather than a substitute for it, the more so as his lips "praised on their own, on their own the feet ran;/ The heart beat strongly; and the tongue proclaimed its adoration."[58] — just as he preferred his language to evoke or lead to reality rather than pretend to self-sufficiency and an ontological status rivalling that of the non-verbal world.

Ultimately the problem of Miłosz's poetic art, as distinct from his achievements as a poet (which are no doubt very substantial), comes down to the following: a poetry, whose main motive force is the search for the real behind the real, for knowledge as distinct from *doxa*, must either allow itself to trust fully the poetic mood, rhythmic possession, and the voice coming "in an unearthly tongue"[59], and be shaped by such direct, even if only apparent, illumination or revelation, or it must be in competition with philosophic discourse. Miłosz, and this is another aspect of his major stature, is aware of the problem. At times he is almost ready to trust the poetic mood, and he states on several occasions that he has felt himself to be in the power of a daimon (and this creates a further difficulty, since "it's an exaggeration to maintain that he must be an angel"[60]; yet he also makes clear that he does not believe himself to have received special illumination.[61] At other times

Miłosz is almost ready to view himself as a philosopher ("Let us say that my philosophising is analogous to the situation of Mr. Jourdain, who didn't know that he spoke prose."[62]), but again he stops short, in the knowledge that he is, above everything else, a poet who thinks, and not a philosopher who is also a poet or who strays occasionally into poetic form, and thus certainly not a Plato, Wittgenstein, Heidegger or Quine. How, then, does he resolve his dilemma? Very interestingly, I think. Miłosz's way is, on the one hand, to trust his experience, meditate on its significance, and *say* in as pure a way as possible the thought that it has become, and, on the other hand, to try to comprehend the answers given by others to the questions to which he himself seeks an answer. He is thus, in the latter case, not "a historical poet of bleak illumination" (a rather lame formula, anyway), but, though of course not exclusively, a modern poet of those moments of historical consciousness which appear, at least to him, to impart illumination. Nor is he, at the same time, a poet of single, unified belief, doctrine or philosophical outlook (though Manichean poisons certainly circulate more insistently than anything else in his system), but of admitted and unresolved contradictions and of unceasing reflexivity, appropriation and gloss on appropriation, approximation, distancing and reconsideration, which means, among other things, that while Miłosz's poetry may be annoying at times, given the gravity and the pervasiveness of its *singularis maiestaticus*, it is almost never uninteresting. Moreover, there is no mistaking of how profoundly human (and that means also comical) are the complexities of the authorial personality behind the authorial *persona* and the relations, if one may put it that way, between them:

> The young man was cleverly constructed.
> He was inhabited by a vulgar and lunatic ego.
> He demanded love, admiration, the murmurs of praise . . . [63]
>
> ★
>
> Confess, you have hated your body,
> Loving it with unrequited love. It has not fulfilled
> Your high expectations. As if you were chained to
> Some little animal in perpetual unrest,
> Or worse, to a madman, and a Slavic one at that.[64]
>
> ★
>
> My lord, I loved strawberry jam
> And the dark sweetness of a woman's body.

Also well-chilled vodka, herring in olive oil,
Scents, of cinnamon, of cloves.
So what kind of a prophet am I? Why should the spirit
Have visited such a man? Many others
Were justly called, and trustworthy.
Who would have trusted me? For they saw
How I emptied glasses, throw myself on food,
And glance greedily at the waitress's neck.
Flawed and aware of it. Desiring greatness,
Able to recognise greatness wherever it is,
And yet not quite, only in part, clairvoyant . . . [65]

*

Now there is nothing to lose, my cautious, my cunning, my hyper-selfish cat.

Now we can make confession, without fear that it will be used by mighty enemies.

We are an echo that runs, skittering through a train of rooms . . . [66]

5. Aleksander Wat's Poetry of Experience

Miłosz had high praise for the poetry of Wat, whom he had befriended in the last years of his pain-ridden life, whose dramatic (not to say demonised) autobiography he helped to record and publish[67], and whose poems he translated into English. He held Wat's poetry in high regard because it was not nihilistic, despite its character of an almost "stenographic record of suffering".[68] Moreover, it had scope, "the scope which was being destroyed both by the 'purity' of the lyric as well as by verbosity", for it ranged in form "from the laments of a biblical prophet to the nearly mathematical wit of gnomic maxims". He also noted that the poems of Wat fascinated "the young people in Berkeley and San Francisco" (and these were the flower children and anti-Vietnam protesters of the mid-1960's and early 1970's), because they were *zany*, but, he typically added, not only because of that: "In reality . . . these young readers are attracted by something which is rather rare in the sad buffoonery of contemporary *zany* literature — what attracts them is the weight of content, the interest in the experienced truth".[69]

Is Wat, then, a lesser Miłosz, whom his early dadaist phase (Mayakovsky apparently called him "a born futurist") fortunately saved from being too much like Miłosz, thanks to the *zaniness* into which it transmuted itself forty years and incredible experiences later?

No, Wat is different from Miłosz in more ways than one, and although he is not as major a poet as Miłosz, he is very much a poet in his own right. Wat does not equal Miłosz either in the size of his *opus* or in the degree of systematic reflection that went into its unfolding. As will be remembered, there is a hiatus of over twenty years in Wat's poetic career, and his later work, although comprising well over a hundred poems, including several longer pieces, has the appearance of a fitful development and unstudied fragmentariness, even sketchiness. At the same time, there is a linguistic inventiveness in Wat, a capacity for poetic flashes of striking imagery and brilliant turn of phrase, for telling deformation, grotesque, queer or quaint, and sharp wit which are rare in Miłosz. If Miłosz is contemporary *with* modernism, with surrealism and the various forms of the literature of the absurd, of naked poetry, *turpism* and the poetry of violence, principally by opposition, because he is concerned to safeguard the dignity and clarity of speech and the voice of affimation, Wat is part *of* modernity, its idiom and its discordancies. He may not be a nihilist, but his experiences have engendered in him such a radical pessimism as to the ability of the human mind to cope with reality, as well as the conviction that "there is no bottom to evil"[70], that it has led him to embrace, fitfully, doubtingly, yet with outbursts of great fervour, not only religious faith (he became a Catholic while in the Soviet Union), but evident superstition (as he did at one point in Italy, in the hope of finding a miraculous cure for his sickness).[71] Nor did he try to make his poetry filter out, or compose into balanced periods his experiences of the terrors, the cruelties, the inconsistencies and incoherencies, and the sheer paltriness of the human condition:

> Heavy testes force them to genuflect,
> they are so grand. Clad in scarlet,
> they play chess. Unceasing tournaments.
> Though the clock from afar strikes their hours,
> and this bell of time falls heavily, depressing.
> "It's gravity," says the physicist.
> "It's levitation," says the metaphysician,
> who has been observing for quite a while a cockroach, which ran
> out
> into the middle of the hall and stopped there as if paralysed,

lost in its metaphysical contemplations . . . *A batons rompus*,
we have been talking of chess:
"Metonymy," said an admirer of Romie Jakobson.
"Metaphor," said Peiper's disciple.
And got so heated up that they are fighting.
While I am merely watching from behind the window-pane,
also, after all, a contender, but too old
to take part in their disputes. And, by God, about what?
For metonymy? For metaphor? Against?
I went back home, to have lunch, without even having some coffee,
which, to tell the truth, is here pretty lousy.[72]

★

"Blood, blood, blood,"
he grated angrily. Adriana got up: "I wanted, master,
to sit at your feet and imbibe the words of wisdom from your
lips. And now . . . " she sobbed, poor, dear Adriana. "Blood,
of blood, with blood," repeated the turtle, obviously unable to
stop.
"You gulped the blood of my cousins, is not that enough? Seizing
them in whole droves in the bulrushes by the river Ili, crushing
and smashing them with a roller on the rough table in the kitchen
of the Prokombinat where you helped the boorish woman cook
to steal food. The blood of my brothers splashed into your eyes,
bespattered your face, your rags, you waded in their blood, still
you had not enough. You have never had enough. Not enough. Not
enough.
Not enough . . . "[73]

Wat's poems are not embarassed to speak with the voice of untransmuted feelings, of horror, disgust, rebellion, pain, anger, wrath, solidarity with fellow human beings, sheer misery, compassion and love, which in his poems is in fact broader than the Miłoszian Eros hungry for the body of the world, or lusting for the sexual act in the glory of male potency, for it desperately needs the touch that momentarily cancels the void and quietens pain, and knows of otherness not only as a metaphysical problem, or as actual separateness, but also in its, however partial, transcendence. If in Miłosz images of "dark triangles of hair," of "convexities of silk," of glances under skirts, of copulation on grass, in thick woods, or high up in a New York skyscraper (like "the mating of birds/ Without intent, reflection,/ Over the splendour of autumn dogwoods and maples") tend to outweigh the expressed desire to learn "some compassion for us people, some goodness/ And, simply, tenderness, dear Y.Z.,"[74] In Wat the image of "Eros with the torch pointing downwards"[75] speaks of the reality of those manifestations of love which arise from vulnerability and weakness, and are personal rather than 'natural'.

It is altogether interesting to observe how certain basic experiences, or lack of them, have influenced the poetic perspective and sensibility of the major post-war Polish poets. Różewicz was a member of a Polish partisan unit which operated against the Germans out of the forests, and while he has not told us whether he shot to kill, he saw death at close quarters and all round him. Herbert experienced both the Soviet and the German occupations, he spent some time in a Soviet jail, and also fought in the Resistance; during the peak years of Stalinism he refused to compromise even slightly his anti-communist stand: he did not publish at all, withdrew from the Union of Writers and eked out a living as best he could, which was at times close to bare subsistence.[76] Miłosz experienced fear and watched from fairly close both the agony of the Warsaw Ghetto and of the Warsaw Uprising, but he did not join the active Resistance; he opposed Socialist Realism, but collaborated with the Communist rulers until the end of 1950, and then chose freedom. Wat spent five full years in Soviet prisons and in exile, and these experiences permeate his entire sensibility and outlook:

> Work is a blessing.
> I tell you that, I — professional sluggard!
> Who slobbered in so many prisons! Fourteen!
> And in so many hospitals! Ten! And innumerable inns!
> Work is a blessing.
> How else could we deal with the lava of fractricidal love towards
> fellow men?
> With those storms of extermination of all by all?
> With brutality, bottomless and measureless?
> With the black and white era which does not want to end
> endlessly repeating itself *da capo* like a record
> forgotten on a turntable
> spinning by itself?
> Or perhaps someone invisible watches over the phonograph?
> Horror![77]

Wat's experience of the consequences of what he calls "fratricidal love" embraces not only the public but also the private sphere:

> This night, well after midnight
> P.B. dropped by.

> This time in the shape of an earth-worm,
> 4 meters 20 centimeters long, I took the measurements
> at a glance. And my room
> barely measures 3 meters across.
> So he contracted
> like a spring pressed by a finger.
> And then he started coiling around me, unhastily,
> in measured movements. Tighter and tighter.
> I felt through his soft hairs his vertebrae
> hard like unvulcanised rubber. I did not shout,
> though it was painful.
> After all: what he does he does for the love of me.[78]

Pressed on every side, and scampering

> (To be a mouse. Preferably a field mouse. Or a garden
> mouse — but not the kind that live in houses.
> Man exhales an abominable smell!)[79]

Between metaphysical and psychological horror, between physical and intellectual pain, Wat fills the poetic space left him with a great variety of forms, among them odes, Hölderlinian, dialectical, nightmarish, witty, and surreal at the same time, parables, gnomic maxims, actual and imagined, whispered tape-recordings, and occasional lyrics or lyrical passages that pierce through the *lumen obscurum* of his other poems with momentary brightness, as if to exemplify the claim he once made in a poem addressed to a friend:

> Believe me, in myself
> I contain my whole self as a bright point.
> Even transparent.[80]

Wat's diction, turns of phrase and inflexion derive both from demotic speech with its idiomatic richness as well as from the speech of the intelligentsia with its various jargons, erudite and ideological, from the Bible as well as from Nietzsche and Dostoyevsky, but there is no attempt to fuse the disparate registers, styles and layers and forge a synthetic or stereophonic voice in which they all are modulated. On the contrary, constant contrast, sudden shifts of tone, clashes of registers, make this poetry dynamic and intellectually dramatic, and even if the long versets do at times get tiresome in the longer poems, the tone is never pontificating or pompous. As in Herbert and Miłosz ("What I'm saying here is not, I agree, poetry", though the statement is probably not meant to apply outside the context of *Ars Poetica?*), one finds in Wat a sense of dissatisfaction with his way of writing:

> And I don't want to write the way I write. I would want to write
> beautifully, with clarity, in the sacred manner, *à la Bach*.
> And in despair that I don't know how to, I jot down this poem
> the way a grass-snake would write
> imprisoned in a jug with milk. At other times:
> the way a crab would write
> when it is pulled out from a basket by the old hand of a black
> woman.
> That's how my fate has arranged it.[81]

Writing the way a crab or a grass-snake would write finding themselves in unnatural, perilous circumstances is indeed a far cry from Leśmian's flower writing the poetry of its unfolding on a nearby leaf. But only perhaps if we conceive the flower 'poetically'. For shouldn't a grass-snake in a jug filled with milk by an experimentally-minded boy, or a crab feeling a dark hand taking it out from a basket, write the poetry of their experience? Wouldn't sacred, dignified, beautifully arranged words, poems "*à la Bach*", syntax hammered in metal, jar by their inappropriateness (which is, after all, an aesthetic category), or, though that is no doubt a lesser evil, be an unnecessarily easy prey for prying 'deconstruction'?

"Rhythm," wrote Leśmian in 1915, "is recurrent and repeatable and this constitutes its joyfulness. The moment sin and crime enter Art's territory, they immediately cease being sinful and criminal."[82] Such transformations occur in Wat inasmuch as the grotesque can be said to delay the realisation of horror, as in this poem entitled 'Easter':

> In a two-horse carriage
> an old Orthodox Jew
> wearing a top hat
> is riding from a synagogue
> rocks and says to himself:
> I am king, I am king, I am king.
>
> Men line the streets
> Women look out of windows
> Children hang garlands of flowers
> Policemen kneel on the pavement

Suddenly the hand of Yahweh
pulls the top hat off his head
and crowns him with a crown of thorns.
Whereupon the old Orthodox Jew
rides in his two-horse carriage
straight to the gate of heaven.

Columns of smoke over the city
Garlands of hanging children
Women lie on the pavement
Policemen line the streets[83]

And in a few crystalline lyrics, of which the following is perhaps the best example:

On a rock of basalt
Hammered into sea-waves
Over celadon waters

A golden statuette:
Maiden Medea
Stands in the wind.

Her hands raised
Not in prayer
But with their palms
Turned to the sun.

So that the fate-chiromancer
Lurking in the ether
May know without hesitation
What he will do to her.[84]

Yet if one were to choose a Wat equivalent of the Miłoszian "sentence as if hammered in metal", one would probably choose one "written as if on skin':

I measured with the skin the uncounted dimensions of time-space, probed with the skin the flights of youth and the falls of the age of defeat.

To be in the skin, in every skin, in every skin of every human, in yellow skin, white skin, black skin and red skin, and that shorn of flesh;

with the skin — I shouted — O reformers! let us begin with the skin, or, differently, O mortals! with the holy — I shouted — command of the covenant "I : you";

and so nothing that had to do with the skin was alien to me, nothing of its perishable matter, ravaged by time and rape, nothing of its indestructible energy. And pure, despite all its erosions and shame.[85]

6. The Poetic Otherworld of Bolesław Leśmian

What did I really want to tell them? That I laboured to transcend my place and time, searching for the Real. And here is my work done (commendably?), my life fulfilled, as it was destined to be, in grief. Now I appear to myself as one who was under the delusion of being his own while he was the subject of a style.[86]

This is of course Miłosz with his indefatigably reflexive ('river of consciousness') intelligence considering his *opus* from some vantage point in the future, how it would congeal into a style, blend with his epoch. Yet he could have remembered Leśmian, who already to his contemporaries seemed to belong to a spent epoch, to a period style, and one at that which appeared ridiculous, even revolting with its poeticisms, concepts and symbols that were fast becoming obsolete ("soul", "reverie", "the deep", "abyss", "caress", "rose", "infinity" and all its synonyms), its unnatural, stylised diction, its thematics, which seemed to some to substitute emotional and metaphysical blackmail (Death, God, the Ineffable, Sin, Lust, Nature, Nostalgia) for poetic originality and true lyricism, and its frequently traditional versification. Few critics noticed how Leśmian's poetry stood out in its originality against this background while superficially appearing to have so much in common with it. And some of those who did recognise Leśmian's distinctiveness, found it a further reason to question his achievement. A highly influential critic of poetry and specialist in versification (who was also a dashing cavalry officer) wrote in 1937:

Leśmian's versification is astounding, while at the same time it often appears artificial, forced, reminiscent of the versification of those poets who lack the talent for versifying: the sequence of words is unnatural; the imagery is entangled . . . , words are strangely deformed — if these are neologisms, then they seem to have been concieved not so much as a result of the poet's loving relationship with language but rather as a test-tube concoction of a

> gloomy alchemist. Their use can best be explained by the requirements of rhythm and rhyme. Here we can perhaps see what largely causes the "strangeness" and grotesqueness of his poetry . . . [87]

Indeed, Leśmian's diction still gives the impression of being strange and unnatural; his neologisms still appear forced and concocted (though quite a few of his unusual words are not neologisms, but archaisms or dialecticisms), or "deliberately slapdash" (as Artur Sandauer called his style), or a distinction is made between "a nonchalantly neologistic fantasy style" and "an exact style that carefully traces the contours of nature" (as Paul Coates put it).[88] What is less readily recognised is the functional character of Leśmian's apparently warped use of language.

In the first place, there was nothing unusual in Leśmian's experimentation with word-formation and morphology in general, or in his use of archaic, regional and dialectal words; on the contrary, it was very much in the spirit of the period: one need only mention Khlebnikov among the Russian poets, the tendency toward extreme stylisation among Polish prose writers in the years preceding the First World War, and the dadaist-futurist experiments of the immediate post-war period. But, secondly, what distinguished Leśmian from many of these attempts at stylistic distinctiveness or lingusitic autonomy was the primarily semantic motivation of his strange usage and neologic inventiveness, the need to find an appropriate idiom for his metaphysical vision, on the one hand, and on the other, the deliberate mimetic-symbol extension of actual deformity or unformedness into linguistic structure, thus exemplifying the creative principle at work in humanity and nature. But his neologisms were definitely not, as Paul Coates asserts, "fetish words", that sought "to restore the penis, the power of fecundation, to the castrated body of language: to the Polish language emasculated by the partitioning powers, and to the poetic language of Romanticism, cheapened by a century's blind repetitions".[89] The explanation, while modish, is merely fanciful: it not only wants to have it every possible way by homologising immanent poetic change, external factors, and depth psychology into a unified interpretive conundrum, but does so in an a-historical fashion, ignoring some fairly well known facts, such as the relative paucity of neologisms in Leśmian's poetry written before roughly 1905, and the quite "virile" or "fecund" state of Polish literary activity both in the Russian part of Poland (where the restrictions of censorship considerably eased after 1905), and under Austrian rule, where Polish literature could develop quite freely at least since the 1860s, as well as the already mentioned general tendency to experiment with language.[90] Coates' imagery would, however, make more sense if he had homologised it with Leśmian's distinction between *natura naturata* and *natura naturans*, although there is no simple identification in Leśmian of the procreative activity and Life-Gale, his Polish equivalent of Bergson's *l'élan vital*.

If there is a 'nonchalance' in Leśmian's style (and anyone who has tried to translate him will have examples at the ready not just of real difficulties of rendering his verse, but of moments of irritation at the seemingly 'unnecessary' complexity of syntax, parenthesis or qualification), then it is not so much a matter of his coinages as of the ease with which he fills his lines and stanzas to their required lengths with what may be described as the formulaic elements of his poetics. From the point of view of Miłoszian intonational-structural tautness, or Różewicz's austerity, such 'fillers' appear as empty, just as the complexities of syntax must at times be regarded as being governed solely by the requirements of rhythmic composition. There is thus a price that even an excellent poet will pay for working in a particular convention and poetics (and in Leśmian this price is semantic redundance).

As the above remarks amply illustrate, Leśmian has remained a controversial poet, and this is borne out by the critical literature devoted to his poetry, not only in Polish (which is now considerable and often very penetrating, to mention only the work of J. Sławiński, M. Głowiński, I. Opacki, Maria Podraza-Kwiatkowska and C. Rowiński), but also in English and French.[91] What makes writing about him for English-speaking readers even more challenging is the fact that no one has yet succeeded in rendering more than a couple of his poems into even remotely comparable English.

In his *The History of Polish Literature*, Czesław Miłosz defined what he called "Leśmian's central problem" as that "of a man who is a born worshipper, *homo adorans*, in perpetual need of contact with God; yet that God is so weak that he seems to depend on the worshipper for his very existence. Or to put it another way, the existence of man and nature is a function of the existence of God and *vice versa*, but both are illusory. Perhaps only man-as-poet maintains both through his creative act". And he went on: "Superficially, Leśmian is mostly fascinated with nature, [which] stands for continuous transformation, since its very essence is a passage from shape to shape, from existence to non-existence. Bucolic images are put to a perverse use, and beneath is the tremor of a religious mind deprived of religion and forced to cope with that lack."[92]

Two things are of immediate interest in this apt characterisation of a poet who, in Miłosz's view, "should be ranked with the greatest figures of modern European literature": firstly, the extent to which Leśmian's "central problem" is defined in Miłoszian terms, and, secondly, how, at the same time, the really significant parallel, and contrast, between his poetry and Leśmian's fails to be brought out. For both are in a very significant way poets of the ontological theme, as is immediately apparent from the fact that both have felt it necessary to reflect in poetic form on Bishop Berkeley's principle of *esse est percipi*: Miłosz's stanza from 'The World'

> Some say that our eyes deceive us,
> That there is nothing, but just seems to be,
> But it is people like these who lack hope.
> They think that wnen you turn your back,
> The world behind you ceases to exist,
> As if a thief had snatched it.[93]

parallels quite closely Leśmian's poem 'Unbelief':

> What happens to the whole world
> When it has vanished from my eyes?
>
> Does it, when I have shut my eyelids tight,
> Snatch the brief moment to transform its charm,
> Worn out with throbbing and with tears,
> Into mere shadows? . . .
>
> No, no! It still endures by your side,
> Mortal, luxuriant!
> Here, where your dread is, and your unbelief,
> And watchful dreaming![94]

but even the juxtaposition of two short excerpts is sufficient to suggest how different the treatment of the theme must be in the two poets. One does not find in Leśmian, for instance, Miłosz's concern over the disappearance from things of their 'materiality' and the disposession of space of its objects;[95] he is not a 'materialist' or a 'somatist', since for him reality is a metamorphic continuum characterised by innumerable gradations of being, all of which are of intense interest to him as a poet; with those entities whose degree of existence is the weakest or most transitory, or whose form appears botched, unfinished or deformed, having a special claim to attention for precisely those reasons, as well as because the weakest ontological status may be said to be existentially especially tantalising. Moreover, not only is there in Leśmian's world constant transformation of one thing into another, but there is also a far-reaching dependency of individual existents as well as forms or levels of being upon one another, which is quite distinct from Miłosz's sense of quiddity. Leśmian's poetic reality is full of existential drama, of active, toilsome, heroic beingness, of arrested effort to come into, and futile resistance to the departure from the sphere of fuller existence, in which the tragic is also graded, depending on the degree of self-consciousness, with God being, paradoxically, the most tragic of all entities, next only to man, the more so as his ontological status seems to depend directly on the strength or weakness of the belief invested in him by human beings. Hence Leśmian's poetic reality is not only literally 'unfinished' but paradoxically gives the impression of being less 'real' than Miłosz's; in fact, it is quite phantasmagoric in comparison, more like a field of throbbing energy assuming various shapes and modes than a relationship of individual things firmly set in space (and in that sense may be said to be more 'modern'). It is characteristic that while Leśmian continued to the very end to "examine the possibility of a dream different from the dream of existence" (as his fascinating poem 'Elijah' shows),[96] though with an increasingly poignant sense of the reality of personal death, Miłosz found himself compelled to admit defeat in the face of a similar aspiration:

> I tried to imagine another earth and could not.
> I tried to imagine another heaven and could not.[97]

One of the earliest statements of the ontological theme occurs in Leśmian's poem 'The Green Hour' (written before 1910), which in addition to the important motif (and concept) of reflexivity as a phenomenon pervading all entities ("Every thing sees and is seen. Everything plenifies/ With the magic of mutual reflection.")[98], contains also his first multiple image of intentionality (called by some critics animism, or anthropomorphisation)[99] transferred onto the natural world and beyond it:

> A fern casts a nenuphar shade, whose faint flower
> Holds the memory of water whispering in the wake
> Of a boat with a butterfly which drank of its ripple.
>
> A willow spreads on grass the shape known to mists
> Of a girl that is wandering somewhere through the gardens
> That are played on a reed-pipe in somebody's dream.
>
> Near an oak in a slanted ellipsis stands looming
> The shadow of a nameless hut open to sunrays
> Which one day will replace here its uprooted trunk . . .
>
> And from my figure, which I see in day-dream,
> Spreads at my feet and suddenly falls upon the flowers
> God's shadow — an excessive, agitated shape.[100]

The fascination of Leśmian's poetry, its poetic as well as intellectual appeal, lie above everything else in the quality and inventiveness (linguistic, structural and mythopoeic) of his imagination as it reveals itself in the treatment of the ontological, and more broadly, of the metaphysical theme. Leśmian's work comprises other types of poems: excellent love lyrics, considered by some as his unquestionable masterpieces, ballads that reinterpret, often in a highly original or perverse fashion, Scandinavian and Polish folk motifs as well as classical and literary myths and *topoi*, and can in turn be interpreted as exemplifying 'Freudian' elements of Leśmian's psyche (although that approach can be misleading, and has been exaggerated)[101], and the distinct group of poems which deal with the theme of the re-intergration of man and nature, such as the frequently anthologised 'The Man Who Drowned in the Green', or the long poem 'Meadow', which narrates in ecstatic stanzas and imagery derived from epithalamia and idylls, but in characteristic Leśmianesque diction, the visit paid the poet by an 'actual' meadow in his modest, but festively adorned house. He also wrote a number of tales (mainly in prose), which present a variety of themes (from love to magic and exoticism), and whose generic character is mixed, including elements of fairy-tale, adventure story, legend, and folk yarn.[102] But the metaphysical theme, even if secondary, or incidental, is evident in almost everything Leśmian wrote, at least indirectly, though always suggestively.

It may take, for instance, the form of an epistemological image, which is so blended with the narrative or descriptive mode that it may be easily overlooked, and certainly does not disrupt the more superficial level at which Leśmian's tales, as well as some poems, can be read. In the 'Polish fairy-tale' *Podlasiak* (Man-by-the-Forest) two travellers decide to rest in a forest:

> But to tell the truth and looking at the essence of it from the point of view of some ruthlessly third person, one should rather surmise that they rested not in the forest itself, but in what other people call "the sight of the forest", having in mind not so much the forest as such than their own eyes.[103]

The theme often surfaces as a reflection on the nature and paradox of time. In the love poem 'Our throbbings have met at the lips', the treatment of the theme is humorous, while being typical of a baroque ('metaphysical') conceit:

> The sun looks at our spirits, unwanted in heaven . . .
> As on living sun-dials, where the hour of love
> Is shown by the moving shadows of cornflowers.
> Our hands . . .
> In their clasp have crushed our mortality,
> Freed of time, freed of partings.
> And yet time has returned. I can hear
> The call of death
> As it leads a troop of spirits upwards.
> Yet its call will be in vain.
> For I cannot die now.[104]

The existential drama may take the form of an urge to existence at a higher ontological level, as in the 'Uninhabited Ballad', where a might-have-been girl is unable to become:

> At the edge, under fool's parsley, something godlike stirred:
> Maiden mist desiring human lips and eyes.
> You could feel her desparate urge to become, to incarnate,
> Shine just once a golden tress, flash the white of breasts.
> You could feel her struggling forth like a heaving, suffering womb,
> Till she lost all strength for ever — and subsided unbecome.
> But the place of that might-have-been went on being, went on
> rustling,
> A place fragrant for that body, a space empty for that soul.[105]

I have quoted Paul Coates' characterisation of one of Leśmian's modes of writing as "an exact style that carefully traces the contours of nature." There are, indeed, descriptive poems in Leśmian's repertoire, but the description is almost never picturesque or painterly. Leśmian's descriptions usually exhibit a fascination with active existence as do his narrative poems, and their mood is that of total visual entrancement. In the excellent poem 'Remembrance', which takes us to Leśmian's childhood years in the Ukraine (where his metaphysical romance with verdure began), the remembered vision is characterised first as a form of almost organic inner awareness rooted in absolute familiarity:

> I would see everything and almost nothing,
> Knowing the whole road as if blindly,
> Since I would follow it as much in myself
> As without myself.

— and only then becomes intensely focussed, not on the landscape, but on the inner life of a meadow:

> Then I would stretch myself across the grass
> To study stealthily and with curiosity
> The familiar meadow, looked at from below,
> Which, understanding such a moment's meaning
> Of its own accord would open its thickness
> To show me how the shadow of a butterfly
> Fell on the flowers later than its wings;
> And how a bumble-bee in tiger fur
> Loomed like a giant, sparkling on a flower,
> Entering it now from this, and now from that direction;
> How through the poppy's darkling scarlet
> A beetle, hiding slyly in its fragrant centre,
> Showed through, a darker and mobile smudge;
> And how a groggy frog, raising its eyeballs
> Circled with yellow rings towards the sky,
> Inhaled with short and rapid gasps . . . .
> The smell of earth.[106]

Catching nature *in actu essendi* can have in Leśmian's poetry the character of witnessing a miracle, the more so as the fact of the witness's own existence is also, in such passages, witnessed by whatever part of nature is within his vision, so that the asserted reciprocity functions as an indication of the primal unity of all creation and thus of the possibility of that union's restoration:

And it seemed to me that all around and everywhere
With their heads as much on fire as my own,
There lay in madness similar to mine,
Silently active with a choral longing,
Beings enveloped in a simultaneous dream,
Hidden in grasses to their golden tip,
Gigantic, wondrous, ominous, erotic,
And that in their harmonious choir they saw
My face in one of the innumerable realms
Of being: an unfamiliar, stranger's face,
But similar to their faces in the burden
Of sunshine falling on the eyes
Lost in contemplation.[107]

But the act of catching being through perception in one of its manifestations has also another function: it provides the proof of the existence of what is perceived.

Now the sun penetrates with light the distant forest,
Giving the pines a secret sign of the approaching evening;
Now the pines burst aflame, as if in the depths of the forest
Something crimson had happened for ever and ever.

Enticed by that sign, I rush there immediately,
To catch at the right moment, before the night enfolds me,
In its tenuous lingering, and to verify visibly
Precisely what the trees had already seen before me.[108]

Of a number of key words in Leśmian's poetic vocabulary, two particularly crucial begin with the prefix *za*, which means 'beyond', 'meta', 'trans' (a 'period prefix', if one remembers, for instance, the Russian futurists' *zaumnyi yazyk*, that is, transrational language, or Przybyszewski's concept of the 'metaword'),[109] but which can also signify the completion of action, its plenitude or absoluteness. One of the Leśmian words with the prefix *za* is *zapatrzenie*, which I have translated as "contemplation", and which stands for enraptured visual perception "of everything at once, yet of nothing separately", and describes a state of visual saturation with Being, something analogous to a *unio mystica*. The term occurs already in some very early poems of Leśmian, but the most effective translation of the concept into image occurs in a later poem entitled 'Evening':

The sun, in its setting, drags across the meadow
A huge shadow of a cloud, pulling it over the hills
To where they touch the sky, which extends life,
Smothered with colour, deeper into dream,
Until it highlights through the empty spaces
The only crimson kerchief in all of this vastness
Of a girl, who has gathered with clasped hands
Her knees under the chin in willing togetherness,
And in this vesperal expanse and weather,
Ever so lonely under the sky's canopy,
Has for a long time now remained completely still
Both in her dream and in her posture,
Absorbing the numb magic of sheer looking
At everything at once, yet at nothing separately.[110]

The other key word is *zaświat* which I have rendered as "otherworld", rather than "the beyond", or, which would not be appropriate in the case of Leśmian, "antiworld". Leśmian did not set his poetic world in opposition to reality, but only to that part of it which he termed *natura naturata*. In that context the otherworld embraced everything that was not mundane, practical, governed by the rules of logic, solidified in form and thought, typical of the 'statistical man' or (another easily recognisable period characteristic) of the bourgeoisie.[111]

Gradually, the concept of the otherworld acquired for Leśmian a wide semantic range: by the sheer force of his poetic imagination 'the beyond' divided into innumerable worlds, each of them constituted principally in accordance with the ontological character of a given sphere of reality. Each sphere of reality, and practically each seperate world, now appeared as external relatively to other spheres of reality and other worlds: all discernible worlds became, in a relative sense, other worlds, and in the end the only world worthy of the prefix would have been the one that transcended the known universe. The poem 'Elijah', which I have already mentioned, describes the prophet's inconceivably daring journey beyond the confines of the universe of precisely such unthinkable magnitude. As he is propelled by the wind on a chariot of fire through space, he leaves behind him not only the earth and the planets, but the entire conceptual, semantic, denotational, symbolic, fancied or imagined framework of humanity:

The world, the otherworld and the soul, death and immortality,

> Everything became pale, and paltry in supernal recollection.
> Like a dream, which doesn't want to, but continues dreaming.

As the chariot continues on its way, the corpse of an angel passes by "with the scale of death in his eye", a death that "increasingly diminishes". A conversation with God ensues in which Elijah, despite his ambivalence, declines God's indirect plea not to leave the world where God has his ambiguous and contingent yet somehow real existence:

> Free, useless to God, all alone he now sailed
> Higher and more dangerously into dusk beyond heaven,
> Where there is no creation and where God is unnecessary.

And as he crossed the boundary of the universe, never to reappear in it again, there is a momentary consummation; but that is all that there is, as he is enveloped by "a numb and diligent Silencium". And so for the absolutely last time he leans out of his chariot of fire as it is flickering out

> To ascertain in the clair-voyance of his final breath
> The possibility of a dream different from the dream of Existence.[112]

But before reaching the boundary beyond which the true otherworld spreads or doesn't spread, Leśmian probed innumerable real and possible worlds and their modes of being: the world of mirrors and other kinds of reflecting media that create doubles or in multiplying images give the semblance of infinite depth (or of time frozen for ever); the world of art and the nature of its reality, nowhere more poignantly and brilliantly than in his unquestioned masterpiece, the long poem, '*Pan Błyszczyński*', that deserves to stand alongside the antiworld of Mallarmé; the world of dream; the world of intentional beings, such as literary characters (e.g. Don Quixote, Cleopatra), mythic and science-fiction figures, characters from folklore and fairy-tales, and even the products of human hands, such as 'A Doll':

> Myself — I am a doll. In my earings a rainy metaworld glitters.
> My dress in its apparent satin recollects a dream.
> I like the faience of my eyes and the sticky smell
> Of paint, enlivening with death's blush my lack-lustre cheeks.

I like lying, when the room is sunning busily,
In the crimson corner of the dressy carpet,
Where an iris beside a doe blossoms plantlessly,
And from plush eternity rise particles of dust.

I am grateful to the girl who plays with my lifelessness,
When, kidnapping my nonbeing with her hands,
She says, pink with inspiration, all that I would say,
And pretends to believe that I am alive . . . [113]

As in the quoted poem, Leśmian's principal poetic method is to spin a narrative out of each mode of existence and dramatise its particular world, so that it becomes an otherworld in a double sense, as the creation of poetic imagination and a transcendence into a particular sphere of reality, with its characterological parameters, as it were, and perspective determined by its 'essential beingness'. In this mythopoeic process, which constitutes a kind of modernist recreation of the fairy-tale (metaphysical, cosmological and theophanic), even the mode of being of corpses is imaginatively investigated and turned into a narrative since, in the world of Leśmian's imagination death does not end completely the existence of a human being, considering that the body continues to be active, and thus tells a tale. Moreover, just as for each mode of being there is a world, so for each mode of being there is a story and a virtual consciousness. When in the poem 'Bees' a swarm of bees, having taken a wrong path among the pathways of existence, flies into an underground nook, "where the corpse, instead of a roof, has nothingness over the head", all the dead in that particular "inhabitable darkness" become understandably excited. They crowd "shadow to shadow" and cry in amazement: "Look — bees! Do you remember? Definitely — bees!" But the bees sense their way back to that other world from which they have strayed, leaving behind an aroused throng that continues to gaze after them for a long time, perhaps for ever.[114] In the poem 'Cemetery', a wanderer enters a graveyard and finds there "death, grass, oblivion, and dew". But this is no ordinary graveyard for he hears underground "the flapping of sails". It is the graveyard of ships, as an inscription on a grave-stone tells him (in the somewhat free rendering by Jerzy Pietrkiewicz and Burns Singer):

I did not die by chance but through the will
Of winds that found in me an easy kill.

They promised me safe anchor in my death,
Death in that anchorage: now they break faith.
The winds persist, and shipwreck underground.
New fears, not those I lost with life, resound.
Though slack with nothingness my buried forms
Are still judged worth their steerage throughout these storms.
Who blows the wind that makes my mainsails pout?
Why is a ship, once started, always out?
I can say only that, without life, this hull,
Plods sleeplessly, and misery bakes the skull.
For more than plain endurance none can pray.
But pray for me to Mary, traveller, pray.[115]

There is no way to avoid the ontological trap, whether in language, whose negations, which Leśmian loved to use, are never devoid of at least a trace of the positive, or outside language.[116] Nor does Leśmian fail to dramatise the fact that there does not seem to be in reality a passage less intentional than imagination or ideation from one sphere of being into another. In the poem 'Country dream' (dated 1916), village girls in the poet's dream walk from the fields, and their walk is strange, as if it was meant to "prove to the one dreaming, that they are walking". The poet knows everything about them, as "usually happens in dreams, when life enters into its own story", but they, in turn, guess that his knowledge "is something different and empty". The somnambulic vision continues with hallucinatory vividness, but neither can the poet fully enter his own dream, nor can the girls leave it except by reaching its end.[117] In Leśmian's poetic summa, the long poem 'Pan Błyszczyński', God visits the wonderful garden created by the protagonist (the metaworld of art, here closest to a poetic antiworld), and while its godlike creator, Mr. O'Glimmer (as we may render his name) is anxious about the consequences of his having tried to rival God with his creative act, his real concern, one that is absolutely critical and vital, and leaves him at the end of the poem "extremely pale", is the fact that he lacks the power to dissolve ontological boundaries, being unable to make a real girl enter his garden.[118]

The increasingly pale Mr. O'Glimmer (a close relative of MacSilver from another of Leśmian's poems about poets[119]) cannot, in the end, escape the ontological trap, as he cannot inhabit the garden of his poetic creation, and must literally pale away. At best he can gain a sort of moral victory, as in the highly ironic yet ballad-like poem 'The Two Matthews', in which two simple-minded peasants find the flower of immortality in the forest, but when, returning with it to their village, they encounter God (who is here called Crygod), they give it to him on the very sensible grounds that "immortality is due to God, and God is due" to humanity.[120] Or, he may gain in a dignity that is close to deeply hurt humanistic (and perhaps Nietzschean) pride which he cannot but lose in every other possible way, by insisting, in 'In Time of the Resurrection', that there will be a human bone which "will say no to being resurrected":

> For what if the trumpet sounds in heaven
> To daze the world with a new being?
> Not every laughter can be woken up!
> Not every tear can be repeated![121]

The stanza should be juxtaposed with Miłosz's:

> Yet I belong to those who believe in *apokatastasis*.
> That word promises reverse movement . . .
> It means: restoration. So believed: St. Gregory of Nyssa,
> Johannes Scotus Erigena, Ruysbroeck and William Blake.
> For me, therefore, everything has a double existence.
> Both in time and when time shall be no more.[122]

The utter simplicity of such a gnostic distinction proved impossible to attain for Leśmian. And it left Miłosz himself despairing:

> I was judged for my despair because I was unable to understand this.[123]

7. In Lieu of a Conclusion

In one of Leśmian's tales a character says: "God! Make it happen that a sudden and unexpected fairy-tale surprises me in the forest! Let that fairy-tale be frightful and sinister, as long as it is engrossing and beautiful."[124]

Had Miłosz written similar lines, they might have run as follows: "And I, having been placed on this earth and not knowing why or by whom, ask that I may penetrate through the veil of all fairy-tales to the innermost garden of reality, so as to be able to say: I know."

And Wat could have put it still differently: "God (do not scoff!), oh God! everything began so promisingly, like a surreal fairy-tale, we set out to change words, and then suddenly a terrifying reality surprised me, full of unimaginable horrors; they said: grotesque, but it was deadly." Or instead he could have quoted a sentence of Baudelaire's (which he actually used in one of his poems as a motto) from *Un Voyage à Cythère*:

> *Ah! Seigneur! Donnez-moi la force et le courage*
> *De contempler mon coeur et mon corps sans dégoût.*

Notes

1. Zbigniew Herbert, 'Do Ryszarda Krynickiego — List', (To Ryszard Krynicki — A Letter) in *Raport z oblężonego miasta* (Paris, 1983), pp.26-27. Translation by John and Bogdana Carpenter in Zbigniew Herbert, *Report from the Besieged City* (New York, 1985) pp.21-22; I have modified some lines in both excerpts.
2. Tadeusz Różewicz, 'Zdjęciecię żaru', (They Shed the Load), in *Poezje zebrane* (Wrocław, 1971), p.508. Translation by Adam Czerniawski in Tadeusz Różewicz, *Conversation with the Prince* (London, 1982), p.95.
3. The fragment beginning with the line "The season in the *Paradis du Langage*" is from a short manifesto-like article entitled 'Sezon poetycki - Jesień 1966' ('The Poetic Season — Autumn 1966'), which was written by Różewicz in response to an announcement that a poetry festival was to be held in Vienna under the slogan: '*Die Lyrik ist nicht tot, die Lyrik kann nicht sterben!*'. It is included in a collection of Różewicz's articles and statements on poetry *Przygotowanie do wieczoru autorskiego* (Warsaw, 1971), from which come most of the other quotations. I am unable to attribute the translation of the fragment, which I have found in a lecture I once gave on Różewicz's poetry, and which may or may not be my own. See also the poem 'I Did Espy a Marvellous Monster', in *Conversation with the Prince* (pp.183-185), which ends: "at home a task/ awaits me:/ To create poetry after Auschwitz" and Czerniawski's introduction to the volume, which contains several quotations from Różewicz's writings on the situation of poetry "after Auschwitz".
4. Bolesław Leśmian, 'Pejzaż współczesny' (Contemporary Landscape), in *Poezje* (Warsaw, 1965), p.358.
5. Bolesław Leśmian, *Utwory rozproszone, listy* (Warsaw, 1962), p.326.
6. Bolesław Leśmian, 'Z rozmyślań o Bergsonie' (From Thoughts on Bergson), in *Szkice literackie* (Warsaw, 1959), p.31. See also 'Znaczenie pośrednictwa w metafizyce życia zbiorowego' (The Significance of Mediation in the Metaphysics of Social Life), 'Rytm jako światopogląd' (Rhythm as *Weltanschauung*), and 'U źródeł rytmu' (The Origin of Rhythm), *Ibid.*
7. Bolesław Leśmian, 'Z rozmyślań o poezji' (From Meditations on Poetry), *Ibid.*, p.81.

8. *Ibid.*, p.86.
9. *Ibid.*, pp. 87 and 91.
10. Aleksander Wat, 'Namopanik charuna', in *Ciemne świecidło* (Paris, 1968), p.210.
11. See Aleksander Wat's *My Century: The Odyssey of a Polish Intellectual* (Los Angeles, 1988) on his involvement in and attitude to communism.
12. Czesław Miłosz, Foreword to Aleksander Wat: *Mediterranean Poems* (Ann Arbor, 1977), p.ix.
13. See Stanisław Barańczak's comments on the stylistic range of Wat's poetry in his 'Four Walls of Pain: The Late Poetry of Aleksander Wat', *Slavic and East European Journal* (1989:2), pp.176-177.
14. Miłosz has written extensively on Oscar de Milosz. See especially *Native Realm* (New York, 1970), chapter 'The Young Man and the Mysteries', *The Land of Ulro* (New York, 1985), chpts.16-20 and 31-36, and *The Witness of Poetry* (Cambridge, Mass.,1983), chpt. 2. See also Miłosz's introduction to the translations of Oscar de Milosz's essays *The Noble Traveler* (1985).
15. Compare Miłosz's own accounts of the war years in *The Captive Mind* (London, 1953); *Native Realm*; 'Strefa chroniona' (Protected zone), in *Ogród nauk* (Paris, 1981); 'Koniec Wielkiego Księstwa' (The End of the Grand Duchy), *Kultura* (1989:5); and in Aleksander Fiut, *Rozmowy z Czesławem Miłoszem* (Kraków, 1981).
16. See the section 'Ameryka' in Miłosz's collection of essays and translations *Kontynenty* (Paris, 1958). The principal essay in the section 'Wprowadzenie w Amerykanów' (Introducing the Americans) appeared in 1947. It contained, *i.a.*, some very pertinent remarks on Eliot and Auden, both of whom Miłosz treated as American poets.
17. Miłosz's only volume of poems to appear in postwar Poland before 1980 was published in 1945, but his poems and translations continued to appear in periodicals until 1950.
18. See Ewa Czarnecka, *Podróżny świata: Rozmowy z Czesławem Miłoszem* (New York, 1983), p.23.
19. *Ibid.*, p.26.
20. Miłosz, '*Ars Poetica?*', in *Collected Poems* (New York, 1988), p.211. Translation by Czesław Miłosz and Lilian Vallee.
21. Ewa Czarnecka, *op.cit.*, p.25. On the multivocal and dialogic character of some of Miłosz's poems see Alexander M. Schenker, 'Introduction', *Utwory poetyckie* (Ann Arbor, 1976); Jan Błoński, *Odmarsz* (Kraków, 1978); Jan Błoński, 'Poetry and Knowledge', *World Literature Today* (1978:3); Stanisław Barańczak, 'Język poetycki Czesława Miłosza' (The Poetic Language of Czesław Miłosz), in *Teksty* (1981:4-5) and 'Miłosz's Poetic Language: A Reconnaissance', *Language and Style: An International Journal* (1985:4); and Aleksander Fiut, *The Eternal Moment: The Poetry of Czesław Miłosz* (Berkeley, 1990), pp.164-181.
22. On the *Skamander* poets see Czesław Miłosz, *The History of Polish*

Literature (London, 1969), and Stanisław Barańczak, 'Skamander after Skamander', *Cross Currents: A Yearbook of Central European Culture* (1990:9). On the *Awangarda* poets, see Bogdana Carpenter, *The Poetic Avant-garde in Poland, 1918-1939* (Seattle, 1983).

23. Miłosz, '*Ars Poetica?*', *op.cit.*
24. Miłosz's changing, yet remarkably consistent poetic "I" would deserve a separate study. For an example of his earlier reticence (and rejection of the confessional mode), see the highly ironic 'Greek Portrait', *Collected Poems*, p.131. Compare also the essay 'Niemoralność sztuki' (The Immoral Character of Art) in *Ogród nauk* (Paris, 1981).
25. See my 'The Idea of Reality in the Poetry of Czesław Miłosz', in Edward Możejko, ed., *Between Anxiety and Hope* (Edmonton, 1988) and Aleksander Fiut, 'The Traps of Mimesis', *op.cit.*
26. Czesław Miłosz, 'On Pasternak Soberly', *Emperor of the Earth* (Berkeley, 1981), p.66.
27. Czesław Miłosz, 'From the Rising of the Sun', *Collected Poems*, p.303.
28. *Ibid.*, p.304. Translation by Czesław Miłosz and Lillian Vallee.
29. Czesław Miłosz, *Wiersze* (London,1967), p.125.
30. Czesław Miłosz, *Collected Poems*, p.78. Translation by the author.
31. Although mainly in the form of reflections on the pre-war years. Compare, for instance, 'Pages Concerning the Years of Independence', *Collected Poems*, pp.365-371; 'La Belle Époque', *Ibid.*, pp.463-476.
32. Czesław Miłosz, 'Przygody poezji nowoczesnej' (The Adventures of Modern Poetry), *Kultura* (1961:7-8), pp.39-40. The translation is my own.
33. Czesław Miłosz, 'O niewiedzy, wyuczonej i literackiej', *Kultura* (1980:6), p.40.
34. Donald Davie, *Czesław Miłosz and the Insufficiency of Lyric* (Knoxville, 1986).
35. Helen Vendler, 'From Fragments a World Perfect At Last', *New Yorker* (March 19, 1984), p.142.
36. Of about 180 poems included in the *Collected Poems*, no fewer than 140 have Miłosz listed as their co-translator.
37. Compare, Miłosz's long and irrate response to A. Alvarez's review of his *Collected Poems* in *The New York Review of Books* (2 June, 1988), in which he expressed his dismay that the author of the review concentrated on his earlier phase, "copiously quoting" from his "old prose books", instead of dealing with his "poetic *oeuvre*". "You may guess my uneasiness [wrote Miłosz] when I saw the long evolution of my poetic craft encapsulated by Mr. Alvarez in the word 'witness', which for him is perhaps a praise, but for me is not. Am I really so exotic an animal that I deserve to be exposed in a separate cage bearing a label 'Far away'? Could not a question be asked what is the place of my poetry in the framework of contemporary poetry in general? And if an author and his co-translators have put together a volume of poems of five hundred pages, are not they right being curious to hear an assessment by a critic?" Alvarez's brief rejoinder (which began:

"Dear, dear . . . ") expressed admiration for Miłosz's poetry but avoided the issues raised by Miłosz. See *The New York Review of Books*, 21 July, 1988, p.42.

38. Joseph Brodsky, 'Presentation and Encomium', *World Literature Today* (1978:3), p.364.
39. See *Collected Poems*, pp.36-55.
40. Helene J.F. De Aguilar, 'A Prince Out of Thy Star: The Place of Czesław Miłosz', *Parnassus: Poetry in Review* (1983-4:2), p.128.
41. D.J. Enright, 'At the Feast of Brief Hopes', *TLS* (2-8 September, 1988), p.955. See also the short section on Miłosz in Enright's *Fields of Vision* (Oxford, 1988), with its concluding: "But to be moved, again and again, is something".
42. Czesław Miłosz, *Selected Poems* (New York, 1973), p.101. Translation by Miłosz and Richard Lourie. The version in the *Collected Poems* is slightly modified (pp.162-163).
43. Andrzej Busza and Bogdan Czaykowski, editors and translators, *Gathering Time: Five Modern Polish Elegies* (Mission, British Columbia, 1983), pp.43-44.
44. The entire passage from which the quotation comes is of interest: "The loss of respect for the individual verse line is cause for reflection. One cannot construct a poem with lines that fall apart in your fingers, just as one cannot construct a house with bricks that crumble. After all, a poem is nothing else than a column of lines, of which each is so strongly moulded that it stands on its own, irrespective of all the other lines. One recognises good poetry by being able to detach from a poem one line and appreciate its fulness ["pełny ładunek"]. It is the quality of the line (rather than the quality of metaphors and similes) that is the yardstick of evaluation even in the case of the most blatantly avant-garde poetry. Without appreciating the value of the line one cannot appreciate the value of a phrase (its extension over several lines, or of enjambment, or of the couplet)." Czesław Miłosz, 'O przekładach' (On Translation), in *Kontynenty*, p.127. First published in 1948.
45. Tadeusz Różewicz, 'Uśmiech Leonarda da Vinci' (The Smile of Leonardo da Vinci), *Poezje zebrane*, p.579. Translation by Adam Czerniawski, *Conversation with the Prince*, p.123.
46. Czesław Miłosz, 'Tak mało', *Utwory poetyckie*, p.346. Translation by Miłosz and Lillian Vallee, *Collected Poems*, p.247.
47. Czesław Miłosz, untitled, *Nieobjęta ziemia* (Paris, 1984), p.145. Translation by Miłosz and Robert Hass, *Collected Poems*, p.441.
48. Czesław Miłosz, 'Wyznanie', *Kroniki* (Paris, 1987), p.16. Translation by Miłosz and Robert Hass, *Collected Poems*, p.451.
49. Quoted after Alexander M. Schenker, 'Introduction', *Utwory poetyckie*, p.xxvi.
50. Czesław Miłosz, 'Gucio zaczarowany', *Utwory poetyckie* p.253. Translation by Andrzej Busza and Bogdan Czaykowski, *Gathering Time*, p.43.

51. Miłosz, 'Gdzie wschodzi słońce i kędy zapada', *Utwory poetyckie*, p.357. Translation by Czesław Miłosz and Lillian Vallee, *Collected Poems*, p.259.
52. Miłosz in Aleksander Fiut, *Rozmowy z Czesławem Miłoszem*, p.86.
53. Quoted in B. Czaykowski, *op.cit.*, pp.101-2.
54. Miłosz, 'Esse', *Utwory poetyckie*, p.207. Translation by Miłosz and Robert Pinsky, *Collected Poems*, p.221.
55. Miłosz, 'Gdzie wschodzi słońce i kędy zapada', *ibid*, p.351. Translation by Miłosz and Lillian Vallee, *Collected Poems*, p.252.
56. Miłosz, 'Czytając japońskiego poetę Issa' (Reading the Japanese poet Issa), *Poezje* (Paris, 1982), vol.III, p.30. Translation by Miłosz and Robert Hass, *Collected Poems*, p.331.
57. Ryszard Nycz, in the very interesting discussion of Miłosz's compositional practice (pp.46-68) in *Sylwy współczesne: Problem konstrukcji tekstu* (Wrocław, 1984).
58. Miłosz, 'Osobny zeszyt: przez galerie luster' (A Separate Notebook: A Mirrored Gallery), in *Poezje*, p.71. Translation by Renata Gorczyńska and Robert Hass, *Collected Poems*, p.363.
59. Miłosz, 'O aniołach' (On Angels), *Utwory poetyckie*, p.347. Translation by the author, *Collected Poems*, p.248.
60. Miłosz, '*Ars Poetica?*'.
61. See, for instance, 'From the Rising of the Sun'.
62. Aleksander Fiut, *Rozmowy z Czesławem Miłoszem*, p.47.
63. Miłosz, 'Gdzie wschodzi słońce i kędy zapada', *Utwory poetyckie*, p.374. Translation by Miłosz, Leonard Nathan, and Robert Hass, *Collected poems*, p.280.
64. *Ibid.*, p.392. Translation by Miłosz and Lillian Vallee, *ibid.*, p.302.
65. Miłosz, 'Wyznanie'.
66. Miłosz, 'Osobny zeszyt: Gwiazda piołun' (The Separate Notebooks: The Wormwood Star), *Poezje*, vol.III, p.78. Translation by Renata Gorczyńska and Robert Hass, *Collected Poems*, p.372.
67. See Note 11.
68. Miłosz, 'O wierszach Aleksandra Wata' (On the Poetry of Aleksander Wat), *Kultura* (1976:9), p.4.
69. *Ibid.*, pp.5-6.
70. Aleksander Wat, 'Z perskich przypowieści' (From Persian Parables), *Ciemne świecidło* (Paris, 1968), p.111.
71. See Wat's *Mój wiek* (London, 1981) and Ola Watowa, *Wszystko co najważniejsze* (London, 1984).
72. Wat, 'W kawiarni literackiej' (In a Literary Café), *Ciemne świecidlo*, p.54. The translation is my own.
73. Wat, 'Żółw z Oksfordu' (A Turtle from Oxford), *Ciemne świecidło*, p.32. Translation by Czesław Miłosz, *Mediterranean Poems*, p.21.
74. Miłosz, 'Elegia dla Ygrek Zet' (Elegy for Y.Z.), *Nieobjęta ziemia* (Paris, 1984), p.97. Translation by Miłosz and Robert Hass, *Collected Poems*, p.431.

75. Wat, 'Z kosza' (From a Basket), *Ciemne świecidło*, p.50.
76. See Leopold Tyrmand, *Dziennik 1954* (London, 1985) for an account of Herbert's life during the Stalinist period; and the claim by Zdzisław Łapiński, in *Jak współżyć z socrealizmem* (London, 1988) that three of Herbert's poems, published in a 1954 anthology, compromised to some extent his intransigence. See also Tadeusz Różewicz's account of the negative reception of some of his poems during the Stalinist period and of his difficulties with various editors, in 'Tożsamość: Wspomnienie o Karolu Kuryluku' (Identity: Reminiscences of Karol Kuryluk), *Przygotowanie do wieczoru autorskiego*, pp.62-73.
77. Wat, 'Przed Breughelem starszym' (Before Breughel the Elder), *Ciemne świecidło*, p.115. Translation by Czesław Miłosz, *Mediterranean Poems*, p.3.
78. Wat, 'Tej znów nocy . . . ', *Ciemne świecidło*, p.44. The translation is my own.
79. Wat, 'Być myszą . . . ', *op.cit.*, p.68. Translation by Czesław Miłosz, *op.cit.*, p.5.
80. Wat, 'Co ja na to poradzę', *op.cit.*, p.59. Translation by Czesław Miłosz, *op.cit.*, p.23.
81. Wat, 'Z kosza', *op.cit.*, p.50. The translation is my own.
82. Bolesław Leśmian, 'U żródeł rytmu', *op. cit.*, pp.73-4.
83. Wat, 'Wielkanoc' (Easter), *op.cit.*, p.101. The translation is my own.
84. Wat, 'Zobaczone z pociągu' (Seen from a Train), *op.cit.*, p.100. The translation is my own.
85. Wat, 'Ody' (Odes), *op.cit.*, p.19. The translation is my own.
86. Miłosz, 'Haftki gorsetu' (The Hooks of a Corset), *Nieobjęta ziemia*, p.22. Translation by Miłosz and Robert Hass, *Collected Poems*, p.401.
87. Karol W. Zawodziński, *Wśród poetów* (Kraków, 1964). See Vasa D. Mihailovich, Z. Folejewski, B. Czaykowski et. al., *Modern Slavic Literatures* (New York, 1976), p.333.
88. Paul Coates, *Words After Speech* (London, 1986), p.101.
89. *Ibid.*, p.106.
90. See, for instance, Norman Davies, *God's Playground: A History of Poland* (Oxford, 1983), vol. II, chpt. 4 on Polish cultural life in the Austrian part of Poland.
91. Cp. the following: Artur Sandauer, 'Filozofia Leśmiana,' *Moje odchylenia* (Kraków, 1956); Jacek Trznadel, *Twórczość Leśmiana* (Warsaw, 1964); Marian Pankowski, *Leśmian: La révolte d'un poète contre les limites* (Brussels, 1967); J. Sławiński, 'Semantyka poetycka Leśmiana', in M. Głowiński and J. Sławiński, *Studia o Leśmianie* (Warsaw, 1971); Ireneusz Opacki, *Poetyckie dialogi z kontekstem* (Katowice, 1979); Michał Głowiński, *Zaświat przedstawiony: Szkice o poezji Lésmiana* (Warsaw, 1981); Cezary Rowiński, *Człowiek i świat w poezji Leśmiana* (Warsaw, 1982); Maria Podraza-Kwiatkowska, *Somnambulicy: Dekadenci: Herosi* (Kraków, 1985); Paul Coates, *Identyczność i nieidentyczność w twórczości Leśmiana* (Warsaw, 1986).

92. Czesław Miłosz, *The History of Polish Literature*, pp.348-349.
93. Czesław Miłosz, 'Świat' (The World), *Utwory poetyckie*, p.90. The translation is my own.
94. Bolesław Leśmian, *Poezje*, p.384. The translation is my own. All translations from Leśmian are my own unless indicated otherwise.
95. Czesław Miłosz, '*Oeconomia divina*', *op.cit.*, p.330; *Collected Poems*, p.235.
96. Leśmian, 'Eliasz' (Elijah), *op.cit.*, p.414. I have translated "jawa" as "dream", although it normally stands for "reality".
97. Miłosz, 'Gdzie wschodzi słońce i kędy zapada', *op.cit.*, p.388. Translation by Miłosz and Lillian Vallee, *op.cit.*, p.297.
98. Leśmian, 'Zielona godzina' (The Green Hour), *op.cit.*, p.38.
99. See, for instance, Rochelle Stone, *Bolesław Leśmian: The Poet and His Poetry* (Berkeley, 1976), p.57. Stone's work, the only book-length study of Leśmian's poetry in English, is unfortunately very uneven and sometimes quite misleading. See also Cezary Rowiński, *op.cit.*
100. Leśmian, *ibid.*, p.35.
101. For instance, by Paul Coates.
102. See Leśmian's *Klechdy polskie* (Warsaw 1978), *Klechdy sezamowe* (Warsaw, 1968), *Przygody Sindbada Żeglarza* (Warsaw, 1972).
103. Leśmian, 'Podlasiak', *Klechdy polskie*, p.134.
104. Leśmian, '*Dreszcze nasze u warg się spotkały,*' *op.cit.*, p.436.
105. Leśmian, 'Ballada bezludna', *op.cit.*, p.179.
106. Leśmian, 'Wspomnienie', *op.cit.*, pp.192-3.
107. *Ibid.*, pp.194-5.
108. Leśmian, 'Oto słońce przenika', *op.cit.*, p.136.
109. See V. Markov, *Russian Futurism: A History* (Berkeley, 1968). On Przybyszewski's concept of the "metaword", see B. Czaykowski, 'Poetic Theories in Poland', *The Polish Review* (1966: 3), pp.51-53.
110. Leśmian, 'Wieczór', *op.cit.*, p.128.
111. Leśmian, 'Znaczenie pośrednictwa w metafizyce życia zbiorowego', *Szkice literackie*, p.59.
112. Leśmian, 'Eliasz', *Poezje*, pp.410-414.
113. Leśmian, 'Lalka', *op.cit.*, p.313.
114. Leśmian, 'Pszczoły', *op.cit.*, p.304.
115. Leśmian, 'Cmentarz', *op.cit.* p.392. Translation by Jerzy Pietrkiewicz and Burns Singer, *Five Centuries of Polish Poetry* (London, 1970), p.85.
116. See M. Głowiński, 'Poezja przeczenia' (The Poetry of Negation), in *Zaświat przedstawiony*, and the earlier study by A. Sandauer, *op. cit.*
117. Leśmian, 'Sen wiejski', *op.cit.*, pp.461-463.
118. Leśmian, 'Pan Błyszczyński', *op.cit.*, pp.404-409. The girl who does appear in Mr. O'Glimmer's garden was created "by no one, since she came lifeless and deathless, and thus neither lived nor died".
119. Leśmian, 'Srebroń', *op.cit.*, pp.310-311.
120. Leśmian, 'Dwaj Macieje', *op.cit.*, pp.415-420.
121. Leśmian, 'W czas zmartwychwstania', *op.cit.*, p.376.

122. Miłosz, 'Gdzie wschodzi słońce i kędy zapada', *Utwory poetyckie*, p.399. Translation by Miłosz and Lillian Vallee, *Collected Poems*, p.310.
123. *Ibid.*
124. Leśmian, *Klechdy sezamowe*, p.41. Quoted after Anna Czabanowska-Wróbel, 'Baśń jako światopogląd: Baśń i baśniowość w twórczości Leśmiana', *Pamiętnik Literacki* (1988:4).

II

A Poem Chosen . . .

George Hyde

Cyprian Kamil Norwid: 'Yesterday-And-I' / *Wczora-i-ja*

A deafness sad and rare
When you hear
The Word, but miss
The accent and stress.

★

For an angel calls . . . But they mock:
"Thunder!"
So you slam the coffin lid over your face under
The rock.

★

You have no wish to cry
"Eloi . . . Eloi . . . " why?
— Ah, God, sails lap the northern gale,
Seas rail.

★

A hum in my ear (I have no theory
Regarding storms)
So I dream and feel a folio of history
Turn to stone . . .

(*Translated by Adam Czerniawski*)

Norwid is one of those poets whose every poem is a sort of Advertisement for Myself (albeit heavily coded). In other words, he is always to a certain extent confessional. And yet choosing a favourite 'representative' poem is hard, because in one you get the Political Animal, in another the Erotic Animal, many give you different versions of the Prophetic Animal, but the 'real' Norwid escapes behind his smokescreen of words. For the English reader, he is like the French Symbolists, and shares Baudelaire's fascination with paradox and dialectic, his duality of Spleen and Ideal (the historical Fall and a tormenting vision of Redemption). His almost paranoid view of language as a dense system of 'correspondences' from which we are necessarily excluded (but by which we are judged) again echoes Baudelaire and Mallarmé. But like a true Pole, he never loses touch with the Romantic images of nationhood, freedom and independence embraced and propagated by his fellow-countrymen and his beloved homeland (from which, of course, he was exiled, a condition which permeates his mind-style). He is simultaneously a political poet steeped in the history of a specific moment, and one of those powerful practitioners of the genre of 'silence' (or a hermeticism bordering on silence) that the 'new' Poland currently rising from the ashes of 'People's' Poland will have to reassess. Throughout this century, his influence, despite his obscurity, has been enormous.

'Yesterday-And-I', like dozens of other Norwid poems ('Narcissus', or 'Word and Word', are just two relevant examples) is to some extent autotelic; in other words it struggles, like many of Hopkins's poems, to articulate its own creative processes, and to relate them by a kind of 'magical' (analogical) thinking to other, comparable, manifestations of the creative will, especially History, and Christ's decisive intervention in it. As with Mallarmé, the poetic 'word' *is* language, and what we hear around us is a kind of distracting babble, unless refined into meaning by art. For Norwid, silence and the blank page thus acquire (again as with Mallarmé) a pregnant virtuality and are infinitely more expressive than mere 'rhetoric'. Moreover, since the poet deals in ambiguities, or creative misreadings, for him the 'sign' is redolent of lost worlds of meaning ('associations', 'connotations') that lend it a density unperceived by ordinary mortals. The poet's prophetic task is to cleanse the doors of perception: but it is a task that he finds hard enough to accomplish on his own account, let alone on anyone else's (which makes the burden of Polish history even harder to bear).

The title of the poem 'Wczora-i-ja' runs the word for "yesterday" (wczoraj) together with the word for "I" (ja) into a catachresis suggesting a superimposition of the writing or speaking subject and its temporal extension; thus 'history' and the way the self is constituted enter into a problematical relationship, much as in Mallarmé's great sonnet about the swan trapped in the ice, dreaming of its 'virtual' (imaginary) flights. The tragedy of fallen humanity split between being and knowing, history and transcendence, the world and the Word, is barely articulated by the deliberately low-key opening of the poem, which expresses the sadness of the inevitable 'głuchota', or existential deafness, that marks humanity's inability to both 'be' and 'mean' simultaneously. There is a scarcely concealed Platonism here of the kind transmitted, or reworked, by the Romantic poets, but again the emphasis is on the opacity of the Word, presented now in almost Christian terms both as what was in the beginning and as what must be made flesh, painfully renewed in every moment through the 'body' of writing where 'accent' and 'stress' reside. Another, almost contemporary, and very comparable, formulation of the same issues is in the philosophy of Nietzsche, and especially his *The Birth of Tragedy*, with its profound dualism and its conviction of the irreconcilable split between the Apollonian, or form-giving, principle ('representation'), and the Dionysiac, or musical world-will, experienced as 'formless'. And, as we have seen, 'yesterday' and 'I' are caught in a symbiotic exchange, anticipating Freud's great tragic philosophy of mind.

Engulfed by 'language', the poet strives to make out the cry of the angel, which 'they' (the ubiquitous others that perennially threaten Norwid's sanity) would have us believe is a clap of thunder. The poet alludes to his retreat from the world into an inner space as if it were burial alive, but with a suggestion also of Christ's entombment (and he is addressed as "you", or "thou", in a familiar process of splitting which allows for the possibility of 'otherness': Rimbaud's schizoid "je est un autre" is the condition of creativity). It may well be the call of destiny (the national theme), or history, that prevents the poet from putting on the mantle of the crucified Christ; or perhaps, like Pasternak's Dr. Zhivago, the role of Redeemer is one that he is not ready for, and prefers to transform into the romantic image of ships sailing the Northern seas (the self extended in time and space). But allegory is a trap waiting to catch the unwary poet: 'theories' are another distraction: the 'real' discourse has fragmented, the 'real' storm is raging in the inner space of the poet's mind and feelings, heard best in dreams, and in the amazing onomatopoeic coinage "Z-marmurza", which seems to murmur but actually sends us violently back to the image of the block of stone or rock (*marmur* is marble) behind which truth hides. Is Polish history doomed to remain a series of powerful monuments? Or will it one day become a process, a flow, an expressive medium where the word meets the World? Adam Czerniawski's translation inevitably loses some of the complex sonic effects of the original, but it firmly resists the temptation to interpret or 'explain' Norwid's Mallarméan opacities, allowing the English reader to breathe the same rarified air that Norwid breathed.

John Bayley

Czesław Miłosz: 'Encounter' / *Spotkanie*

We drove before dawn through frozen fields,
The red wing was rising, yet still the night.

And suddenly a hare shot across our path.
One of us pointed to it with his hand.

That was long ago and both are dead:
The hare and the man who stretched his arm.

O my love, where are they, where do they lead,
The flash of a hand, the line of movement, the swishing icy ground

I ask not in sorrow, but in contemplation.

(*Translated by Adam Czerniawski*)

Horrible Heidegger once remarked that the German language "spoke being", while other languages "spoke of being". Horrible he certainly was, in his personality and *his* being, but he was also a great genius, and — most unusually for a philosopher — he worshipped a poet, the poet Hölderlin. Heidegger considered Hölderlin not only the greatest poet of modern times but the one whose poetry *was* being, which did not express the sense of things, but *was* it. With that amazing primal innocence, that lack of irony which distinguishes his sharpest and clearest words, Hölderlin wrote that "Full of merit, yet poetically/ Man dwells on the earth".

"Merit" had nothing to do with *Dasein*, or with poetry. Any lover of poetry would agree with that, for leaving out the point about the German language, the kind of conviction that Heidegger needed for his sense of his own philosophy, we can indeed surely say that all true poetry *does* speak being. No doubt that is merely a metaphor and an impression, just as the *being* of Hölderlin's — or of Celan's — poetry in German comes from its own expression of itself, its own conviction of language. But that is how language operates in poetry: any great poem, but some more than others, may give the impression that the language in which it is written exists so that it should have been written; that the peculiar genius of a language has found its self in the poem.

Or one of its true selves, for in a sense there are as many languages as there are poems. And some poems may give the impression that they can and do exist in different languages. Frost famously said that poetry was what got left out when the words were translated, but that perhaps is only partly the case. Certainly I would like to think that the Polish language, as written by Miłosz, or Herbert, has a peculiar clarity and power of transmission, a synthesising and synergistic power which comes from Latin and from its position in the heart of an always changing and self-transforming European culture. In a poem by them in English I feel I sense Polish, in a way that one is aware of the nature of French in Racine, of Russian in Pushkin, of English in Shakespeare, German in Hölderlin. It cannot of course be the absolute nature of the language, because it is not the Polish language itself and in any case I am ignorant of it. But poetry like theirs gives one an intimation of it, subjective as it may be, which adds to one's sense that their poetry has not only survived but declared itself in another language, has taken on in this new form the dignity, the absoluteness, of its own being.

That at least is what I feel about such poems of Miłosz as 'Bells in Winter' and 'A Short Recess', to name only two. Of course Miłosz is, as it were, a poet in English as well as in his native tongue, and his translations are in one sense new poems, yet it is vital to their poetry that they could never have been written as poems in English. They carry their singularity with them into the other tongue, and the poem of Miłosz that moves me most is indeed about a single moment, which the poem has kept, and still keeps, in its English words. A.E. Housman said that the test of poetry was whether it made your skin prickle and your hair stand up, brought water to the eyes. Not all great poems do those things — why should they? — for poetry does many and various things — but Miłosz's early poem 'Encounter', dated to 1936, certainly does them to me.

The poem breaks through into being, in Heidegger's sense ("Being's poem is just begun"). But there is no need to be cumbrously philosophical about it, because a lighter, more absent, more unpretending poem, could not be conceived. Someone who hated dogs once said of a friend's well-behaved one that it was almost as good as no dog at all. Someone who hated poetry (although of course no one admits to such a response) might say that 'Encounter' was almost as good as no poem at all. Yet the simplicity is not deliberate, has none of the formal intentionality of a 'little poem', a Haiku, something in Chinese, or a few lines by Ezra Pound. It is as transparent as it is poetically absolutely genuine, and moving. It has all the mystery and the clarity of Hölderlin but none of the afflatus. Miłosz is a learned man, a thinker, a philosopher and historian. But it is deeply true of him what Sir Philip Sidney wrote in his 'Defence of Poesie': "But the poet is the food for tendrest stomacks, the Poet is indeed the right popular Philosopher." I have often thought of that streak of movement, on that cold morning, the red wing that rose in darkness. It has the absolute uniqueness and mystery of the small thing that once occurred and vanished: exactly coincident with the mystery and simplicity of the poem.

Edwin Morgan

Tadeusz Różewicz: ‘Following The Guide’ / *Za przewodnikiem*

To eat drink read live faster
love faster
drive fly farther
speak quicker more
bid farewell go off leave quicker
listen look more
examine touch smell
examine possess relish
love be here and there
and who knows where else
laugh louder shove
run breathe
Quicker
more
faster farther higher lower deeper
quicker broader to live
eat drink sleep
love
live longer

In the Palazzo Ducale a throng follows the guide
the little flock rushes
well preserved old ladies
gentlemen in suspenders mop
their brows with handkerchiefs flowers in their hair

wherever they can they flop
but the guide rushes on little birds in their hair
from his lips gush names
dates anecdotes beautiful
this pietà is the most beautiful
an expression of suffering
please look from this angle there's a better view
the expression on the mother's face
this instrument is called
this is the hall where the court convened here through
    this opening
this slit people could drop secret denunciations
please move on the next group is behind us
flowers bedeck little hats
the armory
swords cannons coats of mail shields
daggers visors armor cannonballs matchlocks
sudden silence roars of laughter
the guide has winked
a knowing eye
whispers lisps
the group surrounds him tightly
a circle
almost at a gallop they have run past
along
to the left Bosch's Inferno
to the right Bellini's Pietà
to the left Bosch's Paradiso
to the right
to the left
in a display case amidst military weapons
hangs a rust-covered belt
in the belt are two openings
the round one studded with spikes
and the oval one
with spikes bent inward
the belt is padlocked
a knight setting off on a crusade
would take the key with him
the gray-haired ladies lean tenderly
toward their husbands' ears

the guide narrows his eyes
gesticulates children try
to break through the circle of grownups
they see nothing
smiles false teeth flushed faces
three nuns stand
hands folded under
eyelids lowered to
their lips
their lips move
outbursts of laughter silence
castles Tristan Isolde the golden-haired
barbarism
the chastity belt with spiked opening
and all around armor cannons crossbows cannonballs
visors matchlocks coats of mail cutlasses
but to this
nobody pays attention

1963
(*Translated by Magnus Krynski and Robert Maguire*)[1]

I have always thought that Różewicz presents a most tantalizing spectacle: when you take away as much from poetry as he has felt forced to do, how do you make the most of what is left? At first sight, his dislike of what he is determined to see as appurtenances rather than essentials — metre, rhyme, metaphor, verbal density, punctuation — seems to undermine the very impetus for writing, since poetry, whatever else it may or may not be, is a special form of words, distinguished from both prose and speech by *something*. That something may be delicate and marginal, as American poets like Williams and Creeley have shown, but Różewicz adds to such marginality a factor of depreciation of the whole art of poetry which even if it is regarded as a rhetorical topos pushes him alarmingly near the position of not believing in what he is doing. What could poetry do for someone who had been a young man in wartime Poland? Postwar numbness of spirit led to deep distrust not only of the high ideals of romantic and symbolist poetry but even of the very basic claims poetry might make to 'speak for a generation' or anything equally noble-sounding. Nevertheless, Różewicz visits the Auschwitz Museum, sees the masses of hair shaved from women's heads before they were gassed — and writes about it.[2] And it is a good poem, classical in its restraint, yet as 'aesthetic' as any poem must be, when it zooms in on a final close-up detail of a ribboned pigtail which evokes the earlier world of a playground and the 'naughty boys' who pulled the girl's hair. To be truthful, there are times when Różewicz is flat and untransmuted, a natural consequence of the risks he takes, but he is admirably clear-sighted about the limits, as also about the necessity, of his art. My poetry, he says,

> does not create new rules of the game
> takes no part in play
> has a defined place
> which it has to fulfil
>
> if it's not a cryptic language
> if it speaks without originality
> if it holds no surprises
> evidently this is how things ought to be[3]

A rather desperate humanism struggles to surface in this poetry. 'Letter to the Cannibals' is a humorous but serious plea for people to show some solidarity instead of buying up all the "candles shoelaces and macaroni" and always saying 'I me my mine'. One positive recurring figure in his poems is that of an old woman, surviving war or poverty, going about her business without fuss, holding things together in continuity as neither art nor human institutions can do:

> that old woman who
> leads a goat on a string
> is needed more
> is worth more
> than the seven wonders of the world
> anyone who thinks or feels
> she is not needed
> is a mass murderer[4]

Such a strong trope as the one in that last line is uncommon in Różewicz, but it points to something basic which can be best illustrated by taking a closer look at one of his notable poems of the 1960s, 'Following the Guide' (1963).

If the old woman's patience, dependableness, unambitiousness, and durability can be taken to be peasant virtues, even though they may be found in an urban context, the unhurried deliberateness of the woman's movements gives a broader human rebuke to the frantic modern world in general. 'Following the Guide', describing an incident with tourists in Italy, opens with a non-syntactical barrage of infinitive verbs and adverbs designed to give the impression that contemporary existence is like a speeded-up film, with all of us doing as much as we can in the shortest time possible:

> To eat drink read live faster
> love faster
> drive fly farther
> speak quicker more
> bid farewell go off leave quicker
> listen look more
> examine touch smell
> examine possess relish . . .

This 'live faster' motif is then illustrated in the main body of the poem, as a professional guide hurries his flock of (largely elderly) tourists round the medieval and Renaissance splendours of an Italian museum. Well-preserved old ladies and perspiring men in braces do their best to keep up, snatching a brief rest whenever they can, but are continually urged forward ("please move on the next group is behind us") by the guide whose practised gabble packs as many names and dates and stories as possible into the whirlwind tour:

> this pietà is the most beautiful
> an expression of suffering
> please look from this angle there's a better view
> the expression on the mother's face
> this instrument is called
> this is the hall where the court convened here
>   through this opening
> this slit people could drop secret denunciations

The pace quickens as they run ("almost at a gallop") past famous paintings towards the armoury where a special treat awaits them, the core of the tour, which will always stick in their minds. It is not Bellini, it is not Bosch, it is certainly not (although from another point of view it equally is) a pietà. The guide tightens his little circle of followers, whispers, winks, gesticulates:

in a display case amidst military weapons
hangs a rust-covered belt
in the belt are two openings
the round one studded with spikes
and the oval one
with spikes bent inward
the belt is padlocked

Silence alternates with bursts of laughter as the guide explains how the crusading knight would take the key of the chastity belt with him; nothing is said about the pain or humiliation of the woman. The grey-haired ladies (unlike "Isolde the golden-haired") "lean tenderly" towards their husbands' elderly ears; three nuns keep their eyes down and mutter a prayer; some children try unsuccessfully to peer through the magic circle of grownups. The contrast between the young medieval wife, forced by the customs of honour of the time to submit to a kind of slavery, and the "smiles false teeth flushed faces" of the tourists — a brilliant image of lewd impotent excitement — is tellingly conveyed in a few sure strokes. What is barbarism? The chastity belt is barbarous; so is the warfare the armed knight engages in; so too (the poet implies) is the well-fed international modern culture-gulping tourist to whom the chastity belt is a music-hall joke, and who in any case, in our sex-obsessed society, fixes on that one object while the rest of history becomes a blur:

barbarism
the chastity belt with spiked opening
and all around armour cannons crossbows cannonballs
visors matchlocks coats of mail cutlasses
but to this
nobody pays attention

The poet's horror of sentimentality prevents him from making any point of comparison between the virgin mother in the religious painting with her "expression of suffering" and the imagined wearer of the chastity belt, but the reader does not miss the analogy, and both women, like the peasant woman with her goat on a string, are images of painful endurance. So what has the modern world learned from all this? Not much. The elderly female tourists are roguish; the nuns seem rather too consciously prim; the conspiratorial guide and the guffawing male tourists are irredeemably filled with the old Adam. Whether this is pessimistic, or stoic, or a plea for us to be angry, is for each reader to decide.

Notes

1. Tadeusz Różewicz, 'Following the Guide', *The Survivor and Other Poems* (translated by Magnus J. Krynski and Robert A. Maguire), Princeton 1976, pp. 83-87.
2. Tadeusz Różewicz, 'Pigtail', *Conversation with the Prince and Other Poems* (translated by Adam Czerniawski) London 1982, p. 43. [See also pp.103–9 — Ed.].
3. 'My Poetry', *op. cit.*, p. 158.
4. 'In the Midst of Life', *op. cit.*, p. 63.

John Osborne

Tadeusz Różewicz: 'Pigtail' / *Warkoczyk*

It was the French writer Fernand Gigon, in a book called *Formula for Death: E=MC² (The Atom Bomb and After)*, who highlighted the case of Major Claude R. Eatherly, pilot of the aircraft that bombed Hiroshima and Nagasaki.[1] According to Gigon, when Eatherly realized the results of his missions he began to suffer "brief moments of madness". Military doctors diagnosed "extreme nervous depression", and Eatherly was honourably discharged from the service with a pension of £237 a month. However, "he seems to have regarded this pension as a premium for murder, as a payment for what he had done to the two Japanese cities, for he never touched the money." Instead, he took to "petty thievery", for which he was incarcerated in Fort Worth prison. Robert Jungk, respected author of those classics of Hiroshima literature *Children of the Ashes* and *Brighter Than a Thousand Suns*, added that Eatherly interpreted his mother's cancer as a sign that "we shall all have to make atonement"; tried to commit suicide when President Truman announced the manufacture of a Hydrogen Bomb; and engaged in robbery (some of the proceeds from which he paid into a fund for the Children of Hiroshima) in order to suffer the punishment he felt to be his due. Seeking a divorce from her husband, Mrs. Eatherly told the judge: "He frightens me. He often jumps up in the middle of the night and screams out in an inhuman voice that makes me feel ill: 'Release it! Release it!' Then after a moment or two, during which my husband seems to be in hell, he shouts: 'Not now, not now! Think of the children! The children are burning!'"[1]

In the late 1950s Eatherly became a media icon, a secular saint whose private agony expiated public guilt. *Newsweek* described him as a "Hero in Handcuffs". Richard Avedon photographed him, hand to brow, as a tortured existentialist. He was praised by Bertrand Russell, the philosopher and anti-nuclear protester. NBC television devoted a programme to his case. A movie, entitled *Medal in the Dust*, reached the scripting stage. And the English writer John Wain produced 'A Song About Major Eatherly', which was broadcast on the BBC. This poem employs diverse styles (strict quatrains, irregular blank verse, *terza rima*, *vers libre* to move its argument through a succession of stages: a précis of Eatherly's career; a moral disquisition on the price of murder; a philosophical meditation on our changing conceptions of hell (the proposition being that by ceasing to believe in the imaginary inferno of Christianity we have come to create real ones); finally, the suggestion that if Eatherly's passion cannot, like Christ's, redeem us, it *can* offer an image of atonement we might care to acknowledge, even emulate:

> But lay a folded paper by his head,
> nothing official or embossed, a page
> torn from your notebook, and the words in pencil.
> Say nothing of love, or thanks, or penitence:
> say only 'Eatherly, we have your message'.[2]

Wain's poem not only set the seal on this peculiarly modern saint by dignifying his fall and rise with the permanency of art, but also set the seal on the poet's career by becoming a favourite anthology piece and school text. As recently as 1985, Anthony Thwaite was praising this as one of Wain's "most impressive poems" — "certainly ambitious, but with an authoritative unifying strength";[3] and two years later it was singled out for respectful attention in John Williams's *Twentieth-Century British Poetry: A Critical Guide*.[4] Yet this much admired poem perfectly illustrates why Polish poetry comes as an antidote to our literary decadence, and also explains why certain translations, such as Adam Czerniawski's Englishing of *Conversation with the Prince and Other Poems* (1982) by Tadeusz Różewicz, might constitute an intervention in British poetry as momentous as Chapman's Homer. For Wain's sonorous rhetoric, moral indignation and historicized eschatology was triggered, not by an acquaintance with its subject, but by a few lines in a newspaper. Unfortunately for the reputation of the poem, the evidence at

Wain's disposal was entirely bogus: far from being a hero, Eatherly went through the Second World War without seeing action; he neither commanded nor participated in the Hiroshima and Nagasaki raids; his penchant for petty crime was not prompted by the Atomic explosions (he had earlier come near to dismissal from the service for cheating in exams); and at his divorce proceedings no mention was made of nightmare cries, Mrs. Eatherly never having heard any. Eatherly was a con-man, and in retrospect Wain's poem is mainly of interest for its part in the sanctification of a charlatan.[5]

Of course many great works of literature are based on false or partial knowledge, but the Eatherly débâcle makes unavoidably explicit a failure of literary decorum which characterizes English poetry addressed to the horrors of our century. Remember Auden's poem 'Spain', with its "acceptance of . . . the necessary murder", and Orwell's famous admonishment that such a phrase "could only be written by a person to whom murder is at most a *word*".[6] Wain's language has likewise not been chastened by the enormity of what it addresses, so that the Hiroshima catastrophe becomes merely an excuse for specious sermonizing. One symptom of this is the high incidence of comatose adjectives (death is cold, blood is rank, hell is a furnace, saints are holy) whose sole use is to pad out the lines in an impeccable but deathly fulfilling of metrical norms. Far from being rendered speechless by the unspeakable, the poem becomes loquacious; but the rhetoric gives itself away, honesty ringing false.

It is Poland's misfortune to be situated on the high road between Berlin and Moscow; and back and forth along that route the eyeless juggernaut of History has trundled, crushing all who stand in its way. An almost exact contemporary of Wain's, Tadeusz Różewicz was born 3 years after the rebirth of Poland following a 100 year partition; he was 18 when Hitler and Stalin sealed their friendship by repartitioning his country; 20 when the Nazis took possession of the whole; and 24 when it was liberated (or, as Heinrich Böll says, 'liberated')[7] by a USSR whose fraternal feelings did not prevent it from appropriating a sizeable Polish acreage. Older poets in many countries (Leopold Staff, Giuseppe Ungaretti, William Carlos Williams, Bertolt Brecht) had already engaged in 'language-washing',[8] attempting to discover how many of poetry's sacrosanct conventions could be dispensed with, and in what combinations, whilst still giving rise to what would indisputably be verse. Behind this drastic asepsis, one senses the desire to arrive at that resistant thing, the undecorated essence of, the bedrock of poetry. Różewicz's generation of Polish poets arrived at an identical simplicity but by the opposite route, not stripping poetry down to the bare essentials, but patiently building it up, syllable by syllable, after the annihilation of meaning at Sobibor, Treblinka and Katyń. There can be "no poetry after Auschwitz", insisted the philosopher Adorno,[9] and these poets have written on the very threshold of silence, testing each vocable against a reality so monstrous it unsinews all utterance. "What I produced", Różewicz said, "is poetry for the horror-stricken. For those abandoned to butchery. For survivors. We learnt language from scratch, those people and I."[10]

The result is a poetry which distrusts its own fictiveness, which teaches language respect for the dead, and which uncovers the ethic in aesthetic. Consider, for example, the following:

PIGTAIL

When all the women in the transport
had their heads shaved
four workmen with brooms made of birch twigs
swept up
and gathered up the hair

Behind clean glass
the stiff hair lies
of those suffocated in gas chambers
there are pins and side combs
in this hair

The hair is not shot through with light
is not parted by the breeze
is not touched by any hand
or rain or lips

In huge chests
clouds of dry hair
of those suffocated
and a faded plait
a pigtail with a ribbon
pulled at school
by naughty boys.

The Museum, Auschwitz, 1948 [11]

This poem consists of 97 words, 83 of which are monosyllables and a further 12 disyllables.[12] The elementary diction (so simple it could be understood by just such a child as it concerns) isolates like an amoeba on a slide the slightest verbal exoticism. How telling, for instance, that the only word to draw attention to itself by exceeding two syllables should be "suffocated", and that it should be repeated for emphasis. How affecting that the metaphor applied to the victims' massed hair should be "clouds", thereby invoking the zyklon B gas by means of which they were asphyxiated. How poignant that the glass behind which it is displayed should be "clean", whereas the hair itself is already "faded" (could any other poet throw the reader's emotions into a commotion by juxtaposing two such unexceptional adjectives?). How unhinging that third stanza, with its series of negations, reminding us of Wittgenstein's point that to understand what something is not (in this case, alive) is to understand what it is. Remark the metonymic sequence by means of which the pigtail personifies a girl, the girl betokens all the shaven women, the women epitomize everyone (male or female) exterminated at Auschwitz, Auschwitz embodies all Nazi death camps, and they in turn epitomize all those institutions of annihilation which eptiomize our era: yet no mention is made of a girl, nor of the Nazis and their millions of victims, and even the name Auschwitz is relegated to a footnote. At the same time it is entirely appropriate that the poem should be female-centred; for while men as well as women were the victims of the Final Solution (no doubt naughty boys suffered as terrible a fate as little girls with pigtails), it is nonetheless true that the victimizers were (in both senses) all male. Yet how impressive is Różewicz's restraint in declining a them and us, Poles versus Germans, Jews versus Gentiles posture (which would have been a gross falsification): this is a poem which communicates the definitive bad news about our species, but which does not cry for vengeance and is too compassionate for nihilism. Even the fact that the sole punctuation is a full stop postponed for four sentences until the very end of the poem, emphatically terminating a text about termination, comes to be expressive.

Few adjectives, hardly a metaphor, one punctuation mark, not a single simile, absolutely no myth, a monosyllabic diction: if, as Ruskin claimed, poetry is the art of using one word to suppress many, then this, assuredly, is poetry — a poetry in which the silences are sounded and the erasures speak, obliging us to read, not just between the lines, but between every vocable. If anything is, this is a poetry whose undeluded lexis speaks for and to we dwellers in the interregnum between genocide and omnicide, between the holocaust that is past and the more devastating one which we have thus far managed to defer.

Notes

1. Fernard Gigon, *Formula for Death: E=MC² (The Atom Bomb and After)*; Robert Jungk, 'Introduction' to *Burning Conscience*, the correspondence of Claude R. Eatherly and Dr. Gunther Anders; both quoted in Malcolm Muggeridge, 'The Passion of St. Eatherly', *Tread Softly For You Tread On My Jokes* (Fontana 1968), pp. 219-227.
2. John Wain, 'A Song About Major Eatherly', *Weep Before God* (Macmillan 1962), p. 40. A typical reprinting of the poem was in Elizabeth Jennings, *An Anthology of Modern Verse: 1940-1960* (Methuen 1961).
3. Anthony Thwaite, *Poetry Today: A Critical Guide to British Poetry, 1960-1984* (Longman 1985), p. 47.
4. John Williams, *Twentieth-Century British Poetry: A Critical Guide* (Edward Arnold 1987), p. 93.
5. Eatherly was first exposed by William Bradford Huie in *The Hiroshima Pilot*. See Malcolm Muggeridge, 'The Passion of St. Eatherly', *Tread Softly For You Tread On My Jokes* (Fontana 1968), pp. 219-227.
6. Auden's 'Spain' appeared as a pamphlet poem in 1937. It was amended in later versions before being entirely suppressed by its author. It is most conveniently available today in *The Penguin Book of Spanish Civil War Verse*, edited by Valentine Cunningham (Penguin 1980), pp. 97-100. Orwell's rejoinder came in his classic essay 'Inside the Whale' (1940); reprinted, *Inside the Whale and Other Essays* (Penguin 1957), pp. 9-50 (see expecially pp. 36-37).
7. See Heinrich Böll, 'Introduction' to *Ashes and Diamonds* by Jerzy Andrzejewski (Penguin 1980), p. vii.
8. Bertolt Brecht, quoted by Michael Hamburger, *The Truth of Poetry* (Penguin 1972), p. 207.
9. T.W. Adorno, *Prisms* (Spearman, 1967), p. 34. For a useful commentary on this theme see George Steiner, *Language and Silence* (Penguin 1969).
10. Quoted in Michael Hamburger, *The Truth of Poetry* (Penguin 1972), p. 272.
11. Tadeusz Różewicz, *Conversation with the Prince and other poems*, translated by Adam Czerniawski (Anvil 1982), p. 43.
12. The original has 25 fewer words, of which, however, only 25 are monosyllabic and as many as 23 are disyllabic. These differences are accounted for by certain different features of the two languages. Thus,

Polish dispenses with definite and indefinite articles and combines into linguistic units expressions which in English are split up, as in the case of "swept up", "gathered up", "shot through" and "had their heads shaved". The monosyllabic terseness of English enhances the restraint and bleakness of Różewicz's poetry. (Ed.)

The aim of this article is to underline the relevance of Polish poetry in translation to the health of British verse. My concern, therefore, is less with that great Polish poet Tadeusz Różewicz, than with the great English poet Różewicz-Czerniawski. (J.O.)

John Lucas

Tadeusz Różewicz: ‘A Tale of Old Women’ / *Opowiadanie o starych kobietach*

I like old women
ugly women
evil women

they are the salt of the earth

human refuse
does not disgust them

they know the other side
of the coin
of love
and faith

coming and going
dictators clown
their hands stained
with human blood

old women rise at dawn
buy meat fruit bread
clean cook
stand in the street
arms folded silent

old women
are immortal

Hamlet rages in the net
Faust's role is comic and base
Raskolnikov strikes with his axe

old women are
indestructible
they smile indulgently

a god dies
old women get up as usual
buy fish bread and wine
civilization dies
old women get up at dawn
open windows
and remove the filth
a man dies
they wash the corpse
bury the dead
plant flowers
on graves

I like old women
ugly women
evil women

they believe in life everlasting
they are the salt of the earth
the bark of trees
and the humble eyes of beasts

cowardice and heroism
greatness and pettiness
they perceive in true perspective
scaled to demands
of common day

their sons discover America
perish at Thermopylae

die on crosses
conquer the cosmos

old women go out at dawn
to buy milk bread meat
they season the soup
and open the windows

only fools laugh
at old women
ugly women
evil women

for these are beautiful women
good women
old women
they are the embryo
mystery devoid of mystery
the sphere which rolls

old women
are the mummies
of sacred cats

they are tiny
shrivelled
parched
spring's fruit
or plump
oval Buddhas

when they die
a tear
flows from the eye
and joins
the smile
on a young girl's lips

1963

(*Translated by Adam Czerniawski*)

A few years ago I spent rather more than twelve months living in Greece. Greece, I soon came to realise, was a nation of aged women.

They were everywhere, and to judge from the habitual black headscarf, black dress, black stockings and shoes, the majority of them were widows. And so it proved. The explanation for this was tragically simple. Over a period of some twelve years — from the Italian invasion of the Greek mainland at the outset of the Second World War until the conclusion of the civil war — almost two million Greek men went to early and violent deaths. Many were killed in battle. Others, non-combatants, were butchered by the Nazis, innocent victims of reprisal or terrorist tactics. Still others died in prison camps or in villages and on hillsides where, after 1944, communists fought against collaborationists and royalists. Given that the entire population of Greece could not at that time have exceeded eight million, it will be apparent that what happened to the nation's male population in those dreadful years was far worse than decimation. No wonder there were so many widows.

One evening I watched a television programme which brought a group of them together. They were from the same small village in the north of Greece, and they had been invited in front of the cameras in order to talk over their experiences of the civil war. One had lost her husband and two sons. Another had tried to hide her fiancé from royalist soldiers, only to see him dragged away. Did she ever set eyes on him again? Oh yes, she said, his body was returned to her for burial. She could tell from the marks on it that before being shot he had been tortured. Other women had similar, or worse, tales to tell. As any one of them spoke the others would nod their heads, vouching for the truth of what was being said. Yes, yes, terrible things had been done. Deaths and burials every day. Hardly a family but had been directly affected.

The women's faces were deeply lined and they all looked very old. It was tempting to see in them a reincarnation of Sophocles' women of Troy, helplessly protesting against war and brutalities. But this would have been wrong, a mere literary indulgence. As the programme ran its course I was increasingly struck by the fact that the most remarkable feature of the women's tales was not what they had to say but how they said it. Appalling as were the stories they had to relate, each woman told hers in a manner that implied its inevitability. These things had happened. This was the way things were. They spoke without visible rancour. It was as though nothing they had witnessed or experienced retained the power to shock or even surprise them. These women had outworn tragedy.

Not surprisingly, then, their image came back to me when, a year or so later, I re-read Różewicz's 'A Tale of Old Women'. The following lines in particular seemed to be about the old women I had seen and heard on that television programme.

old women are
indestructible . . .

their sons discover America
perish at Thermopylae
die on crosses
conquer the cosmos

old women go out at dawn
to buy milk bread meat

Yeats comes near to this kind of statement in his accounts of beggar and tinker women, but he gives them a gaiety which Różewicz's, old women lack. The Greek women I had watched didn't have it either, although they had the "ancient glittering eyes" which Yeats ascribes to his Chinamen. But Yeats would have understood why Różewicz should call his old women "ugly women/evil women." Such women — crones, witch-like — seem to *know* about life in a way that affronts and discomforts male assurance. If they can cope with such knowledge there must be something wrong with them, something — well, "evil".

In *Conversation with the Prince and Other Poems*, 'A Tale of Old Women' has on either side of it poems about not-so-old men. I assume that the three poems are to be read in sequence. At all events, to do so deepens the meaning of each one and to take them together gives them greater collective strength. The first is called 'he tears easily . . . '. It is a bleak, mordant fable in which "they" rip a paper man to shreds in an effort to fit him to an appropriate size and shape. Finally

they crammed a 'philosophy'
down his throat
then cleared up and removed
the paper porridge[1]

Then comes 'A Tale of Old Women', with its account of those indestructible survivors down whose throat no philosophy could ever be forced and who could never be fitted into an acceptable shape. It is followed by 'Précis'. Here a man tells his son about *Hamlet*, a play which understandably haunts Różewicz. 'Précis' ends:

> I pass over in silence
> the question which
> the Danish Prince had asked himself
> it's a joke too cruel and vulgar
> for modern man[2]

Hamlet's questioning of the worth of existence involves or requires a degree of self-awareness which, the poem says, modern man cannot afford. The implication is that where there is no choice there can be no tragedy. This feels in some ways close to the experience of the Greek women.

There are, however, differences. The world of 'Précis' is one of utter aridity, of bleak, unending determinism. It is also the world as perceived by men, a world in which they are denied the possibility of the tragic experience which has always seemed a largely male experience. To say this is not to make a fashionable feminist point. It is simply to observe what happens in Różewicz's three poems. The old women know all that is contained in the experience of 'he tears easily . . . ' and 'Précis', but they are still able to function, whereas the men cannot do so or, it may be, cannot bear to confront the full truth. They lack the capacity to be "evil". The old women embody this capacity and they are quite without the self-pity that dances attendance on male self-consciousness. (Hamlet's as much as, if not more than, any other man's.)

> a god dies
> old women get up as usual
> buy fish bread and wine
> civilization dies
> old women get up at dawn
> open windows and remove the filth

One can of course imagine a feminist argument against the poem, which might run along some such lines as the following: Różewicz is fixing the old women in a type image; let them be symbols of endurance and survival, he says; meanwhile men will get on with being gods and making (as well as destroying) civilizations. But

Różewicz is saying that the old women are not taken in by any of this:

> cowardice and heroism
> greatness and pettiness
> they perceive in true perspective
> scaled to demands
> of every day

There is nothing reductive about this essentially comic view of life. (Comic in the sense that it is concerned with social rhythms of recurrence.) Heroism and greatness are given their due, but there is also, as there have to be, the quotidian demands of every day. And these produce an intimate understanding of the possibilities of life and death which encompass the worst as well as the best. This is the "evil" of true knowledge, without which life could not continue.

Accordingly, the poem concludes by saying that when any of these old women die

> a tear
> flows from the eye
> and joins
> the smile
> on a young girl's lips

There is a sombre yet wry wisdom about this, a visionary understanding which it would be reductive, even sentimental, to call tragic. Such understanding forms the deep, unyielding core of Różewicz's remarkable poem.

Notes

1. Tadeusz Różewicz, 'he tears easily', *Conversation with the Prince and other poems*, translated by Adam Czerniawski (Anvil 1982) p. 144.
2 Tadeusz Różewicz, 'Précis', *Ibid.*, p. 148.

John Pilling

Zbigniew Herbert: 'Mr. Cogito and the Imagination' / *Pan Cogito i wyobraźnia*

1

Mr Cogito never trusted
tricks of the imagination

the piano at the top of the Alps
played false concerts for him

he didn't appreciate labyrinths
the Sphinx filled him with loathing

he lived in a house with no basement
without mirrors or dialectics

jungles of tangled images
were not his home

he would rarely soar
on the wings of a metaphor
and then he fell like Icarus
into the embrace of the Great Mother

he adored tautologies
explanations
idem per idem

that a bird is a bird
slavery means slavery
a knife is a knife
death remains death

he loved
the flat horizon
a straight line
the gravity of the earth

2

Mr Cogito will be numbered
among the species *minores*

he will accept indifferently the verdict
of future scholars of the letter

he used the imagination
for entirely different purposes

he wanted to make it
an instrument of compassion

he wanted to understand to the very end

— Pascal's night
— the nature of a diamond
— the melancholy of the prophets
— Achilles' wrath
— the madness of those who kill
— the dreams of Mary Stuart
— Neanderthal fear
— the despair of the last Aztecs
— Nietzsche's long death throes
— the joy of the painter of Lascaux
— the rise and fall of an oak
— the rise and fall of Rome

and so to bring the dead back to life
to preserve the covenant

Mr Cogito's imagination
has the motion of a pendulum

it crosses with precision
from suffering to suffering

there is no place in it
for the artificial fires of poetry

he would like to remain faithful
to uncertain clarity

(*Translated by John and Bogdana Carpenter*)

In spite of believing that man "destroyed the order of nature by his thought and labour" — a judgment prompted by his visit to the Lascaux caves — Zbigniew Herbert has nevertheless chosen to adopt an essentially humanist stance in his quest to establish whether the cultural products of thought and labour can provide any kind of substitute order. Yet while passionately committed to the continuance of civilization, Herbert has conducted his inquiries into what threatens it in a diffident spirit, typically manifesting a wry scepticism which refuses to align itself with comfortable dogma and ideology. In the keynote essay of *Barbarian in the Garden,* for example, Herbert identifies Paleolithic palimpsests as equivalent in status to "poetry and fairy-tales": relics no-one could seriously be expected to believe in. But the description of *Homo sapiens* that follows reads oddly like a blueprint for his own practice: like primitive "barbarian" man, Herbert has "craved a new discipline through a sequence of self-imposed prohibitions" and often worn masks, "as if trying to appease his own treason". It seems oddly apt in this connection that, by the kind of twist to which Herbert is temperamentally attracted, his most frequently employed *persona* — Mr. Cogito — should possess a surname derived from the most famous sequence of self-imposed prohibitions in the history of philosophy: the unsuccessful but immensely influential attempt by Descartes to eradicate doubt and to establish thinking as the fundamental human labour.

Ergo sum, one feels impelled to add on Mr. Cogito's behalf, since he is so much more than a mere *alter ego* that it seems impossible for him not to exist independently of his creator. So much so that to align him with *Homo sapiens* and Descartes — the cave-dwelling architect of the ancient world and the prototypical model for the modern — seems a poor tribute to his individuality. As Mr. Cogito insists, in a splendidly imaginative repudiation of the heroic enterprises undertaken at Imagination's behest, in any event he belongs to the "species *minores*" and "won't inhabit history", either now or in the future. In this respect he resembles J. Alfred Prufrock, who is "not prince Hamlet, nor was meant to be"; and it is no surprise to find Herbert in an essay on Siena quoting from Eliot's 'Tradition and the Individual Talent'. Much like his predecessor, Mr. Cogito is always obliquely re-establishing his entitlement to membership of the human race. A diligent (if sometimes misguided) observer of life, Mr. Cogito is repeatedly implicated in the dramas it generates, and painfully aware that whatever afflicts the actors on the stage applies equally to the spectators in the auditorium. Encountering Mr. Cogito on the portico steps, as it were — ham-fistedly concocting an effective exit-line, doffing his hat to the assembled company besieging him (as he imagines) on all sides — one accustoms oneself to seeing him make off down the street and then, conscience-stricken, turn and return to the focal point of the action. Though the Lascaux essayist cuts a comparable figure under the guise of providing neutral information — "I returned . . . by the same road as I arrived" — the motif of renewing contact with reality (something of an *idée fixe* with Mr. Cogito, as 'Mr. Cogito — The Return' illustrates) is clearly freighted with a more than casual significance. In the Lascaux context Herbert carefully avoids suggesting that this might be a version of the Orpheus myth; it is the "warm touch" of a hand extended across an "abyss" of space and time that prompts him to claim the right to be considered "a citizen of the earth".

Though Mr. Cogito rarely feels confident enough to sum things up in quite so euphoric a fashion, it is precisely as a humdrum citizen of earth that he makes his mark. No wonder "the piano at the top of the Alps" (a phrase adapted from the first of Rimbaud's *Les Illuminations*, 'Après le déluge') impresses him much less favourably than what was accidentally discovered — a far cry from any "dérèglement systématique de tous les sens" — beneath the hills of Montignac by a teenager already almost forgotten, whom no-one seems to have heard of since. But "the joy of the painter of Lascaux" is only one of the items Mr. Cogito treasures from his travels, armchair or otherwise; forewarned by Rimbaud's predicament, and loath to abandon creative labour altogether, he decides — in the age-old dispute between the one and the many — in favour of the latter. In Mr. Cogito's scheme of things there is really no room for solo recitals; extreme individualism is, for him, simply the obverse of extreme conformity. Hence his insistence (found in many other poems) on the virtues of a strategy which hardly seems to demand any artistic skill at all. Herbert, at Lascaux, acknowledges shamefacedly that "all inventories are useless"; Mr. Cogito boldly demonstrates that this despised genre may legitimately be considered an appropriate mode for conveying spiritual utilities.

'Mr. Cogito and the Imagination' reflects the creative tensions in Herbert that have led him to use this persona more than any other, after many years of virtuosic ventriloquism. Indeed, a bi-partisan stance conditions the very structure of the poem. Reluctant to offend against the Aristotelian law of non-contradiction which makes A = A the test of an entity, Herbert initially dramatizes his conviction that everything not a tautology is a kind of treason. The principal casualty of this discourse on method is undoubtedly imagery — the stock-in-trade of the Imagination. But the second half of the poem exposes this radical prohibition as minimalist not only in manner but also in meaning. A distinctively human effort must, it would seem, keep covenant with an "uncertain clarity" — analogous to the doubt that has been perceived as fundamental — more expressive than *idem per idem* could ever be. Even if a grain of untruth creeps in under this rubric to sow disorder, this is to be preferred over an order that is merely a closed system. Poetry, Herbert seems to be saying, is a compromise that is always at the risk of being compromised still further — but not when, as an art like any other, it enables a practitioner to fashion an "instrument of compassion" capable of maintaining a human presence.

Tom Paulin

Zbigniew Herbert: 'Elegy of Fortinbras' / *Tren Fortynbrasa*

Now that we're alone we can talk prince man to man
though you lie on the stairs and see no more than a dead ant
nothing but black sun with broken rays
I could never think of your hands without smiling
and now that they lie on the stone like fallen nests
they are as defenceless as before The end is exactly this
The hands lie apart The sword lies apart The head apart
and the knight's feet in soft slippers

You will have a soldier's funeral without having been a soldier
the only ritual I am acquainted with a little
There will be no candles no singing only cannon-fuses and bursts
crepe dragged on the pavement helmets boots artillery horses
    drums drums I know nothing exquisite
those will be my manoeuvres before I start to rule
one has to take the city by the neck and shake it a bit

Anyhow you had to perish Hamlet you were not for life
you believed in crystal notions not in human clay
always twitching as if asleep you hunted chimeras
wolfishly you crunched the air only to vomit
you knew no human thing you did not know even how to breathe

Now you have peace Hamlet you accomplished what you had to
and you have peace The rest is not silence but belongs to me

you chose the easier part an elegant thrust
but what is heroic death compared with eternal watching
with a cold apple in one's hand on a narrow chair
with a view of the ant-hill and the clock's dial

Adieu prince I have tasks a sewer project
and a decree on prostitutes and beggars
I must also elaborate a better system of prisons
since as you justly said Denmark is a prison
I go to my affairs This night is born
a star named Hamlet We shall never meet
what I shall leave will not be worth a tragedy

It is not for us to greet each other or bid farewell we live on
archipelagos
and that water these words what can they do what can they do
prince

(*Translated by Czesław Miłosz*)

The corny, the overexposed, the anthology piece, the national heritage sign or shrine — we can all list examples of these revisited boredoms. *Hamlet* and the Mona Lisa are two of the most outstanding, and Zbigniew Herbert has confronted them both.

In 'Mona Lisa' he crosses "seven mountain frontiers" —

> barbed wire of rivers
> and executed forests
> and hanged bridges[1]

in order to stand in front of Western Europe's supreme cultural cliché. What he sees is a frightening image "hewed off from the meat of life/ abducted from home and history." The displaced transcending image is "smothered with a scarf of glaze" and is entirely outwith and beyond its original social moment.

Matthew Arnold performs a similar action in his essay, 'The Study of Poetry', where he simultaneously witholds canonical greatness from Chaucer and then confers it upon him:

> His poetry transcends and effaces, easily and without effort, all the romance-poetry of Catholic Christendom; it transcends and effaces all the English poetry contemporary with it, it transcends and

> effaces all the English poetry subsequent to it down to the age of Elizabeth.

This idea of art expresses a secure idea of national grandeur and it flattens social, political and literary history. The critical act of affirming the one great author, the single perfect image, wipes out generations of artists. To the writer who is not imbued with national confidence the historical void which this act of canonization designs is threatening, like a piece of weaponry:

> between the blackness of her back
> and the first tree of my life
>
> lies a sword
> a melted precipice[2]

The Mona Lisa is separated from Herbert by a huge historical gap. His lines register that sinister hole with enormous bitterness because this ahistoricism, or anti-historicism, is really a trope which conceals the heavy artillery of empire, of successful power. And his attitude to the image and the trope is complicated because he both envies and despises the Western bourgeois enjoyment of art, leisure, historical absence.

Sensing that attitude, I approach 'Elegy of Fortinbras' warily — tempted in the face of so much inattention to Herbert's work to call it 'great', but knowing how that much-derided adjective drains history from texts.

My first sense of *Hamlet* as a twentieth-century political drama came from seeing the haunting Soviet film of the play in Belfast in the mid-1960s (the film was directed by Grigori Kozintsev, the script was by Pasternak, the score by Shostakovich). In the — with hindsight — unreal quiet of that city, the film threw the spectre of Stalin's terror across the screen. And after that experience, Olivier's film was a hollow embarrassment. Later I learnt from Shostakovich's memoirs that the censors banned *Hamlet* in the 1930s because Stalin hated it. Reading Pasternak's poem, 'Hamlet in Russia', we can see how the stage-fright of the actor playing Hamlet is a symbolic code for the relationship of the artist to the Stalinist state, and Herbert's poem develops this theme. Clearly, the Soviet Union, the figure of Stalin, his successors, are central to Herbert's poem, but to locate it we need to consider Hamlet in Poland. Here, the distinguished Polish drama critic, Jan Kott, must be our guide.

Kott notes the play's canonical similarity to the Mona Lisa and then describes its stage-history in Poland where it was staged for the first time in Lwów in 1797, two years after Poland lost its independence. The actor who took the title role and also directed the play, Wojciech Bogusławski, had been a prominent participant in the Kościuszko insurrection three years earlier. The failure of that insurrection brought about the fall of Poland. In this production, Denmark was Poland and Claudius was Catherine the Great/Frederick/Maria-Theresa, the three monarchs who partitioned Poland.

The first Polish Hamlet, Kott notes, appeared in *Horsztyński, a historical drama* by Słowacki written in the 1830s:

> This Polish Hamlet, Szczęsny-Kossakowski by name, is the central figure of the play. He has a fine aristocratic lineage; his father commanded the Polish army and his uncle was a bishop. Both the father and the uncle are authentic historical figures. Both were hanged during the Kościuszko Insurrection for treason and servitude to Catherine of Russia. The time of the play is the eve of the Insurrection. Szczęsny hates his father, the traitor to Poland, but his Hamlet-like "To be or not to be", "To act or not to act", is, at the same time, the choice between the long tradition of the nobility of old Poland and joining the mob of cobblers and tailors who, in their admiration for the French Revolution, are only too eager to hang the aristocrats. The first Hamlet in Polish drama is unable to make the choice.

These versions of *Hamlet* must inform the figures both of Hamlet and Fortinbras in Herbert's poem.

In 1904, Kott notes, Stanisław Wyspiański described Hamlet as "Poor boy with a book in his hand". Wyspiański — a painter, dramatist and designer much admired by Gordon Craig — made the Polish Hamlet walk round the renaissance galleries of Kraków's Royal Castle:

> The scenario of history imposed on the Polish Hamlet at the turn of the century a duty to struggle for the nation's liberation. That particular Hamlet used to read Polish Romantic poets and Nietzsche.

Herbert's Fortinbras might be a tough-minded anti-romantic, an exemplar of what James Joyce termed "the classical temper". He might be rejecting Hamlet's elegant romantic posturing, his nationalistic excess.

In 1956, Kott attended the opening night of *Hamlet* in Kraków. This production took place at the time of the 20th Congress in Moscow, three years after the death of Stalin, and just before what Kott terms "the stormy October in Poland", the period of the thaw. Evoking the atmosphere of that moment, Kott remarks:

> The lines that everyone knew by heart, that were until now only literature, suddenly sounded frightening, almost shocking . . . *Hamlet* became from the first scene to the last, a political drama. Of all Shakespeare's words the most audible was "watch". At Elsinore someone is hidden behind every arras.

Kott describes how Rosencrantz and Guildenstern behave like secret police agents and suggests that this is how Shakespeare saw them: "He certainly knew well who murdered Marlowe and why." In Kraków Hamlet's "To be or not to be" may signify "To act or not to act" because the Polish Hamlet of 1956 was both "an angry young man and a rebellious communist."

For Kott, Fortinbras is central to a political *Hamlet*. He has broken the chain of crime and revenge, and restored order to the Danish kingdom. This order may be understood as "the restoration of moral law, or as the '*neue Ordnung* in Europa'". Fortinbras may be one thing, he may be the other — this uncertainty of interpretation is the adhesive irony which holds together the character of Herbert's Fortinbras. As Kott points out, the difficulty is that in Shakespeare's text Fortinbras — "man of the strong arm" — is only broadly sketched:

> Who is this young Norwegian prince? We do not know. Shakespeare doesn't tell us. What does he represent? Blind fate, the absurdity of the world, or the victory of justice?

Reading Herbert's poem, we have no producer to impose a definite meaning on the text — instead, we need to float various meanings. Is Hamlet an insurrectionary idealist? Is Fortinbras a positivist, a pragmatist? Is this a version of the young, romantic Joseph Conrad's correspondence with his sceptical uncle, Tadeusz Bobrowski? Is Hamlet merely Fortinbras's biased view of the prince?

For Kott, the rest is not silence: "The rest, or at least, the very end, is the coming of Fortinbras." And here Kott would seem to be echoing Herbert's "The rest is not silence but belongs to me". Maybe Fortinbras is the politician who has to pick up the pieces? He embodies two political clichés — 'the bottom line', 'at the end of the day'. He is nothing if not a realist. Perhaps he will reform the prison system? Or perhaps he will build bigger prisons and fill them with more and more detainees?

Fortinbras knows that Hamlet's state funeral will be an excellent propaganda opportunity which will help create the myth of Hamlet, that "star named Hamlet". And in English, *hamlet* is a little village like Bethlehem. The prince's charisma is both secular and religious. His canonization will assist Fortinbras's control of the state.

Perhaps for the reader who views *Hamlet* as securely embedded in a literary canon that is above politics, this may seem a merely idiosyncratic and peripheral reading of the play? Here, we may note that Coleridge seized on its propagandist possibilities when he was making notes for his lecture on the play. Commenting on the opening scene, he noted "Shakespeare's tenderness with regard to all innocent superstition: no Tom Paine declarations and pompous philosophy". He then wondered

> whether it will not do to speak of the honest pride of our Englishmen — Milton, Shakespeare, Bacon, Newton, and now Wellington — and how the glorious events of the day all are (as?) deducible from the attack on England.[3]

At the time — it was May, 1809 — Wellington was beginning his invasion of Southern France, after driving Soult out of Spain. Perhaps Wellington is Fortinbras? His name looks out of place, like the odd name out in a quiz or intelligence test. But for Coleridge writing under the pressure of war, he is another great name to add to the list of national greats.

Herbert's Fortinbras, like Wellington, is both soldier and politician, but at moments his voice has a lyric cadence which makes him more than the tough terse man of action and cynical operator:

> but what is heroic death compared with eternal watching
> with a cold apple in one's hand on a narrow chair
> with a view of the ant-hill and the clock's dial

Like an apostrophe to the office furniture, this is power seen from the inside, without the self-regard of the megalomaniac who reminds us that it's lonely at the top. The last poignant lines are religious in their cadence and texture:

> It is not for us to greet each other or bid farewell we live on
> archipelagos
> and that water these words what can they do what can they do
> prince

The trailing incomplete close is reminiscent of the beginning and end of Eliot's 'Marina':

> What seas what shores what grey rocks and what islands
> What water lapping the bow
> And scent of pine and the woodthrush singing through the fog
>
> What images return
> O my daughter.
> [. . . . .]
> What seas what shores what granite islands towards my timbers
> And woodthrush calling through the fog
> My daughter.

Perhaps in the end Fortinbras sounds romantic and mystical, not armourplated? Perhaps he, too, has succumbed to the dream and the myth? He and Hamlet are kin, they need each other.

Notes

The Jan Kott quotations are taken from his *Shakespeare Our Contemporary*, (London 1967) pp.48-60 and from *Theatre Notebook 1947-1967*, (London 1968) pp.18-21.

1. Zbigniew Herbert, 'Mona Lisa', *Selected Poems*, trans. Czesław Miłosz and Peter Dale Scott, (Harmondsworth 1968), pp.85-7.
2. *Op. cit.*
3. Thomas Middleton Raysor (ed.), *Coleridge's Shakespearean Criticism*, Vol. 1, p.40.

III

Donald P.A. Pirie

Engineering the People's Dreams: An Assessment of Socialist Realist Poetry in Poland 1949-1955.

Engineering the People's Dreams: An Assessment of Socialist Realist Poetry in Poland 1949-1955

> Why do you write these poems?
> Life is more beautiful than poetry.[1]

There has, in the mid-1980s, been a resurgence of interest in the social phenomenon of Stalinism in general, as well as its traumatic effect on post-war Polish culture. Usually these studies concentrate either on the vilification of those writers who compromised themselves in participating in the Stalinist lie[2], or on the ludicrous aspects of the ideological doggerel that was published in mass editions, a ridiculous sympton of a hated, frightening system[3] that has now virtually disappeared from public awareness. The approach here will be to deal with the mechanism and themes of a discredited but sorely misunderstood era.

The political framework of Poland in the early 1950s is fundamental to an appreciation of the poetic works published between 1949 and 1954, acclaimed by the Stalinist 'cultural establishment'. Political reality dominated all areas of public and private life, and censorship suppressed and falsified history, sociology and psychology.

The infiltration of Soviet culture into Poland began slowly after the end of the Second World War. Of course, the mere presence of the Red Army and Soviet advisers, and the hands-off policy of the Western 'allies' gave the Soviet-sponsored Polish Workers' Party (PPR) enormous advantages over other political groups with which it first cooperated. Much as in Western Europe, there was genuine public enthusiasm for socially oriented political solutions to rebuild a devastated economy and society. But the 'gentle revolution' promised by the coalition government that emerged after elections in October 1947 was redirected within a year, after the isolation and criminalisation of all opposition, towards the 'building of socialism' on the Soviet model in line with the 'innovative' works of Comrade Stalin. A unification Congress in December 1948 forced the rump Polish Socialist Part (PPS) to merge with the Stalinist PPR: this was little more than a ritual to mark the founding of a single vanguard Party (PZPR — the Polish United Workers' Party) that supposedly embodied all the political aspirations of the victorious Polish working class. The leader of the new 'people's democracy', Bolesław Bierut, held all key posts of President of the state, First Secretary of the Communist Party and Head of the Armed Forces. The principle of the Party's 'leading role' in society, exercised well before the unification Congress, was finally formalised in the Constitution passed on 22 July 1952, the zenith of Stalinist terror and paranoia in Poland.[4]

The transformation of Polish society was from the start to be synchronised with a 'cultural revolution' that would do battle with those remnants of 'bourgeois' morality that threatened the evolution of the 'new, socialist man'. Bierut declared as early as October 1947 the Stalinist conviction that the arts have a central role in the political education of the nation:

> It is an artist's obligation, in forming the spiritual sphere of a nation's life, to insert himself into the pulsating heartbeat of the working masses, into their longings and aspirations, to draw creative inspiration from their emotions and experiences, and thereby expand his efforts the main purpose of which is tc raise and celebrate the standard of living of those masses. Creative work bereft of this aim, art for art's sake, is the consequence of asocial tendencies. Of the various means of affecting people, it is art that probably has the most profound and universal impact on society, improving it, enlightening and nurturing it. A work of art can profoundly affect the mind as well as the feelings and the imagination, can electrify people, persuade and captivate them. It is enough for us to remember the enormous role played in the history of the formation of our national spirit, in the mobilisation of the whole of Polish society during the period of slavery by Mickiewicz and Słowacki. Our contemporary artists must imprint on their memories their duty to improve, nurture and enlighten the nation in their works.[5]

Socialist Realism, the Stalinist method of producing a 'socialist culture', was formally endorsed, only weeks after the consolidation of the Communist Party, by a congress of the Polish Writers' Union (20-23 January 1949). The organisation's nominated leadership was to prepare a production plan for literature to be enforced through its control of paper distribution, publishing houses and editorial staff in accordance with the government's national Six Year Plan (1950-1955). The centralisation of culture and its subordination to the grandiose Stalinist vision of an industrialised state was advanced in the endless meetings, conferences and congresses organised by Party activists whose actual artistic talent was less in evidence than their politically correct rhetoric. From 1949 it was impossible to publish anything that did not conform to the rigorous logic of Marxist-Leninist dialectics (as modified by Stalin) or the 'aesthetics' of Socialist Realism. Poetry, now merely a sub-committee of the Union of Writers within the whole cultural edifice, was just another appliance in the writer-worker's toolbox. Poetry was not permitted to be 'neutral' in this crucial period of the 'heightened class struggle', or escape from the realities of politics and the contemporary world any more than the other arts.

The war had decimated the ranks of elder artists and writers, except for those who had managed to emigrate to the West, or those who had survived Soviet captivity. Thus the majority of the Union's members were young enthusiasts and fanatics. Those of the older generation who were sympathetic to the new ideology but unable to write (produce) satisfactory texts were sent to live (and work) with the nation's soul, the workers and peasants. The Party suspected the older generation to be contemptuous of the 'people': these expeditions 'to the masses' were the basis of tedious eulogies of the collective farms, steelworks and shipyards, and those employed there. The young were encouraged to contribute poetry by the countless poetry competitions, prizes and the founding of 'poetry circles' in factories, on farms and in schools. The appearance of a festive literary scene was given, which hid a robotic discipline of talent and work.

All the arts suffered as compliance in the system extended to virtually all the writers, artists, film-makers and actors in Poland. Guilty complicity in the imprisonment of culture added to a spiralling paranoia, each writer publicly declaring his greater commitment to the cause, and denouncing others whose writing fell short of unbridled enthusiasm for the Party, the Soviet Union and

Socialism in the search for 'class enemies'. All these factors led to the disappearance of creative writing for the whole of the period of the Six Year Plan, and its replacement by repetitive, cliché-ridden 'schematic' works that soon embarrassed even the foremost figures in the Party's cultural leadership.

Yet the Party's literary taste was not openly questioned, and the 'loss of production' was explained in terms of human inefficiency or sabotage by alien ideology. A degree of dissatisfaction was voiced in late 1952, which led to the toleration of a broader interpretation of Socialist Realism. After the inevitable dirges to his greatness and genius, Stalin's death in March 1953 inaugurated the slow shift away from the excesses of the 'cultural revolution'. In February 1954, Minister of Culture Włodzimierz Sokorski was expressing distaste for "any attempt to direct the arts" or "intervention in the creative process". Within the next year, as the leadership admitted to its misuse of power within the state, open criticism was voiced about cultural policy, and Socialist Realism attacked.

Then the twentieth Congress of the Communist Party of the Soviet Union heard Nikita Khrushchev attack Stalinism and its cult of the personality, the 'period errors and deformations' of socialism, which led to the total discrediting of Socialist Realism among artists. Its one-time spokesmen recanted and explained they too had been misled by the utopian promises of the Stalinist system. Bierut suffered a stroke on hearing Khrushchev's attacks on his political idol, and died in Moscow in March 1956. For Poland, Stalinism in pure form had come to an end, though the dismantling of the Stalinist contraption (particularly censorship and the control of publishing) was to take thirty more years.

From the perspective of the 1990s, the arts in the early 1950s and poetry in particular, appear to be extraordinarily vulgar and inept. But it must always be remembered that the very real threat of police repression or redundancy made the ridiculous 'socialist culture' of the Bierut era a deadly serious affair. However hilarious the unskillful imagery and poetic forms, public criticism of the works of this new culture was interpreted as waging war on the political system and was quickly suppressed.

Under the Six Year Plan, it would be possible to ignore the names of poets or the titles of works, since personality and individuality was reserved exclusively for Stalin himself. Poets, like other artists, dreamed of merging into the victorious masses:

One single light pours over our faces
And in the steps of all there is the step of each and every one.
On to the parade of people and countries![6]

The poetry devoted to Stalin's 'genius' is a sourcebook of unself-conscious nonsense, illustrating the extraordinary personality of the 'Father of Nations'. As Bierut wrote on the General Secretary's seventieth birthday:

> The incomparable development of the first workers' and peasants' state in the world, a socialist state, its development attained in the sweat of the five-year plans guided by the unshakable will and all-knowing planning of Joseph Stalin has epoch-making significance for progressive forces throughout the world.[7]

These sentiments are repeated in the sublime lines written by the Party's greatest poetic asset, Władysław Broniewski (1897-1962), a self-confessed practicing Communist already before the war. Broniewski wrote his rapturous epic 'A Word About Stalin' in 1950 setting a 'norm' for poetic production:

Millions of people in the Union of Soviets and the countries moving down
the road to socialism are creating a new world, carrying in their hearts and on
their lips the name of STALIN
The Chinese People's Army marches ahead and expels the alien force and the
slavery of money from its territory, shouting STALIN!
Striking French miners hold out and reach out their hands to the East with the cry STALIN!
A poet, exiled from his own land for loving freedom and social justice,
a beautiful Chilean poet writes a poem about STALIN.
Warsaw, horrendously destroyed, raises its blood-stained bricks on top of each
other all the faster with the name of STALIN.
Everywhere in the world where the violence of money, the bayonet of the
mercenary and the policeman's truncheon have reached, the people are struggling
and will win with the name of STALIN.
Hundreds of millions of people are crying out: STALIN, STALIN, STALIN![8]

What is particularly striking in this sloganistic prose poem is its articulation of a collective mass's faith and trust in the God-like generalissimus who is omnipresent and omniscient. The sublime and ridiculous are welded together in one poem on Stalin's birth, translated especially from the Georgian of poet Giorgi Leonidze in celebration of the General Secretary's seventieth birthday as a model worthy of emulation. It depicts in pastiche form the scene of Christ in the manger, adored by shepherds, with the proud mother looking on:

> The child was born in a small hut
> And the neighbours come running up
> To see Vissarion
> And to wish him well.
>
> Upon the bedding there smiles
> His mother, silent and happy,
> And stringed sweets —
> As required by custom — arrive too.
>
> His grandmother, gleaming with joy
> Looks down enraptured at the child . . .
> Then on a mountain slope there shines
> A maple tree, illuminated in the sunset.[9]

It hardly matters that this is not by a Pole: a fundamental principle of Socialist Realism is its cultural interchangeability, in keeping with the ideological slogan that the arts should be "national in form and socialist in content". (Though what the socialist content is here I cannot hazard to guess.) Leonidze's Polish poet comrades reached equal heights of the personality cult's fawning sycophancy, as illustrated by the following celebration of Stalin's supernatural powers penned by Krzysztof Gruszczyński (b. 1925):

> He who kept watch over the revolution like an eye,
> He who led the nations to victory,
> He can redirect the course of rivers
> He founds nature's laws.
>
> It is Stalin who commands the forests to march,
> And orders rivers to flow into the deserts,
> Stalin — our comrade, Stalin — our leader,
> Stalin the engineer of our dreams.[10]

Yet Stalin's cultural engineering demanded of poets ever more ridiculous leaps of the imagination to outdo (much as among

Stakhanovite workers) their fellow 'workers of the mind'. Again it is an old stalwart of the inter-war period who succeeds where others fail:

> History's train speeds on,
> As the semaphore of the centuries shine out.
> Revolution needs no glories,
> Needs no pompous metaphors.
>
> It is the train-driver who is vital,
> And that is HIM:
> Out comrade, leader and communist —
> Stalin — a word clear as a bell![11]

Even more embarrassing in later life must be the genre of poems pleading directly to a patron for attention, advantages or mercy. A jewel of this type of self-criticism is by Jarosław Iwaszkiewicz (1894-1980), entitled 'Letter to President Bierut'. In it the effete poet declares his master always to be right, much as the Party was infallible:

> For while, my President, you knew well
> which road to take and how to lead us,
> I trusted too much in my own out-of-date wisdom,
> feeding my tired eyes on the views of beauty —
> and illumined by rainbows I had not noticed
> the common man bent underneath the yoke.
> I know, now I understand so much,
> and I am trying to comprehend what has been,
> though I do not turn back, since I do really miss
> those 'radiant sunsets' and 'roses' and 'marble' . . .
> And so you see, my President,
> how difficult it is for me today,
> I am no longer young, and we must speed on,
> I had thought I had achieved something in life,
> and yet I must learn it all anew.
> You know that I did not praise the great men of this world,
> and I do not write this letter to you
> because you seem in the sharp light to be standing on a plinth;
> everyone watches you, everyone praises you,
> but when it's too much for me or when I feel lost,
> I always think of you, and I know that you also
> love Poland far and wide, and its simple people,
> who are building their homeland up at great effort,
> and I know that you are right. And that thought of work
> is like a spring breeze on a snow-covered plain,

it is like being dazzled with light on an autumn morn.
And I know that you understand that fate has condemned me
to write verse: to compose words for Poles;
that I know little else. And that this also contributes to
the building of new things and the way towards the light.
And that like weavers at their looms, I with my pen,
and you bent low over an enormous map of Poland:
we all breathe because of extraordinary love for the reborn world
and faith in man.
So forgive me the daring of writing to you in this tone,
but in you I always perceive a model of such simplicity,
that I am given courage to send you modest greeting.
This is not the time for great words;
this is the time for great deeds.
I therefore turn to you to express ordinary words in an ordinary
way:
"Live long, work hard — we shall all help!"[12]

Poets were thus quite aware of the disciplined response expected of them and that the primary objective was to present their patrons with work that praised the achievements and personalities of their leaders, and confirmed the Stalinist world as one of harmony, order and natural, historical justice.

Yet a central problem of Socialist Realism, which supposedly reflected the struggle to build a socialist society in Poland objectively, was that not only was culture *for* the peasant and working-class masses, but it should ideally be produced *by* them. This gave many writers a guilt complex: the 'real' actors of history were the working classes, but their voice had to be filtered through artists whose origins were not proletarian at all. The poet Konstanty Gałczyński (1905-1953), criticised and silenced for his petit bourgeois attitudes, paradoxically wrote some of the best 'commissioned' attacks on his own 'false consciousness':

Blocked nose. No interest in politics.
Always pained. Ever nostalgic.
Minces around. It's the utter end.

He'd like to. He would. He could. He might.
He wipes his eyes. Looks through the window.
A white charger? No, it's snow falling.

It's all gone wrong. It's just not right.
Signs on the ground. Signs in the heavens.
But, pardon, where's the comet?[13]

Gałczyński's rejection of the post-war émigré threatening to return on "a white charger" and the pre-war liberal intellectual unwilling to take a clear position in what to Stalinism was the clear choice between fascism and socialism condemns persons like himself to the dustbin of history, unless total submission (conversion) to the cause, its doctrines and aesthetics follows from the Marxist illumination of his past errors:

> People, forgive me, if
> in these songs I gave so little,
> that I did not offer the sort of songs,
> that would have been correct.[14]

Tragically for him (in that his attempted compromise actually failed), Gałczyński could not actually write in praise of the new with unequivocal optimism: he was frequently criticised for this at Writers' Union meetings until he was forbidden to publish. His talent lay in satire, and redirecting it against his own past was hardly a problem for him. More shocking is the following workers' marching hymn for the First of May composed by the equally respected Antoni Słonimski (1895-1976), whose total submersion in the collective "we" of the people's will is reflected in the following lines:

> We come from the factories and workshops,
> Marching as we did each year,
> Our steps beat out in time
> The victorious rhythm of history.
>
> We come from the mines and steelworks,
> Coming here because it's better to sing while marching
> And the flags flutter more colourfully,
> And this song reaches the sky
> When the people of Warsaw sing it out.[15]

The Socialist Realist 'method' is a prescriptive system intended to codify for the arts the dogmas of 'diamat' (dialectical materialism, the philosophical basis of Marxism-Leninism) whose aesthetic consequences are obvious from the works quoted thus far. The theory went as follows: Socialist Realism demanded *optimism* from the artist in his rendering of man and history based on the inevitable victory of socialism in the building of communism (since the theory claimed to be 'scientifically' proved). The somewhat tautologous terms include: typicality (*typowość*), the portrayal of characters 'typical' of the struggle to build socialism; democratisation of language (*demokratyzacja języka*), meaning that the masses must be able to understand and respond to the language of the work (hence use of military and building-site imagery); class consciousness (*klasowość*), a dogma that concluded that each artist's class origins determine the view he or she holds of the world, an attitude that could be measured according to the rigorous standards of socialist ideological correctness (*ideowość*). This ideological rectitude was confirmed by the artist's emphatic expression of the leading role of the Party and its infallibility in all things, especially in placing the Party at the hub of plot, character and imagery: Party consciousness (*partyjność*). No apology is made by Socialist Realist theory for the resulting prejudicial attitudes in its model works: indeed this is enshrined in the principle of justified bias (*tendencyjność*). All these terms which overlap in applicability were used to judge a novel's, play's, poem's, film's or ballet's eligibility in the task of "demonstrating the greatness of the times."[16]

Perhaps the most misleading word in Socialist Realism is 'realism'. The theory of Socialist Realism insisted on the applicability of Hegelian determinism to culture. Hegel's concept of a dialectical relationship between the struggle of a thesis with its antithesis leading inevitably to a synthesis reappears as Socialist Realism being the synthesis of Romanticism and Realism. On its own, realism, when applied to the construction of the new utopia, was never enough. The heroic, epic battle with the elements and with history demanded another dimension which was to be provided in the accessible form of Romanticism, a movement which in both the Russian and Polish cultural spheres has been a crucial part of the patriotic education of the average citizen, whatever the governing ideology. This led to numerous unintended self-parodies such as the following war-time tale of a courageous girl who stood alone against the Nazi tanks, totally contradicting its early nineteenth-century model by Adam Mickiewicz[17] in which a seemingly mad girl's imagination had served to reassess superstition as an insight into the unknown:

> "Listen, young girl! She will not listen . . .
> It's clear daylight, it's a small town."
> But there is no small town, there's not a living soul,
> Over the ruins runs naked, red-haired Ryfka,
> Thirteen-year old girl.

> The fat Germans drove over in a fat tank.
> Run, run, little Ryfka![18]

Socialist Realism was scientifically proved to be the logical culmination of earlier ideas and shifts in the cultural history of humanity. Whereas Realism provided the writer with a technique of an artistically 'scientific' or material, real basis for his work by detailed and exacting description and psychology, Romanticism gave the artist the imaginative vision to represent the utopia which the people were struggling for. Furthermore, Romanticism, in its rhetoric of freedom and a revolutionary future, was seen as having criticised the inequalities and hypocrisy of nineteenth-century middle-class society whose values were the mortal enemy of socialism. In this context, again, Realism was seen as complementing the aspirations of the Romantics in its penetrating exposure of the injustices and exploitation of man in industrial Europe (whether or not intended by the author). More importantly, Socialist Realism, in its application of Marxist-Leninist dialectics and in its verifiability through class-consciousness, had overcome the individualist rantings of the Romantics and the criticism for the sake of criticism typical of mere realism.[19]

Andrey Zhdanov, Stalin's cultural commissar, detailed these ideas most clearly in a speech to the All-Union Congress of Soviet Writers in 1934:

> Comrade Stalin has called our writers 'the engineers of human souls'. What does this mean? What obligations does such an appellation put upon you?
>
> It means, in the first place, that you must know life to be able to depict it truthfully in artistic creations, to depict it neither scholastically nor lifelessly, nor simply as objective reality, but rather as reality in its revolutionary development. The truthfulness and historical exactitude of the artistic image must be linked with the task of ideological transformation, of the education of the working people in the spirit of socialism. This method in fiction and in literary criticism is what we call the method of socialist realism.
>
> Our Soviet literature is not afraid of being called tendentious, for in the epoch of the class struggle there is not and cannot be any classless, non-tendentious or apolitical literature.
>
> Soviet literature must be able to portray our heroes and see our tomorrow. This will not be utopian since our tomorrow is being prepared by planned and conscious work today.[20]

Linked to this last premise is the view that Socialist Realism proclaimed what was termed 'objective truth', in other words the scientifically observable fact that all societies strive for the higher level of social development called socialism and will ultimately attain communism. Without knowledge of diamat's laws of history, it therefore follows it is impossible to reproduce objective reality. All writers instinctively betray their class allegiances (subjectivism) which can prevent them from drawing the obvious conclusions, if they do not wholeheartedly, passionately and intellectually accept these incontrovertible truths. The ideological content of a work, whether objective or subjective, always serves the interests of a particular class, but must only serve the interests of the Party. The artist has an obligation to portray only objective truth, or unmask that which hinders progress towards it.

Literature, in the nineteenth-century view of both Marx and Lenin, has a powerful impact on those who read; it must therefore adopt a 'responsible' position now that the natural audience has become the masses in their millions. Unlike mere realism, Socialist Realism has a task to perform: it must educate its readers in the laws of history and teach them how to spot the class enemy:

> He told us in books and pamphlets, Lenin told us in reading rooms
> That we were to be the sparks of a conflagration — the red ray of the sun.
> But that we have to destroy the evil in this world, rescue the world from slavery,
> This was told us at assemblies and meetings by comrade Stalin![21]

As the Soviet Socialist Realist critic Timofieyev observed: "Writers are neither viewers nor observers but active participants in the Socialist system"[22]. Thus writers, artists, film-makers and sculptors are campaigning activists of the Party, for it was considered impossible to both be a member of a society and to be independent of it. Where the artist has doubts or concerns, the Party can provide solid support and ideology. These are his ultimate, infallible inspiration and guide, not the deceptive traditions of fictional literature.[23]

This reorganisation of aesthetic, philosophical, social and political ideas into one whole system was made attractive because the Communist state gave the artist a crucial role in society, rendering into artistic form his testimony of the "glorious forward march of history". Not only, as mentioned above, does the artist merge with the masses, but his work reaches millions:

> If one day I will write a work
> That will be read by many.[24]

The subjects available to the poet were clearly defined: the struggle for the victory and foundation of the socialist system, the struggle for peace, the collectivisation of the countryside, socialist construction, Stakhanovite competition in the workplace, rationalisation of industry, the struggle to fulfil economic plans, and the creation of a new 'socialist' culture. Furthermore, Socialist Realism's educative function required 'positive' heroes (particularly in prose) as models for the masses: not only do such heroes and heroines overcome tragic situations, but they always succeed in attaining their goals. These are not characters with doubts; they are not enclosed in their alienated worlds, obsessed by their own psychological and physical decay. The positive hero always places the interests of the Party, the working class, the fatherland, above his own. This is because only man's participation in the collective effort saves him from alienation. The positive hero is transformed into the new 'socialist' man who progresses to his ultimate aim the complete transformation of human society, and thus overcomes history itself.

Given the grandeur of the task, the literary forms most suited to Socialist Realism were the novel (to show the vast panorama of history and human progress) and drama (where the superiority of socialism could be demonstrated in scholastic speeches). Poetry, a medium used for more universal reflection was the least able to cope with the demanding precision of the theory. On the other hand, the ideologists hoped that the tenets of Marxism-Leninism, if expressed in short memorable versified form, might most easily penetrate public opinion which had traditionally set a great premium on poetry. The constant complaints about 'schematism' (the over-rigorous emphasis on ideological correctness, the use of typical, positive heroes) indicate the total failure to produce more than a few poems 'typical' of their time. The following lines by the pre-war constructivist poet Adam Ważyk (1905-1982) are indicative of the absurdities that followed from ideological correctness:

> At dawn, impatient,
> Unsatiated with its own beauty,

The locomotive hissed
Above a girl, kneeling before it.

Someone seeing
The girl's pagan profile in passing
Wrongly concluded
That she was praying to the machine.[25]

The achievements of the Six Year Plan in poetry are best represented by the anthology *Poezja Polski Ludowej* (The Poetry of People's Poland), finally published in 1955, just as Socialist Realism was being phased out. It remains the most comprehensive guide to the 'method' available, though its print run of ten thousand copies implies a certain hesitancy. A second edition never appeared. Nevertheless it contains model examples of the incorporation of Socialist Realist techniques into Polish poetry, and proposed a new canon of modern poetry that it termed 'socialist literature based on realism'. As the rousing introduction states, "This anthology stands at the end of an unbreakable strand that runs throughout the Polish nation's poetry, the continuous strand of revolutionary thought which is the living tradition of the struggle for progress and justice".[26] The authoritarian editors know what the public wants best: "Contemporary readers want to see the reflection of their thoughts and the aspirations of their lives in today's poetry"[27]; but they concede that some contributors' enthusiasm is not matched by their ability: "Not all are mature and precise in their use of words, but they all aspire to one and the same thing — the expression through their verse of the truth of the world in which they live".[28]

Most of the younger poets were as enthusiastic 'socialist poets' as the twenty-seven year old Andrzej Braun (b. 1923, aged 30 on Stalin's death), their work mosaic reworkings of political axioms determined by their fanatical Party consciousness. His work embodies perfectly the rules and ideals of Stalinist culture, as canonised by the older Broniewski's agitprop demand for "Equality! Education! Tractors!"[29] and so we read in Braun's poeticised political analysis that:

The poor can only be aided
With tractors and the thought of Lenin.[30]

In a confident statement of industrialisation as the assurance of human progress, Braun's 'What It's About' cannot be beaten:

I wage the battle with steel
with words hotter than the breath in my lungs.
For the longed-for classless beyond
it is the free bird of the heart that crashes itself against my ribs.

I agitate for the struggle with nature —
in the song bathed in the waterworks —
for apples in the snow, for the youth of girls,
growing grey in battle at the side of the river.

I describe the battle with time,
for I should yet like to live to see communism.
Rocking in the victorious march-past
in that one world, where creativity is possible.

Before the stars will bow before man
through those days multiplied by planning
I shall sing those oh so hard struggles with ourselves.
Know then how to pass away, as the struggle will pass
oh poem, be ready to die in victory,
and then you shall survive on human lips
you — the veteran of the class front.[31]

The intensified class struggle of the early 1950s easily identified those against the thought of Lenin as the enemies of the people, and demanded ever greater effort by the ranks of the Party's youth groups. A younger colleague of Braun's was Andrzej Mandalian (b. 1926), who pleads in typically military language to be allowed to defeat the 'kulak' (rich peasant exploiter of the poor) in the countryside:

Secretary,
send me out into the country,
there are difficulties there,
there are kulaks at work.
In the country there is hunger, illiteracy, no health provision,
alien truth deceives the people;
I want
my father to cease his toil,
as he has toiled all these years
on others' land;

I want the peasant, in his small corner
free from cobwebs,
to understand for whom he ploughs the land,
I want the land to
buzz with co-operative grain
wrested
from the hard ground.[32]

The one-sided (black and white) view of the world was promoted and justified by the doctrine of "justified bias" which confirmed the Party's interpretation of reality. A true "communist poet" must first be a committed activist determined to destroy the class enemy standing in the path of time. The metaphorical range here is simplistic in the extreme — time and history represent growth, progress, development, life and freedom, vanquishing the static, conservative and exploitative denizens of the regressive bourgeois hydra in a battle to the death. This creates a progressive version of the mythological domain in which the age-old conflict between good and evil can continue to attract the attention of immature minds:

Weakness in the revolutionary task
brings on disaster.
Let the degeneracy of the enemy
be stripped bare before the eyes of our class.
Let the hundred-headed hydra come out of the darkness into the
daylight.
May burning hearts and pure hands reach it (to vanquish it).
This is the will of our class, this class cause
glistens like a bayonet.
The steel-powered enter the factory hall.
And industry is set in motion.
And time, until recently rusty and dying, comes to life.
We have the hammer, plough and grapevine in common.
The Family. The Party.
Human will, human work,
human life.
Stalin has said that this is the 'eternal flame'.
Freedom after many ages.[33]

The hatred of the class enemy is given cathartic expression in images of the behaviour of exploiters in their evil homes:

Under an orange sun-roof, at a small table there sits
A mannekin wrapped exactly in a coat.

The Daily Mirror shields this dismal shadow of humanity,
This retired hyena, with the banner of daily life.
Drink your coffees, you murderers — the aroma suits you.
Women dressed in gaudy flowers.
Criminals were returning from their distant travels,
While a filthy cat gobbled the remains from a tin.
This is a set of the most savage barons,
Unknown even in France or Britain.
They have sardines with lemon as mid-morning snacks!
[...................]
She is the not badly-paid agent of New York.
What do they talk about? Do memories revive
At the greenish outline of the dead dollar?
Papal servants whose fingers glisten with amethysts
Watch the captain of all robbers.
Such necrophilia can even make profit on corpses.
The frilly *soutanes* draw the sweetness of the wine.[34]

The contempt for all that is alien to the experience of the working-class verges on the xenophobic: outside the peoples' democracies the animals of capitalism, murderous female mannekins (with no practical dress sense) wait to tear apart the humans lucky enough to live in socialism. The puritan aesthetic of Stalinism, promoting the positive values of rationing and self-sacrifice, easily reviles such luxuries as sardines and coffee, symbols of debauchery.

The manufacture of a mythology to replace the regressive traditions of national Polish culture can be seen in the following excerpt from Tadeusz Śliwiak's eulogy on the activities of early twentieth-century Communist hero Ludwik Waryński. It uses an emotive phrase from the 1943 wartime Communist Party manifesto (*What Are We Fighting For?*) to introduce the idealism of these mythical heroes of the workers' movement:

What are we fighting for?
Not for gold,
but for earthly, human happiness.
Injustice forces those of us bent over our work
to clench out hands into fists.
The unjustifiably divided
fruit of the land arouses anger,
and brings us all beneath the red standard —
covered in working-class blood.[35]

But it is the 'typical' worker (embodying the requirement of 'typicality' of subject) who is more often the hero of such verse, carrying out his task for the good of the community, as in these immortal lines by Jan Baranowicz (b. 1906) on the co-operative's book-keeper, who feels no distance or alienation from the peasants just because of his responsibilities:

> O book-keeper of the Progress Co-operative
> Francis Balawendra!
> Straighten up your lean shoulders,
> bogged down in your books like a wise man!
>
> Like a tree-stump — impervious to everything — you murmur,
> adding
> up the figures endlessly.
> And yet — I know — you were
> first to dare to dance with the girl tractor driver.
>
> Every so often people stand and nod or shake their heads —
> understanding what it is you bend over
> morning and evening.
>
> The seeds are now golden. The winter corn
> has grown into a green epic poem.
> The wind has ascended the stalks like a cricket,
> joy has carried it for acres![36]

The gross artificiality of this versified government information campaign clashes so obviously with the flexibility, reflection and distance of the truly poetic, that it is reasonable to suggest that no further investigation of the 'method' is necessary. Yet closer inspection reveals this conveyor belt of poetry to be in defensive mode; the young rarely stray outside the strict class-conscious rules, and the older generation returns to approved models from the nineteenth-century. Where doubts occur among the young, the most reliable models are those of the older Polish craftsmen with 'bourgeois' class consciousness, like Iwaszkiewicz or Słonimski, rather than truly revolutionary innovators like Mayakovsky.

This is why the closest model for Socialist Realist practice, whatever the theory claimed, was in fact an academic Classicism and not any 'synthesis' of Romanticism and Realism. The early nineteenth-century Classicists believed that once advanced values of civilisation, based on man's intrinsic goodness, had been defined and taught through their academies, humanity would be led out of the 'dark ages' into 'enlightenment'. This sentiment is echoed in Broniewski's 'Tamburlaine's Tomb':

> Man is good, wise and self-controlled
> Trusts in his reason, in his independent mind,
> He does not want hunger, air, fire or war
> And lays one brick after another.[37]

The dominant themes of the literature of Polish Classicism that lasted from the last quarter of the eighteenth to the first quarter of the nineteenth-century were subordinated to the needs of the socio-political order that the last King of Poland, the enlightened Stanisław August Poniatowski (ruled 1764-1795) hoped to construct, and reflected the ideology of the State's rulers and philosophers. It stressed the citizen's obligations to uphold 'order' and 'law', contrasted with the selfishness and acquisitiveness of provincial gentry mores.

This social idealism led writers far away from personal or inventive, witty self-expression, and as a result of poets accepting their 'duties' their social status (at least in the eye of the State) was significantly raised. It was part of the academic credo that the arts were primarily intellectual, and were easily categorised according to hierarchies, defined by such absolutes as 'beauty', 'perfection', or 'truth', and expressed in terms of perspective, proportion or harmony.

Classicist academicism insisted on the acceptance of definable limits to the subjects treated and to the manner in which they could be presented: "Academicism is a movement in art based on the rules of Classical aesthetics and on the principle of eclectic emulation of artists and works considered as 'perfect'. Academicism is thus a willing limitation of the freedom of individual artistic investigation, whether in the selection of themes or the use of formal techniques."[38] The Socialist Realist poet, much like the classicist, aspired to no greater heights than imitating the achievements of an acknowledged master of his trade, and hoping to equal the model set. The attitude is essentially normative (what poetry should be), allowing little scope for deviation, and criticism was limited to the definition of the 'correctness' or 'inappropriateness' of the finished work according to something vaguely called *decorum*, a sophisticated and demanding aesthetic norm.

Important Classicist subjects included: preference for grandiose mythological canvasses; reflection on the lessons of history and the allegorical lessons it taught (so appropriate for Marxism-Leninism); the stereotype of the virtuous, yet uneducated peasant, happy with his lot because of his sense of harmony with the natural world (the pastoral as a genre that need not correspond to the real hardships, poverty and oppression of the peasantry would almost beg for emulation in the 1950s); whatever the good-natured peasants might feel, however, change was not to be initiated from below, but granted from on high, since otherwise chaos might ensue; the ennoblement of work, though possibly well intentioned, inexorably led to the justification of the status quo. Common to both academic Classicism and Socialist Realism is also the unrequited desire to see 'great works' reflecting these great times: the writing of a tragedy or epic poem.

One such representative epic vision of the Stalinist mythology is by Słonimski, in which he deftly popularises the Marxist interpretation of the redundancy of earlier history and the classes that then held sway by implying that the present is the return of the golden age when man was at one with the universe, and all problems are resolved by philosophers:

> At school, from the frame of a portrait, eyes clean and kind
> Look down on your youthfulness. They do not want it destroyed.
> Do not regret past aeons, today you have better managers.
> Your Poland expands to the noisy song of axes.
> Here where once there ruled pride, or the enemy's money, sword
>   or club,
> It is now reason that holds sway, the heart and thought of the
>   philosophers.
> The grand lord used to strut, his nose held high in the air,
> While low did the peasant bend over the fallow, mean earth.
> Peasants were born, died, mown down next to their ancestors,
> falling like leaves from a tree, manured the land with their sweat.
> A thousand years the land slumbered, fettered by injustice.
> Man was an enemy to his fellow man, and the elements were hostile
>   to him too.
> But now, behold! Though the way is difficult and shrouded in mist,
> Yet it smells of spring, the warm East wind blowing down its course.
> There is still mud and snow, but the frosts will not return.
> The heart is lighter as the first breeze wafts.
> Now it is easier for eyes and hands, for lungs to breathe.
> Listen, oh, listen! how the wind of the approaching centuries
>   bellows out![39]

Socialist Realism has in common with its predecessor a clear preference for didacticism, and works not reflecting the aesthetic and moral order are seen to be undermining and destroying the achievement of the establishment. Literature has to set good examples, since man falls easily into bad habits. The Classicist theoretician Franciszek Dmochowski typically warned against studying the "book of nature" too closely, since the answers to all man's dilemmas were to be found in books.[40], much as the solutions to socialist man's problems were to be found in the writings of Marx, Engels, Lenin and Stalin.

Mieczysław Jastrun (1903-1983), a poet whose pre-war work was dominated by philosophical and Romantic concerns, during the Stalinist period used socialist rhetoric expertly but always as if it were an academic exercise. The emotional distance of the poet from his subject is both obvious and disturbing in the following most classical of works, an 'Ode to May':

> O, guardians of springtime, defenders of the light!
> Mouths open wide for the May day song.
> This day has mirrors in our eyes,
> and commands the words to be mirrors.
> May the leafy tree serve as our shade
> Just as I serve you with my poetry.
> Carry before you the red star,
> carry before you the red rose.[41]

Socialist Realism was not of course a mere copy of the ideals of Classicism. It was an eclectic aesthetic brew that allowed all styles from realism to 'high culture', excluding only the self-centred experimentalism of modernism. Yet in its centralist and prescriptive attitudes, Socialist Realism functioned in more or less the same way as its spiritual ancestor.

The implementation of the Socialist Realist 'method' on a national scale in Poland for even the short period of six years had a traumatic influence on subsequent intellectual and artistic life, and nowhere is this more obvious than in poetry. Socialist Realism had demanded the complete submission of its representatives, and their vocal declaration of commitment to the irrealities of the class struggle, the falsehood of historical inevitability, the lie of the Party's national support and the violence of the totalitarian state. These morally crippling fantasies were too much for persons of very different outlooks such as Czesław Miłosz and Zbigniew Herbert.

The first of these was branded an enemy of the people after his emigration in 1951, while the second retreated into the security of almost total obscurity for the whole period. However, most were willing, for their own comfort, to play the game of fabricating culture. In the period of somewhat half-hearted "de-Stalinisation" (1956-80) in which Stalinist practices were condemned, while socialism was still to be built within more or less the same institutional and economic framework, the consequences of the imposition of Socialist Realism remained an embarrassing "blank space" (*biała plama*) that was censored out of existence. Socialist Realism continued to exist as a negative model that haunted the imagination and the writing of the better poets, such as Broniewski, Iwaszkiewicz, Gałczyński, Jastrun and Ważyk; while the lesser ones, dependent on official approval for their careers, embarrassedly ignored either their own involvement in the period of 'distortions and deformations' or their patrons' responsibility during the purges and repressions.

The crisis of values of the 1980s demonstrated in recent poetry has its origins in the wilful vandalism and falsification of both the plurality of views and collective ethics that had accumulated and formed Polish culture over many centuries. The suppression of open discussion of the Stalinist period and its legacy thus became a moral issue, and poetry over the next quarter of a century reflected the willingness of individual writers to come to terms with the destructive and demoralising effects of the 'method'. As a poetry of resistance to the State's economy with the truth blossomed, poets felt obliged to speak for those unable to identify with socialist culture: this silent majority of disenfranchised, dissatisfied citizens (a term first used by Classicist philosophers) which gradually encompassed most social groups in Poland. The Party's policies first alienated the peasantry through collectivisation and the attacks on the Church during the early 1950s; then isolated the intellectuals and artistic community in the early 1960s. The student population was dealt a symbolic and permanent blow during the repressions of 1968; and the working classes, represented supposedly by the Party in this workers' state, were disgusted by their leaders' callousness and contempt during the 1970s. As most of Polish society found itself unable to articulate its aspirations and anxieties through the official media, it was often poetry that accepted the role of a forum in which to articulate the true concerns of "the unrepresented world", as the New Wave poets of the 1968 generation called the reality in which their alienated society lived.

The verse of the 1970s and early 1980s was moralist and yet anti-ideological, but as the poet reflected on his obligations to a gagged society, in identifying himself as yet another citizen oppressed by a political system, a new ethos of 'solidarity' emerged. At its most basic this ethos allowed artists to regain a lost self-respect by demonstrably protesting with the population at large against injustice (paradoxically reminiscent of what Bierut had termed "drawing creative inspiration from the emotions and aspirations of the working masses" in his speech quoted earlier).

As a result of the trauma of Socialist Realism, poetry led the search for reliable ethical standards and confronted the moral implications of living in a dishonest system. From the 1960s onwards it attempted to rebuild its readership's self-confidence, and slowly but surely to reconstruct a ravaged Polish identity and tattered national tradition. This longing for personal integrity is summed up in Zbigniew Herbert's poem 'The Power of Taste' in which he asserts that people never surrendered to the nightmarish engineering project of Stalinism and its apparent satisfaction of people's dreams. The aesthetic as well as the moral truth was obvious for those willing to see. And paradoxically, the horrendous, kitschy falsity of the "all-knowing planning of Joseph Stalin" had in the long term only reinforced precisely those elements of the national consciousness it had planned to destroy. Thus the last (poetic) word on Social Realism by Herbert is not directly an ethical, but an aesthetic rejection:

> No our refusal dissent and obduracy
> didn't require great character
> we had a pinch of indispensable courage
> but basically it was a matter of taste
> Yes taste[42]

Notes

1. St. R. Dobrowolski, 'Czemu?', *Poezja Polski Ludowej* ('The poetry of People's Poland'), ed. R. Matuszewski & S. Pollak, (Warsaw, 1955) p.290.
2. The predominant line in criticism of the literature of the Polish Stalinist era has been to name those artists, intellectuals and functionaries responsible for the impoverishment of national culture and to hold them to account for their speeches and publications of this period. An example is

an article by M. Danielewicz-Zielińska, 'Gorzkie żale przybywajcie . . . ', *Kultura*, Paris, 1987, no.5, which emphasises the political indoctrination of poets such as Broniewski, Ważyk and others in Lwów, occupied by the Soviets from September 1939, and notes their speedy rise through the Party's cultural ranks after the war. Another significant recent contributor is the ex-Communist Youth member Jacek Trznadel, who recorded conversations with writers who lived through the early 1950s in *Hańba domowa* (Paris, 1986). Other recent writing that does not merely ridicule includes the serious study of post-war prose (many of his comments are of relevance to poetry) by Z. Kubikowski, 'Szklany mur', a cycle of articles published in *Odra* 1983 nos.10-12 and 1984, nos.1-6.

3. Interesting with regard to a more formal discussion of the themes and ideas of Socialist Realist poetry are: A. Zieniewicz's 'Wiersze z marmuru', and B. Urbankowski's 'Poeci i dworzanie', both published in *Poezja* in 1986, nos. 1-2 and 3 respectively; mention must also be made of the enormous synthesis of post-war Polish poetry to 1964 in two volumes by E. Balcerzan. An invaluable assessment of Socialist Realist prose by Wojciech Tomasik, *Polska powieść tendencyjna 1949-1955*, (Wrocław, 1988) complements the range of work done recently in this subject, and as so many of the titles quoted, provides valuable insights.
4. General books on the Stalinist period in Poland are not easily available in English other than obvious general histories of Poland in the twentieth century, but a superb recreation of the atmosphere of the period was made in the collection of journalistic and propaganda articles in three volumes edited by L. Lachowiecki, L. Markiewicz and M. Paczkowski *Polski socrealizm: antologia publicystyki społeczno-kulturalnej z lat 1948-1957*, (Warsaw, 1988).
5. *Materiały do Studiów i Dyskusji z Zakresu Teorii i Historii Sztuki, Krytyki Artystycznej oraz Badań nad Sztuką*, 1952, no.1, p.8-9.
6. M. Jastrun, 'Oda majowa', *Poezja Polski Ludowej* (*PPL*), p.203.
7. B. Bierut, 'Zwycięski wódz nowej epoki', *Twórczość*, 1949, no.12.
8. W. Broniewski, 'Słowo o Stalinie', *Twórczość*.
9. G. Leonidze, 'Narodziny', *Twórczość*, 1949, no.12, p.7.
10. K. Gruszczyński, 'Stalin — inżynier naszych marzeń', *Po prostu*, 1953, no.11.
11. W. Broniewski, 'Słowo o Stalinie'.
12. J. Iwaszkiewicz, 'List do Prezydenta', *PPL*, pp.60-61.
13. K.I. Gałczyński, 'Śmierć inteligenta', *PPL*, p.213.
14. K.I.Gałczyński, 'Pieśń X', *PPL*, p.233.
15. A. Słonimski, 'Pierwszy maja', *PPL*, p.106.
16. K. Brandys, *Listy do Pani Z*, (Warsaw, 1960) p.65
17. J. Berman, 'Pokażcie wielkość naszych czasów', *Nowa Kultura*, 1951, no.48.
18. W. Broniewski, 'Ballady i romanse', *PPL*, p.119.
19. A. Hutnikiewicz, *Od czystej formy do literatury faktu*, (TNT, Toruń, 1965).

20. A.A. Zhdanov, *On Literature, Music and Philosophy*, (London, 1950) pp.15-16.
21. I. Fik, 'Armia Czerwona mówi', *PPL*, p.210.
22. A. Hutnikiewicz, *Od czystej formy do literatery fahtu*, (TNT, Toruń, 1965) pp. 206-207
23. Jastrun pleads to be able to write "without the lies of literature" (bez kłamstwa literatury), 'Dedykacja', *PPL*, p.191.
24. M. Jastrun, 'Dedykacja', *PPL*, p.190.
25. A. Ważyk, 'Widokówka z miasta socjalistycznego', *PPL*, p.251.
26. 'Nić nierozerwalna przez dzieje narodowej poezji — nieprzerwany ciąg myśli rewolucyjnej — żywa tradycja walki o postęp i sprawiedliwość', *PPL*, p.6.
27. 'Czytelnicy współcześni chcieliby widzieć w poezji dnia dzisiejszego odzwierciedlenie swoich myśli i marzeń swojego życia.' *PPL*, p.5.
28. 'Nie wszystkich jednak cechuje dojrzałość i celność słowa . . . dążą do jednego: do wyrażania swymi wierszami prawdy świata w którym żyją', *PPL*, p.6.
29. W. Broniewski, "Równość! Oświata! Traktor!" in 'Do domu', *PPL*, p. 122.
30. A. Braun, 'Front w Kozietułach', *PPL*, p.510.
31. A. Braun 'O czym', *PPL*, p.507.
32. A. Mandalian, 'Dzisiaj', *PPL*, p.555.
33. T. Kubiak, 'Serce Partii', *PPL*, p.517-518.
34. Z. Radek, 'Kawiarnia', *PPL*, p.492-93.
35. T. Śliwiak, 'Waryński w Krakowie', *PPL*, p.580-581.
36. J. Baranowicz, 'Spółdzielnia nad jeziorem', *PPL*, pp.259-60.
37. W. Broniewski, 'Grób Tamerlana', *PPL*, p.118.
38. Maria Poprzęcka: *Akademizm*, Wydawnictwa Artystyczne i Filmowe, (Warsaw, 1977) p.11
39. A. Słonimski, 'Portret Prezydenta', *Autograf*, 1988, no.2.
40. F.K. Dmochowski: *Sztuka rymotwórcza*, (Warsaw, 1788).
41. M. Jastrun, 'Oda majowa', *PPL*, p.204.
42. Z. Herbert, '*Potęga smaku*', *Raport z oblężonego miasta*, (Paris, 1983) p.75; trans. Adam Czerniawski: *The Burning Forest*, (Newcastle upon Tyne, 1988) p.118.

A. Alvarez

Noble Poet

Noble Poet

Zbigniew Herbert has had an exemplary Central European education. He was born in 1924 in Lwów in eastern Poland, the son of a lawyer and professor of economics whose great-grandfather spoke only English (hence his literary British surname). In September 1939, when Herbert was fifteen, Lwów was swallowed by the Russian whale. Twenty months later, the Germans marched in and Herbert finished high school underground, fighting in the Resistance. At the end of the war he went to university to study both his father's disciplines: he took a master's in economics at Kraków, then a master's in law at Toruń, where he stayed on to study philosophy. In 1950 he moved briefly to Gdańsk, then on to Warsaw where for six years he held down a series of menial, Kafkaesque jobs: in a bank, in a shop, as a clerk in the management office of the peat industry, in the department for retired pensioners of the Teachers' Cooperative, and in the legal department of the Composers' Association.

During the Nazi occupation his poems had been published irregularly in underground magazines and they continued to appear more or less in the same unofficial way during the grim Stalinist period after the war. Although he was a precocious poet, he had to wait until Khrushchev's thaw in 1956, when he was thirty-two, to publish his first book of poems. The second appeared the following year, two large collections representing a decade and a half of work, which established him as the leader of his exceptionally gifted generation. It is typical of his ironic indifference to success that he celebrated this recognition with an apologetic poem dedicated to the desk drawer which in sterner times had been his one true audience; his "rebel's fist stiff in dissent," he wrote, had given him a subject and an excuse, and his new liberty to publish what he wants is only reponsibility in another guise:

> such is freedom one has again
> to invent and overthrow gods[1]

He has been inventing and overthrowing gods ever since, a party of one, permanently and warily in opposition. Although he lived abroad from 1965 to 1971, when the conditions in Poland were relatively relaxed, and was abroad again in the late 1970s — he was awarded the Petrarch Prize in 1979, Germany's greatest cultural accolade — he returned home immediately after the troubles started in Gdańsk in 1980. His international reputation had become too secure for the Communist authorities to harm him, yet he refused to accept their embrace. *Report from the Besieged City* was first published by internees in the Rakowiecka Prison in Warsaw in 1983.

To understand modern Polish poetry it is necessary to understand also something of what the country went through during the Nazi occupation: 6 million killed out of a population of 30 million; dozens of villages destroyed and their inhabitants massacred, in the style of Lidice and Oradour; Warsaw razed and emptied of its million inhabitants, the Nazis boasting that they would turn it into "a second Carthage"; Governor General Hans Frank's infamous Operation AB which aimed at the total elimination of the country's intelligentsia — and succeeded in murdering 3,500. There was an old historical grudge between the Germans and the Poles, and it was settled by twentieth century totalitarian methods. All this instilled in the survivors — among other things — a distaste for rhetoric and artistic pretension that amounted almost to a hatred of poetry itself. Tadeusz Różewicz, who is three years older than Herbert, looked on art as an offense against human suffering and reduced his poems to a minimalist notation stripped of meter, rhyme, even of metaphor. "Modern poetry," he wrote, "is a struggle for breath." Herbert, too, eschews all punctuation and every unearned gesture. "He lowers his voice rather than raising it," John and Bogdana Carpenter wrote in the introduction to *Report from the Besieged City*, "the rhythm of his poems sometimes approaching the level of a whisper, or silent thinking."[2] Yet despite the lack of punctuation, the argument of his poems is unfailingly lucid and the voice, however low, is clear and precise.

This clarity is the core of everything Herbert has written. Despite the historical catastrophes he has lived through, he is a classicist, like Eliot, whom he reveres, like Valéry, like Piero della Francesca, about whom he has written eloquently in his collection of essays, *Barbarian in the Garden*.

Or perhaps he is a classicist because the continuing Polish catastrophe has placed such curious burdens on its writers. It is a nation that has held itself together for the past two centuries only by a collective effort of will. For 150 years Poland was partitioned between Russia, Prussia, and Austria, re-emerging between the world wars, then swallowed up again, first by the Germans, then by the Russians. All this puts a special strain on writers, for in an occupied or one-party nation literature takes on the patriotic, educative and moral burdens normally assumed by the state. It becomes, for instance, a forum for national debate in which political issues are discussed in the guise of imaginative writing. Whence the Polish penchant for allegory and what they call "Aesopian language". Whence, too, the strange phenomenon of the underground presses, during both the Nazi occupation and the subsequent troubles, continuing to print poetry and fiction along with political leaflets. In the Polish context, a poem or story can seem as rousing and urgent as a fighting handbill, and is probably as effective.

One of Herbert's earliest poems, written when he was in his teens, first appeared in this clandestine way. It is called 'Two Drops' and is prefaced by a quotation from the nineteenth-century poet Słowacki — "No time to grieve for roses when the forests are burning" — which the young Herbert, writing at a time when all of Poland was on fire, then proceeded to turn on its head:

The forests were on fire —
they however
wreathed their necks with their hands
like bouquets of roses

People ran to the shelters —
he said his wife had hair
in whose depths one could hide

Covered by one blanket
they whispered shameless words
the litany of those who love

When it got very bad
they leapt into each other's eyes
and shut them firmly

So firmly they did not feel the flames
when they came up to the eyelashes

To the end they were brave
To the end they were faithful
To the end they were similar
like two drops
stuck at the edge of a face[3]

It is a beautiful poem; given the circumstances in which it was written and the poet's age at the time, it is extraordinary. The theme is one that Herbert has repeated, in one form or another, throughout his work: that the feeling that can flower between people, however frail, is somehow a match for history, however violent. Most young poets would have been satisfied with that ultimate existential gesture — making love while the bombs fall, as if a kiss could annihilate annihilation. Herbert, however, uses it to affirm less obvious, more abiding virtues: bravery, faithfulness, restraint (grief becomes merely, "two drops/ stuck at the edge of a face"). In the end, the poem is not about a gesture of defiance but about dignity; it is classical in the true Roman sense.

Herbert has never deviated from this passion for *virtù*. The hero of many of his later poems is Mr. Cogito, a battered descendant of Valéry's luminously intelligent M. Teste, and also a descendant of Descartes who exists because he thinks about his existence. In other words, Mr. Cogito is a witness whose duty it is to serve truth not art, to think dispassionately about what he has seen, and to speak up for morality, however inappropriate it may seem:

• go upright among those who are on their knees
among those with their backs turned and those toppled in the dust

you were saved not in order to live
you have little time you must give testimony

be courageous when the mind deceives you be courageous
in the final account only this is important . . . [4]

This is from 'The Envoy of Mr. Cogito', Herbert's stern and moving last testament that ends his 1977 *Selected Poems*. But independence and courage, like clarity and restraint, have little chance against what he calls "the babble of the speaker's platform the black foam of newspapers." The best he can do is elevate plainness into an aesthetic and moral principle. In an early poem, 'A Knocker', he wrote wryly of his style, as though it were a limitation beyond his control:

my imagination
is a piece of board
my sole instrument
is a wooden stick

I strike the board
it answers me
yes — yes
no — no[5]

In the latest collection, 'Mr. Cogito and the Imagination' repeats the same theme less hopefully, but as an article of faith:

he wanted to make it
an instrument of compassion

he wanted to understand to the very end

. . . .

and so to bring the dead back to life
to preserve the covenant

Mr. Cogito's imagination
has the motion of a pendulum

it crosses with precision
from suffering to suffering

there is no place in it
for the artificial fires of poetry

he would like to remain faithful
to uncertain clarity[6]

Early and late, Herbert has avoided "the artificial fires of poetry" by using irony, that most classical of instruments, the enemy of rhetoric, of inflation, of distortion. But irony is also the weapon of the powerless, as Herbert himself pointed out—ironically, of course—at the end of a prose poem called 'From Mythology':

> Then came the barbarians. They too valued highly the little god of irony.
> They would crush it under their heels and add it to their dishes.[7]

For Herbert, irony has always been a two-edged instrument that turns on the poet as readily as on the outside world. But in earlier poems he used it playfully to rewrite his beloved classical myths in modern, deflationary terms — Arion, for instance, becomes "the Grecian Caruso"—and even, in some of his love poems, as an improbable way of expressing sensuality without being victimized by it:

> Inadvertently I passed the border of her teeth and swallowed her agile tongue. It lives inside me now, like a Japanese fish. It brushes against my heart and my diaphragm as if against the walls of an acquarium. It stirs silt from the bottom.
>
> She whom I deprived of a voice stares at me with big eyes and waits for a word.
>
> Yet I do not know which tongue to use when speaking to her—the stolen one or the one which melts in my mouth from an excess of heavy goodness.[8]

But the playfulness has seeped away over the years as his confidence in the power of truth and intelligence, as well as of irony, has weakened. The tone of his recent poems is grim, like the situation of his country and the civilized standards on which his work is based. "I avoid any commentary I keep a tight hold on my emotions I write about the facts," he says in the title poem of *Report from the Besieged City*.

"Then came the barbarians": when he called his prose collection *Barbarian in the Garden* he was implying that he himself was the barbarian outsider reacting to the civilized gardens of France, Italy, and ancient Greece. Yet these elegant, meticulous, oddly passionate essays return continually to the theme of vanished cultures and their violent destruction—the Templars, the Albigensians at Montségur, the Greek colonists at Paestum — as though his underlying concern was always the modern barbarians from East and West who have erupted into the precarious culture of his own country.

In the poems, too, the focus constantly shifts backward and forward between past and present. 'Report from the Besieged City' is both about Poland after December 1981, when General Jaruzelski declared "a state of war", and about Poland as it has been through the centuries, a crossroad for invading barbarians:

> in the evening I like to wander near the outposts of the City
> along the frontier of our uncertain freedom
> I look at the swarms of soldiers below their lights
> I listen to the noise of drums barbarian shrieks
> truly it is inconceivable the City is still defending itself
> the siege has lasted a long time the enemies must take turns
> nothing unites them except the desire for our extermination
> Goths the Tartars Swedes troops of the Emperor regiments of the
> Transfiguration
> who can count them
> the colors of their banners change like the forest on the horizon
> from delicate bird's yellow in spring through green through red to
> winter's black[9]

Invading armies have become so much a condition of Polish life that Herbert describes them as if they were manifestations of nature itself — that is, dispassionately and with an eye for their "delicate bird's yellow" beauty.

It is this objectivity — the rigorousness with which he avoids the easy outs of self-pity, melodrama, even nostalgia — that preserves the classical spirit in Herbert's work. Mr. Cogito's imagination may cross "with precision from suffering to suffering", but as it does so the precision matters as much as the suffering. Whatever his subject, the steady light of his intelligence imposes on it a kind of serenity of which the classics themselves are part, since they enable him to view the unruly present in the long, cooling perspective of history. What he wrote of his idol, Piero della Francesca, is also true of his own work: "Over the battle of shadows, conclusions and tumult, Piero has erected *lucidus ordo* — an eternal order of light and balance."

Czesław Miłosz once wrote that Herbert survived the war and Stalinism because of "his personal qualities — good health, toughness, an orderly mind". Those qualities have also kept him from being abstract in his classicism, or pedantic, or superior. His poetry is founded on a belief in ordinary human values — love, dignity, intelligence, common decency — as the only true defense against the barbarians. "History teaches us that nations and their achievements can be destroyed in an almost total manner," he said in an interview quoted by the Carpenters in their introduction to the 1977 *Selected Poems*. "During the war I saw the fire of a library. The same fire was devouring wise and stupid books, good and bad. Then I understood that it is nihilism which menaces culture most. Nihilism of fire, stupidity and hatred."

Herbert has steadily opposed nihilism with neither rhetoric nor anger, but with sanity — wakeful, ironic, evenhanded, intransigent:

> The pebble
> is a perfect creature
>
> equal to itself
> mindful of its limits
>
> filled exactly
> with a pebbly meaning
>
> with a scent which does not remind one of anything
> does not frighten anything away does not arouse desire
>
> its ardour and coldness
> are just and full of dignity
>
> I feel a heavy remorse
> when I hold it in my hand
> and its noble body
> is permeated by false warmth
>
> — Pebbles cannot be tamed
> to the end they will look at us
> with a calm and very clear eye[10]

Herbert is the only contemporary poet I know who can talk about nobility and, more important, sound noble without also sounding false. It is a note that is rare in the arts of any period. The Romans had it, so did Shakespeare, Donne, and Milton. But it hasn't been much in evidence in recent years and perhaps it took someone who has witnessed close up — "with a calm and very clear eye" — some of the worst horrors of this century to speak out for *virtù* and endurance without sounding sentimental.

The strengths Herbert praises in his poems — steadfastness and independence, imperviousness to cant, contempt for the bullies — have their corollary in the purity of his style. He has been marvellously served by his translators but perhaps his persistent lucidity has made their task a little easier. All of them remark on how much is lost in translation. Despite that, his poems, even in English, seem to me finer than anything currently being written by any English or American poet.

Notes

References to the publications have been abbreviated as follows:

SPH: Zbigniew Herbert, *Selected Poems* (translated by Czesław Miłosz and Peter Dale Scott), Harmondsworth 1968.

SPO: Zbigniew Herbert, *Selected Poems* (translated by John and Bogdana Carpenter), Oxford 1977.

RBC: Zbigniew Herbert, *Report from the Besieged City* (translated by John and Bogdana Carpenter), Oxford 1987.

1. SPH, p. 89.
2. RBC, p. vii.
3. SPH, p. 21.
4. SPO, pp. 79-80.
5. SPO, p. 45.
6. RBC, pp. 17-19.
7. SPH, p. 93.
8. SPH, p. 117.
9. RBC, pp. 77-79.
10. SPH, p. 108.

Paul Coates

Gardens of Stone: The Poetry of Zbigniew Herbert and Tadeusz Różewicz

Gardens of Stone: The Poetry of Zbigniew Herbert and Tadeusz Różewicz

I

There are several possible ways of describing the tremendously subtle mechanism of checks and balances that regulates Herbert's poetry. One could say that in it the incidental becomes central, or — in the terms of his book of essays on European art and culture — the barbarian enters the garden.[1] Here the word 'barbarian' bears spruce inverted commas, and is as dapper as pinstripes: the man classified as a 'barbarian' (a denizen of 'Eastern Europe', for instance, from the forested edge of the steppes) is perhaps 'one of us'. And yet Herbert himself ironically doubts this: Mr Cogito loses the battle with his face, whose inherited medieval desires defeat the educative applications of Mozart and Veronese.[2] The barbarian, however, is also modern man, a quizzical interrogator of the heritage of nineteenth century museum culture, and of such Judaeo-Christian relics as the Mona Lisa ('Jerusalem in a frame', the philosophy of Spinoza and angelology.[3]) It is a garden of stone, that ever-present element in Herbert's work ("if he had a sense of identity, it was probably with stone"[4]): the garden graveyard of stored culture, as strangely impressive and useless as the treasures of Xanadu in *Citizen Kane*. It is the place of culture as interpreted by Walter Benjamin, its every monument built on barbarism. For Herbert, the garden of culture clearly remains open, despite the cataclysms of this century, but the significance of its inventory is problematic (as Stanisław Barańczak notes, it is a mistake to term

Herbert a classicist).[5] What should one do with these objects, which are no longer manufactured? Why and how should one recount stories already known? (In 'Jonah', Herbert's knowledge that we know the story already causes a certain weariness: "then the well-known things occurred".)[6] In order to find a niche for himself amidst the angels, for instance, the poet has to invent one characterized by incompetence.[7] For Różewicz, meanwhile, there is no longer any garden. If World War Two can be seen as the catastrophe that threw all previous European culture into doubt, aesthetic education having signally failed to prevent the eruption of barbarism from civilization's midst, then for Herbert it was an explosion that created a Pompeii, full of frozen, once-human forms, whilst for Różewicz it submerged the old world's surface under level ash. Herbert's garden may lie west of Poland rather than East of Eden, but it is not the West of whose relative political freedom so many Poles dream, as the otherwise intelligent Polish critic Artur Sandauer was to claim in a piece neatly trimmed to a tendentious Party line; nor is it a place preferred through snobbish affectation. For Herbert, the West is rather an enclave of the past, whose inhabitants have as yet been spared the full force of the twentieth century's lesson in the appalling fragility of human life. For the Pole whose compatriots were decimated by war, and whose liberation meant the imposition of a further cage, the West becomes a museum dreamworld: he rubs his eyes, unable to be sure such a place still exists. His own being seems so unreal before the imperturbable complacency of the Gioconda that he pinches himself to make sure he really is standing in front of it.

Another description of the dialectic of Herbert's work might speak of semi-allegorical dramatizations of the confrontation of the real and the ideal, the human and the ethereal: Fortinbras and Hamlet.[8] In 'Revelation', the essence of things is obscured by the postman's visit, prompting a resolution to hold fast the exquisite moment when next it occurs.[9] Similarly, Spinoza yearns to see God, and on succeeding discourses to Him on the nature of man. In an ironic, poignant reversal, the poem presents misunderstanding as the bedrock of experience, with man absorbed in absolute philosophy while God has an entirely different notion of the "Really Important Things".[10] One might be tempted to see God's interest in the trivial as a rebuke to the philosopher's fury for the absolute; Różewicz would doubtless have presented the material thus. It is more accurate, however, to identify this God as a careworn wife, another version of the woman whose preoccupations never intersect with those of the men in Herbert's verse (the fusion of lovers in 'Two Drops'[11] is atypical). In 'Silk of a Soul', for instance, her concerns (a silk stocking) have a simplicity the poet considers poignant:[12] she is like a more distanced version of Tereza in Kundera's *The Unbearable Lightness of Being*. The shadow of the unattainable girl ghosts its way between the lines of Herbert's work, which is perhaps limited by its inability to bring the theme into direct focus. Thus in 'I would like to describe'[13] he says he would give everything for an expression "extracted from my breast like a rib",[14] whilst "an absent girl's fingers"[15] below his rib are said to disturb Mr. Cogito's quest for the pure thought.[16] If there is an unstated yearning for love here, for the woman who might grow out of the rib, it acquires pathos from the inability or reluctance to grasp that love is the object of longing. Similarly — though the presentation is more detached and ironic — the housekeeper-muse of 'Routine of the Soul',[17] does not dream of the poet but, as she looks down from her balcony, of her moustachioed gendarme.

It is Herbert's interest in the encounter of the ideal and the everyday that prompts his recurrent concern with angels, those figures of mediation. Describing Arion's song in a poem accorded the important strategic final position in his first collection, Herbert writes that no-one knows exactly what the angel sings;[18] it is like the most beautiful object in another poem — the one that does not exist.[19] Herbert becomes a frustrated Platonist: as Arion rides away on a dolphin's back, the poem becomes 'Sailing from Byzantium'. He wanders an Eden whose current ghostly persistence (in the phantom form of those inherently alienated objects, *works of art*) barely recalls its once-ideal state.

If for Herbert Eden's ideal trees have turned to stone, it is because of their rootedness in suffering: the cry of Marsyas petrifies the tree to which he is attached.[20] Stone, however, is of ambiguous import. On the one hand, it is the pebble whose isolated perfection and self-sufficiency rebuke humanity, rather as does Rilke's torso of Apollo.[21] But although Herbert is tempted by the aesthete's project of transforming life into a work of art, conferring upon it the stoical perfection of stone, the moralist in him abhors the stone's inhumanity. The result is an extremely subtle, unresolved dialectic of the aesthetic and the ethical. Warmth transmitted to a pebble by a human hand would be false.[22] To warm the pebble is to be like the children in 'Painted Bird',[23] whose hot hands give life to the bird and — in so doing — condemn it to torture and existence "on an impossible border".[24] No wonder the poet is loath to deliver up the pebble to a similar fate. At the same time, the alienated human being can seem stony in his own eyes.[25] Mr. Cogito likens his head to a pebble; and when Herbert notes in another Mr. Cogito poem,[26] that everyday speech tends to exaggerate the motility of thoughts, he is not simply commenting on his own tendency to revert again and again to such motifs as the stone (so that the exquisite texture of his work may be criticized as stemming from too intimate a knowledge of, and respect for, its own limitations), he is also noting the affinity between human thoughts and stones. Observing a dead friend, Mr. Cogito remarks that it would be a relief if the body became a stone.[27] The relief would surely be due to the friend's safe removal into the distance of a work of art, dispelling the eerie distance of a human being deprived of life. Art turns things to stone; but art is not guilty, for this effect is the inadvertent result of its own suffering ('Apollo and Marsyas'). Artur Sandauer, in an effort to discredit 'Fortinbras' Lament',[28] has termed 'Apollo and Marsyas' the superior work, but it seems to me to have a worrying final flaw. Towards the poem's end Apollo walks away, musing that Marsyas's scream may provide the basis for a "new branch / of art — let us say, concrete".[29] Is the use of the word "gałąź" (branch) here a sign of Apollo's insensitivity, or Herbert's? (Marsyas has been tied to a *tree* petrified by his screams.) The witty dismissal of concrete poetry unwittingly identifies with Apollo (as does the classical stylization), trivializing the poem's own insight into the appalling effect of an art adequate to the suffering from which it stems. It corresponds to the poem's reduction of Apollo to almost a fop. And it is here perhaps that one encounters Herbert's one real limitation: a perhaps understandably self-protective refusal to be as evidently horrified by the mid-century's catastrophes as he surely is. It is as if the calculated art of outwitting the censor had muted some aspect of his sensibility (and that of his entire generation), a constant resort to classical allusion filtering out direct feeling in a manner that comes perilously close to aestheticism. To deem Herbert's tactic both understandable and probably self-protective is to argue that the alternative would be a career and fate resembling those of Paul Celan (a poet I will be referring to again in connection with Różewicz) — or, closer to Herbert's Polish home, the ambiguous, tortured figure of Tadeusz Borowski. The fact that Herbert can sustain comparison with Celan is indicative of his stature, but in its light Herbert's irony does seem finally (*pace* Alvarez)[30] to be somewhat dandified. Attempts at more impassioned utterance (e.g. the *envoi* to 'Mr. Cogito'[31]), result merely in extremely accomplished rhetoric.

Stanisław Barańczak has termed Herbert's poetry "a 'tragic vision' related in a classical style".[32] The tell-tale inverted commas represent Barańczak's own identification with the tone of 'Apollo and Marsyas': like Herbert himself, they hold tragedy at a slightly queasy distance. Barańczak's reading of the devastatingly bitter irony of the following lines from 'Substance' is usefully symptomatic of the difficulty critics have in locating Herbert's position. The lines are "they perish / who love beautiful words above fatty smells / but fortunately they are few".[33] Barańczak maintains that the irony is all-but imperceptible: "there is almost nothing that would provide us with a sufficient clue to the irony: read as an isolated and anonymous text, 'Substance' could easily be misunderstood as unequivocal praise for the survivors."[34] The dissonant middle line, however, adopts two contrasting voices in order to criticize both: "piękne słowa" — beautiful words — is part of the dismissive vocabulary wherewith the devotees of common sense pass their verdict upon the idealists, while "tłuste zapachy" — fatty smells — is the beautiful loser's denunciation of those Shelleyan nineteenth century Polish poet Słowacki would have termed the "zjadacze chleba" (the breadeaters). The pervasive mood is one of disgust with language and society. Where Różewicz sits disgustedly *outside* language, Herbert registers his unease from within. The result is the extraordinarily painful sense of disinheritance Andrzej Kijowski once isolated as the central feature of Herbert's work: the dislocations bespeak an alienation from everyday discourse, and perhaps even from the possibility of meaningfully expressive discourse in general (whence Herbert's use of such distancing devices as dramatic monologue, *personae* and classical allusion and stylization). The same discord is present in the final lines of 'Substance': "the nation goes on / and returning with bags fully laden from the paths of its flight / erects a triumphal arch / for the beautiful dead".[35] These lines are harder to misunderstand, but it is still possible for an intelligent critic to do so. Thus Sandauer interprets the calculated dissonance (a term that is, I think, more useful than irony here) as a logical contradiction, tartly correcting Herbert: "as for the triumphal arches, it [the nation — PC] does not raise them for the "beautiful dead" (whom it fobs off with monuments) but — as the name itself shows — for the victors".[36] In actuality, Herbert's discord emphasizes the selectivity of historiography, and of the collective memory: he reconnects parts of the mind society hypocritically separates. But he does not do so for political reasons. Herbert is less a political poet than a moralist; Barańczak's confusion of the two being a very common one in recent Polish ideology. 'Fortinbras's Lament', for instance — legible from both ends of the political spectrum as an allegory of the crushing of Polish ideals, and idealists, under Stalinism[37] — is both political and apolitical: Fortinbras is a *model* of the tyrant, a fusion of baroque and totalitarian ruler, and so Herbert establishes the type as perennial, and opposition as perennially quixotic. Herbert's disgust is less with a particular form of power than with the Darwinism of a history in which the strong always defeat the weak. A party of one, he has no aspirations to power himself; his Mr. Cogito is not — *pace* Trznadel — one more in the line of Polish Hamlets,[38] but a bystander even in his own life, closer to Prufrock than Prince Hamlet. Herbert's comments in Trznadel's own *Domestic Disgrace* giving his reaction to the verse of the younger generation, bear this out:

> When I read their poems — very patriotic and correct ones, for they oppose violence and force — I want to say: life is more complex, mysterious and knotty than the Party, the army, the police; let us step slightly to one side of an everyday reality that truly is appalling and try to write out of doubt, alarm and despair.[39]

Fortinbras' lament, as Sławiński has shown,[40] is a pseudo-threnody: the new ruler pays lip service throughout to *de mortuis nil nisi bonum*, but his every remark about Hamlet carries an undertone of the pragmatist's thinly-veiled contempt for the dreamer. But the poem's most subtle effect is found in the closing lines, which dissolve the apparent absoluteness of the division between the conqueror and the dead Prince: their lyrical cadence shows the strong-arm man capable of pity and poetry. The pity, however, is exclusively for himself, and so is quite compatible with ruthlessness. But the deliberate dissonance, the simultaneous exposure of two different tonalities, is highly reminiscent of the way Herbert closes 'Substance'. The contradictoriness of language — its *political* nature — is the very thing that compromises it in Herbert's eyes: every word is shot through with party spirit. If Herbert is a fugitive from Utopia, it is not simply the self-proclaimed ideal of 'real socialism' that he is fleeing; if this were the case, he could have remained in the West, where Barańczak and Trznadel now work. The interweaving of opposed voices by his dialogic imagination serves instead to rebuke the notion that any human society is bearable as now constituted. The lesson of Herbert's work is not an Aesopian political one, but the agonized one of Adorno's: there is no true life in the midst of the false.[41]

II

To touch on Adorno is to reach an appropriate point of passage from Herbert to Różewicz. After all, was it not Adorno who famously declared Auschwitz an impassable obstacle to poetry's resumption after the war, and does not Różewicz describe his task as that of "creating poetry after Auschwitz"?[42] It can indeed be argued that a meditation on the conditions that made possible the concentration camps is central to all Różewicz's finest poems, from the taut, shocked description of the dead Jewish girl's pigtail[43] to his enumeration of the unfulfillable tasks his poetry confronts.[44] It is also, however, at the heart of his dilemma: how to strip language naked, in quest of fidelity to extreme experience (*Grenzsituationen*) without reducing it to cliché? (Różewicz's valorization of the common man, his identification with the 'Głos Anonima', the voice of anon that furnishes the title of one of his collections, adds to this danger.) One way to do so is to surround one's poem with negations, admitting that it is not what it should be. Even here, though, *cliché* threatens, as the intensity of negation generates a desire to swing back into affirmation; and so where Herbert clamps negation and affirmation together in dissonance, Różewicz oscillates between them. Thus Adam Czerniawski's useful anthology of translations[45] can include the fine 'The Survivor' on one page,[46] and opposite it the banal and lachrymose (and perhaps self-parodistic) 'Purification'[47] ("Naive you will come to believe in beauty / moved you will come to believe in man").[48] Sometimes the shift in gear occurs in mid-poem. An interesting example is 'In the midst of life';[49] a less complex one, 'In connection with a certain event'.[50]

'In the midst of life' begins very impressively, and its first six verse units are powerfully stark, evoking the poet's attempts to reconstruct a life, beginning with the simplest things, after the cataclysm. As he then tries to reconstruct *value* the poem falters:

"that old lady / leading a goat by a rope / is needed more/ more valuable / than the seven wonders of the world / whoever thinks or feels / she is not needed / is a mass murderer".[51] The stanza is problematic because its words are no longer identified as something of which the speaker is striving desperately to convince himself, and so one is compelled to view him as believing them. The moment one has a self-assured speaker, the poem's doubting persona is ruptured. Moreover, little old ladies are recalcitrant literary properties; so automatic is the sympathy they receive that their use can border on demagoguery.[52] At its best, the poem recalls a convalescent Borowski. The shift out of the first person near the end, where we are told that "the man talked to the water",[53] can be read as a sign of the self-alienation that made possible the earlier rupture of the doubting persona. The ending (if he heard a voice . . . / it was the voice of another man [my ellipsis — PC][54]) has things both ways: nature is harshly silent, but contact has been established with another human. But is this other voice merely his own, the fruit of the relinquishment of the first person, so solipsism and isolation persist, albeit disavowed? Had the poem been shorter, Różewicz might not have succumbed to the forlorn and self-contradictory quest for new certainties, resting content with the powerful bleakness of the majority of the poem's lines.

'In connection with a certain event' is a far inferior work. When the poet demands why he and his fellows failed to impart "new feelings" to the young man who leapt from the window of his "boring home", his own phraseology gives the answer. To say, as Różewicz does, that the young man he has depersonalized ("that which fell out") "died of the poison / a festering world / left inside him"[55] is to use language incapable of sparking genuinely new feelings. The poem evinces an unholy mixture of existentialism and socialist realism (fused by the interest each has in the denigration of the bourgeoisie, and by their shared *Schadenfreude* in the degradation of 'high culture') — a mixture that is surely the basis of Różewicz's enormous prestige in official Polish culture (the existentialism appeals to self-styled intellectuals, while the socialist realism fulfils Party demands). Since the poets of 'In connection with a certain event' are not so much individuals as members of a Brechtian committee or *Sprechchor* dutifully concerned for their worker comrades, it is hardly surprising that the suicide lacked individuality too. The poem's mixture of depersonalization and compassion is found also in 'The Prodigal Son':[56] "that peasant beyond the inn's corner / with back turned / is my friend":[57] the turned back is a sign of the world's indifference, and of the indifference of opposites (turned back and friend), a theme to which I will return. The poet identifies with this depersonalized figure because he too is depersonalized ("the world / all around / is complete without me").[58]

The element of socialist realist turpism in Różewicz's work may be concentrated in the volumes from the Stalinist period, but it is not restricted to them. One can find it in the 'Appendix to the notebooks of Malte Laurids Brigge written by "life itself" ',[59] with its jeers at Rilke and pervertedly aestheticized interpretation of the suicide of his daughter in 1972 as an "anti-Rilkean gesture" (*sic*!): her death interests Różewicz only as a source of munitions in a polemic over poetics. It is in fact quite possible to dissociate oneself from Rilke whilst acknowledging his greatness (and for reasons quite similar to those of Różewicz, who sees how the degradation of life in Auschwitz questions Rilke's metaphysics of death) — as is shown by the work of Paul Celan. In one frightening poem Różewicz even adopts the voice of the hangman: 'Head in the void'[60] describes the elitist intellectual and concludes menacingly: "you are a head / which will be removed / and cast away".[61] The poet lays his pen aside and takes up the mightier sword.

If the Różewicz of these poems (and others, such as 'Spring planting in Korea',[62] 'A meeting in Nowa Huta'[63] or his sanctimonious elegy on the death of Gałczyński)[64] is little-known in the West, it is because they have mercifully been spared translation. One need not seek any conspiratorial causes; they have remained untranslated because they are not very good. Thus objections to Różewicz's work should direct themselves against its quality, not its philosophy. Attacking the poetry for its philosophy is the tactical mistake made by Jacek Trznadel;[65] if the philosophy is to be attacked it should be at its true weak point, its linkage with the highly variable *quality* of the work. The key difference between Różewicz and Herbert becomes one of consistency, to achieve which Herbert paid a high price: the decision to write for the drawer during the Stalinist era. Where Herbert's work is all of a piece, that of Różewicz is highly uneven. 'Reply'[66] banally rejects negative poetry and discovers the golden mean; the tasks the plan has set for poetry include "let it remove from man/all that is animal or divine".[67] These lines ought to be juxtaposed with the conclusion of 'A bourgeois death' — a far superior poem:[68] "when you discover the golden mean / dying begins".[69] Różewicz's failure to perceive the contradictions in his work, and to drop poems like 'Reply' in the dustbin, is surely linked to the tendency to destroy opposites that pervades even his best poems, such as 'The Survivor': man and beast, love and hate, friend and foe, dark and light are termed "empty synonyms".[70] It is fed by the despair inculcated by the war. Thus, in a perversely self-fulfilling prophecy, the sense of the paltry worth of poetry can lead on occasions to the writing of worthless poems. Różewicz's work is tainted by an atrophy of choice which issues alternately in cynical, sub-existentialist biologism, and sentimental socialist realist exaltation ("the coming of age will be more beautiful").[71] Fortunately for his international reputation (his Polish reputation is another matter — as Trznadel rightly notes, Różewicz has had little influence on the New Wave Polish poets),[72] when it comes to translation others have chosen for him.

Postscript

When evaluating Różewicz's work, however, the fairest, most valid and illuminating comparison is not with that of Herbert but with the prose of that other great Polish exponent of the vision of the stony world, Tadeusz Borowski.[73] The central question seems to be whether nihilism or negation is dominant in their work. The distinction between nihilism and negation is outlined by Greil Marcus:

> The nihilist, no matter how many people he or she might kill, is always a solipsist: no one exists but the actor, and only the actor's motives are real. When the nihilist pulls the trigger, turns on the gas, hits the vein, the world ends. Negation is always political: it assumes the existence of other people, calls them into being. Still, the tools the negationist seems forced to use — real or symbolic violence, blasphemy, dissipation, contempt, ridiculousness — change hands with those of the nihilist.[74]

As Marcus notes, the one category tends to flow into the other. The distinction may be sharpened however by describing negation as always *concrete* and particular, the rejection of a specific historical moment or experience, and nihilism as the pessimistic generalization about history in its entirety derived from that single experience or moment. The difference between Różewicz and Borowski, then, would be that although the *oeuvre* of each partakes both of nihilism and negation, negation prevails in the former, and nihilism in the latter. For all his tendency to project a world of pure brutalism and chaos — of which his fascination by 'Mondo Cane' is symptomatic — Różewicz is able to focus his poetry on something other than negativity, even if only intermittently and (paradoxically) by negation, through outlining the tasks poetry will never fulfil. Yet at the same time he is satisfied that his own negation has fulfilled them, through the programme of anti-poetry. Both Borowski and Różewicz strive to overcome post-war despair by adopting the socialist realist litany of accusations, directed primarily against fascists and imperialists. But the hysterical frenzy with which the later Borowski propagates this view (particularly in his journalism) indicates a fundamental inability to believe it. What preserves Różewicz from the suicide that claimed Borowski (and those other temporary survivors of the concentration camps, Paul Celan and Primo Levi) is his refusal to implicate himself in the all-too-human inhumanity the camps fostered: 'l'enfer, c'est les autres' is an existentialist maxim that can also be pressed into socialist realist service. Horror does not rage in his blood, for in the end he is a tourist, staring through glass at the evidence of evils other people wrought. The time-traveller leaves the garden of stone, a survivor, having shaken the nightmare and successfully called it past.

Notes

1. *A Barbarian in the Garden* is the title of Herbert's book of essays on Western art and culture (*Barbarzyńca w ogrodzie*, Warsaw: Czytelnik 1973).
2. *Wiersze zebrane* (Warsaw: Czytelnik 1982) pp.203-4, henceforth abbreviated to WZ. All references to Herbert's poems are to this edition.
3. 'Jeruzalem w ramach'. *Ibid.*, pp.137-8, pp.238-40, pp.78-9.
4. "Jeśli miał poczucie tożsamości to chyba z kamieniem" *Ibid.*, p.207.
5. See Barańczak's *Uciekinier z utopii: o poezji Zbigniewa Herberta* (London: Polonia 1984), chapter one. (This chapter is largely omitted from the English version of Barańczak's study, *A Fugitive from Utopia: The Poetry of Zbigniew Herbert* [Cambridge, Mass.: Harvard University Press 1987].)
6. 'Potem byłyrzeczy wiadome', *Wiersze zebrane*, p.146.
7. *Ibid.*, pp.78-9.
8. *Ibid.*, pp.148-9.
9. *Ibid.*, pp.162-3.
10. *Ibid.*, pp.238-41.

11. *Ibid.*, p.7.
12. *Ibid.*, pp.83-4.
13. *Ibid.*, pp.55-7.
14. 'Wyłuskane z piersi jak żebro', *Ibid.*, p. 7.
15. 'I czuł pod żebrem palce nieobecnej', *Ibid.*, p. 213.
16. *Ibid.*, p.213.
17. *Ibid.*, pp.220-1.
18. *Ibid.*, pp.49-50.
19. *Ibid.*, pp.154-8.
20. *Ibid.*, pp.133-5.
21. *Ibid.*, pp.158-9.
22. *Ibid.*, pp.158-9.
23. *Ibid.*, pp.126-7.
24. 'Na niemożliwej granicy', *Ibid.*, p. 9.
25. *Ibid.*, pp.217-8.
26. *Ibid.*, pp.215-6.
27. *Ibid.*, pp.218-20.
28. See Artur Sandauer *Głos dzielony na czworo: Rzecz o Zbigniewie Herbercie* (*Poeci czterech pokoleń*, Kraków: Wydawnictwo literackie 1977, pp.313-41). Sandauer's reservations about 'Tren Fortynbrasa' may well be motivated by an unconscious reaction to the *tone* of the conqueror's lament, which uncannily resembles that of Sandauer's own essay on Herbert: apparent praise, undercut throughout by insinuation. The extreme deviousness of Sandauer's essay has rendered it a very difficult object to skewer; Sandauer himself mocked Izydora Dąmbska's failure to do so (see *Jak fał szować-teksty, czyli moralność Pani Dąmbskiej (Pisma zebrane*, Vol. IV, Warsaw: Czytelnik 1985, pp.236-42, and Dąmbska's *W sprawie artykułu profesora Sandauera pt. "Głos dzielony na czworo*, in *Tygodnik powszechny* 1976, nr 19). It is Dąmbska's failure to pinpoint the slipperiness of Sandauer's style that allows the latter to wriggle off the hook. Again and again in the Herbert essay Sandauer will formulate an accusation and then modify it, apparently seeking the *mot juste*, but really in order to have his cake and eat it (for instance, if he truly felt that "syncretic" more precisely described Herbert's work than "wtórny" (secondhand), then he would have cancelled "wtórny" at the stage of composition — rather than allowing it to stand, and then appending an apparent correction). Vanity may also have co-operated in the generation of this critical stream-of-consciousness: every thought that impinges on the great brain merits transcription.
29. "nowa gałąź / sztuki — powiedzmy — konkretnej", *Wiersze zebrane*, pp.133-5.
30. Al Alvarez, *Introduction to the Poetry of Zbigniew Herbert*, in: Herbert, *Selected Poems* (Harmondsworth: Penguin 1968), p.11.
31. *Wiersze zebrane*, pp.255-6.
32. Barańczak, *Uciekinier . . .* , *op. cit.*, p.17. (This remark is absent from the book's English version.)

33. "Giną ci / którzy kochają bardziej piękne słowa niż tłuste zapachy / ale jest ich na szczęście niewielu", *Wiersze zebrane*, pp.97-8.
34. Barańczak, *Fugitive . . . , op. cit.*, p.96.
35. 'Naród trwa / i wracając z pełnymi workami ze szlaków ucieczki / wznosi łuk triumfalny / dla pięknych umarłych'.
36. Sandauer, *Głos . . .* , op. cit., p.341.
37. It is read thus both by Sandauer and by Jacek Trznadel (*Polski Hamlet: kłopoty z działaniem*, Paris: Libella 1988, pp.282-310). Sandauer, it should be noted, gingerly avoids the use of the term 'Stalinism'.
38. Trznadel, *op. cit.*, pp.308-10.
39. Interview with Jacek Trznadel, in *Hańba domowa* (Paris: Instytut literacki 1986), p.222.
40. J. Sławiński, *Tren Fortynbrasa*, in: T. Kostkiewiczowa, A. Okopień-Sławińska, J. Sławiński, *Czytamy utwory współczesne* (Warsaw 1967).
41. T.W. Adorno, *Minima Moralia: Reflexionen aus dem beschädigten Leben* (Frankfurt a.m.: Suhrkamp 1978 [1951]), p.42: 'Es gibt kein richtiges Leben im falschen.'
42. All references to Różewicz's poems are to the *Poezje zebrane* (Wrocław-Warszawa-Kraków-Gdańsk: Zakład narodowy imienia Ossolińskich 1976), p.695.
43. *Ibid.*, p.136.
44. *Ibid.*, p.327.
45. Tadeusz Różewicz, *Conversation wtih the Prince and other poems*, introduced and translated by Adam Czerniawski (London: Anvil Press 1982).
46. *Poezje zebrane*, p.19.
47. *Ibid.*, p.52.
48. 'Naiwni uwierzycie w piękno / wzruszeni uwierzycie w człowieka'.
49. *Poezje zebrane*, p.331.
50. *Ibid.*, p.224.
51. 'Ta staruszka która / ciągnie na powrozie kozę / jest potrzebniejsza / i cenniejsza / niż siedem cudów świata / kto myśli i czuje / że ona jest niepotrzebna / ten jest ludobójcą'.
52. Perhaps only Baudelaire has succeeded, in *Les Petites Vieilles*, in avoiding sentimentality when referring to them. [In the original the reference is to "that old *woman*" - Ed.]
53. 'Człowiek mówił do wody '.
54. 'Jeśli usłyszał głos / . . . to był głos drugiego człowieka'.
55. 'Umarł na truciznę / którą zostawił w jego wnętrzu / gnijący świat'.
56. *Poezje zebrane*, p.269.
57. 'Ten chłop za rogiem karczmy / tyłem odwrócony / to mój przyjaciel'.
58. 'Świat ten / dokoła / jest pełen beze mnie'.
59. *Poezje zebrane*, p.702.
60. *Ibid.*, p.146.
61. 'Jesteś głową / która zostanie zdjęta / i odrzucona'.

62. *Poezje zebrane*, p.199.
63. *Ibid*, p.208.
64. *Ibid*, p.227.
65. Trznadel, *Polski Hamlet . . . , op. cit.*, pp.285-93.
66. *Poezje zebrane*, p.152.
67. 'Niech odejmie od człowieka / wszystko zwierzęce i boskie'.
68. *Poezje zebrane*, p.207.
69. 'Kiedy odkryjesz złoty środek / zaczyna się konanie'.
70. *Poezje zebrane*, p.19.
71. *Ibid.*, p.178.
72. Trznadel, *Polski Hamlet . . . , op cit.*, pp.292-3.
73. To compare Różewicz's poetry with the *poetry* of Borowski — as does Adam Czerniawski (*Conversation with the Prince . . . , op. cit.*, p. 15) — is to load the dice in Różewicz's favour. Borowski's major work is his prose.
74. Greil Marcus, *Lipstick Traces: A Secret History of the 20th Century* (Cambridge, Mass.: Harvard University Press 1989), p.9.

Krzysztof Karasek

Mozartian Joy: The Poetry of Wisława Szymborska

Mozartian Joy: The Poetry of Wisława Szymborska

In the twentieth century the Word has become — like it or not — a dramatic battleground. At the same time, a shrinking of art's domain and the annexation of this area by knowledge (in the case of the avant-garde) and politics (in the case of committed art) — just as in the Middle Ages it had been annexed by religion — has contracted the territory of autonomous poetic reality, the reality of a poetry which draws strength from its own resources; it has in effect contracted the realm of true poetry, and therefore of what can be called poetry. Nevertheless, it remains a territory sufficiently large to express within it the reality of human fate on earth, the reality of humans immersed in time and aware of it, without recourse to any other categories beside the Word. Pursued by the Chimera of reality or metaphysics, mutilated by the Erynies of history and the demons of internal contradictions, poets dedicate less and less space to poetry as art, to poetry perceived as a perfect shape, a fulfilment. A sketch, a hasty drawing, a barely-pronounced expression of the mouth, a line of the lips, convey the fullness of the world. A curtailment of the intellect, a curtailment of the imagination, specifically excludes elements of thought. Linguistic and epistemological density replaces form. Contemporary poetry at its best has embodied itself most completely in forms that are hurried, sketchy, full of drama and tensions. And yet the deeper we plunge in time (or rather, the deeper time plunges us), we discover all the more certainly that the Chimera of obsessions cannot be tamed; we cannot cure the imagination by fighting it. The Chimera gorges herself at our expense, and the more we struggle with her, the more we define her symmetry, the more we confirm her domain.

So we are overcome with nostalgia for art in its fulness and distinctiveness, in which it would again be possible to grasp 'the totality' of art — not of the sketch, but of the full shape, of plenitude. An art which is not a morass but a hard, rocky base — which instead of a quagmire offers something more durable on which to stand, or even (who knows?) — parhaps even build a house. Something not lacking either joy or tragedy, but retaining in our human dimensions a full warmth of the dramatic. Art which offers something on which we lean, in which one might take shelter during "a pestilential time", "a wretched time" ("what use a poet in wretched times?"), a hostile time. And time is indeed hostile to man and his reveries, above all those focussed on the Word.

There are very few figures in Polish poetry who achieve this, poets who create such a world-house — among them only Zbigniew Herbert and Wisława Szymborska (poets of wise maturity) have tried to create a language which keeps pace with elementary human needs. But they each lead us to very different world-houses: Herbert's is inhabited from cellar to roof; from floor to ceiling with gods and memories of history — both of history happening within us and of that which precedes us, with the relicts of a ruined and defeated world, though its artefacts survive and preserve its name. Here precisely in its human-historical and sacral dimensions lies the saving strength of objects. Szymborska's is the world-house of our daily lives, our ordinary life and death. A world where tears are salty and rain is wet, in which 'love' — in Herbert's words — "means love, and death means death".

Poets of wise maturity find their true voice late. How high a price they pay for the moderation of their passions, for the defeat of the Chimera, can be known only by someone who had himself pitted his strength against hers. We, who are the true offspring of Dionysus, that is of Chaos, are well aware that the secret extorted from Apollo is rarely won without punishment. 'Apollo and Marsyas', one of Herbert's most personal poems, portrays this quarrel between logic and imagination, rules and exceptions, and between the known and the incomprehensible, in a way that is moving and accessible even to a novice.

A poet of obsession discharges his tensions and fears, while the Apollonian poet suppresses them by an effort of will and intellect. But they constantly live in him, return to him; if he choked them he would cease to be a good poet and become a didact, a rhetorician, a fiddler constantly scraping the same old tunes. These tensions and fears return at the most inappropriate moments. Chimeras, Harpies, Erynies and Maenads return to mutilate the poet's flesh, the flesh of Orpheus, Orestes and Marsyas; for extorting secrets from them, they tear him to shreds. Poets of wise maturity are a fixed point of reference in our bustling, excessively bustling world. The very fact that they exist lightens our own existence and strengthens us in our identity and in the certainty that the world nevertheless exists and not merely is. Can our world become a house? If we ask that question when reading Szymborska, then perhaps we are already on its threshold.

Most importantly, we must first know what is most important in the house, we must establish a hierarchy of values. A hierarchy for us. Our own hierarchy, verifiable by us, because those others were fixed without us, before our arrival in the world, and are therefore not sufficient for us. They include father and mother as basic categories, a common point of departure. This is best seen in Herbert, whose world begins with a description of his own (and thus first) parents. Father, a first visible god (or a substitute for God), the giver of values, a signpost through the world's dark byways; and mother, the earth's warm embrace, always ready to welcome the errant wanderer. Then the world of objects: table, chair, bed, a glass on the table, a window, a view onto the street ("Eyes are hands", says Voltaire), a door; these are the elements defining the boundaries of our visible world, our home. A bond grows between objects and people; and thus language is born. It is created by a need to give expression to the drama of existence. A drama occurring between men and objects. A drama also of language, since words are objects in motion and like objects they undergo destruction, corruption, erasure, are insufficient, transient, and in their deepest essence betray men and choose the world.

Wisława Szymborska belongs to *this* world. She is a poet of material objects, of insignificant everyday events, commonplace conversations, everyday reality; the theme of myth, of culture, only rarely enters her work, usually only as a justification of ordinariness. Perhaps her option is realistic (if such a term has any sense whatever in poetry) because in poetry, as nowhere else, the illusoriness of the real world manifests itself. In some sense, everything here is at once the same and not the same; the character of Szymborska's vision is comparable to representational painting. Her deformations do not exceed either Picasso's Cubism or the Impressionists' diffused colour (in relation to objects this means either polarisation or valuation). Reality in her poems is undoubtedly 'objective', but this objectivity is illusory: while undergoing deformation, it does not in any sense turn into meta-reality, a reverie of the imagination; it does not cross boundaries drawn long ago by Horace in his 'The Art of Poetry':

> Suppose some painter, as a tour de force,
> Should couple head of man with neck of horse,
> Invest them both with feathers, stead of hair,
> And tack on limbs picked up from here and there,
> So that the figure, when complete, should show
> A maid above, a hideous fish below:
> Should you be favoured with a private view,
> You'd laugh, my friends [. . .]

Szymborska's poetry sprang from the poetics of the poster. Posters are images with simplified interiors. For years she has been enriching her perception of the image, deepening her perception of things. Like the Old Masters, she has studied sketches and nature, spotting the ever-new complexities, discovering ever-new by-ways and possibilities of the visible. Until the image became an icon: that is, something which by its links with objective reality began to take on magical — or religious, in the pagan sense — characteristics. But it did not turn into a calligramme, a sign stretched between writing and the heavens, even though Szymborska does gravitate towards calligraphy. Is not the title-poem of her collection *Ludzie na moście* ('People on a Bridge') evidence of this?

The image is her primary, basic and most natural form of expression; during the creative process it came to be questioned and subjected to revision, as in 'Lot's Wife', 'Utopia' or 'Mediaeval miniature' in *Wielka liczba* (A Great Number). But the process actually began earlier in Szymborska's first important collection: in 'Atlantis' and 'A Midsummer Night's Dream' in *Wołanie do yeti* (Calling the Yeti). It wasn't the case that words began to be surprised by words or sentences by sentences, or that language itself, like a snake, began swallowing its own tail; it was rather that the image began to swallow the image.

This questioning of the image first began when a conviction arose that eyes are an illusory means of uncovering the truth; a revelation which had great formal consequences. The image is now subjected to an intellectual scrutiny and therefore distanced. Attitudes to it become cooler, less ecstatic — admittedly hers was never such in the fullest sense — more critical. They are saturated with irony, the duality of vision and of sight, they follow a zig-zagging course along which truth moves, with the dialectical 'yes' answered by the dialectical 'no'. The poem becomes an object in the game of intellect and imagination; feelings are around to be played with cat-and-mouse, revealing their mild, though unavoidable disablement. Scepticism and relativism direct the imagination, whose tool becomes the "snake language", as in the Icelandic *Gunlaug's Saga.*

The way language functions in Szymborska's work might be called semantic flirtation. The imagination never moves in a straight line, but rather 'bi-laterally', like the joystick of an aircraft. This corresponds to the movement of thought which in Szymborska's case simultaneously places under suspicion everything she says. Whatever the poet asserts is almost immediately called into question. Imagination is thus compelled to incessant mobility, incessant attack and defence, dualities of meaning are 'forced' out of her: mirrored, twinned, mutually matched non-Baudelairean "correspondences". At every moment the poet seems to withdraw everything she has asserted. One can detect here both an intellectual quality and a spectacular exploitation by the poet of her femininity, fashioning from it a tool of both formal and epistemological inquisitiveness. It is in this extraordinary mobility — already noticeable at the level of 'small' images — that I would look for the fullest realisation of femininity in poetry: the idea of constant change as the most permanent characteristic of feminine nature.

Jerzy Kwiatkowski has already pointed out the malleability of this language. For each poem Szymborska creates a distinct linguistic code, employs different styles, depending on whichever she deems appropriate. But it is difficult to agree with Kwiatkowski when he claims that in Szymborska's work language therefore fulfils an ancillary or subordinate function, though not an utilitarian one. Although this may not seem obvious — due to an illusion created by formal perfection — in the case of a true poet language always performs a creative function and is the driving force. The *a priori*, both in relation to the object and to the intention, is the expression which orders the reality of the poem, though with such an excellent poet as Szymborska one is left with the impression that, precisely thanks to her stylistics, things are here very different from Rimbaud's case — which does not mean that I consider Rimbaud less perfect: he is quite simply unique. Here Szymborska is not alone. The arch-poet Adam Mickiewicz once dreamt of "a pliable language that would express everything the head thinks". But mercifully he confined himself to dreaming; otherwise, would we have had his 'Oda do młodości' ('Ode to Youth') or *Dziady* (The Forefathers' Eve)? In any case, Mickiewicz amended his postulate; the formula of "fervent reason" in some sense defines an extreme possibility of the participation of the rational in poetic activity and cognition. After all, it was Plato — at once the greatest rationalist in human thought and the greatest dreamer — who claimed that "the gods speak through the mouths of poets"; in other words, the powers which transcend poets and which establish the Categorical Imperative of their language. Irrespective of whether the result of this Imperative is a seemingly objecive description, speech pregnant with meanings or a narrative epic like *The Illiad* or *Pan Tadeusz*; or even a Rimbaudesque vision, an "illumination": it amounts to a break-in both into the areas of cognition and into the mystery of fate.

Szymborska's poetry has many opponents. Particularly among poets. I understand their criticisms, but I don't share them. They say: Szymborska doesn't offer cognitive revelations — puzzlement as a cognitive category isn't enough. How mistaken this judgment is! By aiming at puzzlement, Szymborska aims at the very heart of poetry's cognitive energy, at the very source of its life. Indeed, it's from there, from that 'small' or 'great' puzzlement, that 'everything' comes — that first and last glimmer of cognition. It accompanies the birth of a child's language and therefore of its world; and it's there when a man closes his eyes in death: "So that's all? So nothing more? Now's the end ?" — he asks himself; it is the last basis of his cognition. This is primary in poetry, and primary means both first — and thus, simplest; and last — thus, chief and fundamental.

Isn't this the source of poetic mastery: To give an original expression to one's own puzzlement? Not even posing questions: this is a secondary characteristic for a poet — though primary for a philosopher. And poetry is not philosophy. What separates it from simple philosophical schemes is language which sparkles, shines, lives, burns, freezes and never leaves one indifferent; which reanimates the dead structures of the image, fills it with living contents, empathetic puzzlement. Yet also from this perspective Szymborska is under fire: aren't questions indicative of philosophical puzzlement? The questions Szymborska raises concern existence rather than redemption. Historically speaking, one might say that her poetry concerns the 'here' rather than the 'now'. Another reproach: Szymborska's poems are devoid of mystery, as if for her metaphysics didn't exist. Certainly, the author of *Sto pociech* ('A Hundred Joys') and *Wielka liczba* isn't a metaphysician, and certainly not a mystic; that simply isn't her area. And if one is to categorise her in these terms, she is rather an epistemologist or a phenomenologist of revelation. Her patrons are Descartes and Pascal — and speaking of Pascal I don't have in mind his paradoxes of division but the sensation of sudden experience, of epiphanies. So, on the one hand, a rational, investigative, almost scientific relation to the object — this brings Szymborska close to the Age of Enlightenment, and also to the cognitive passions of the twentieth century: Ponge's dispassionate descriptions or the ideas of the French Nouveau Roman; and, on the other hand, Pascal with his celebration of cognition: "I am incompetent in truth and goodness" and: "Man is nothingness in the face of infinity, everything in the face of nothingness and a mediator between everything and nothing". Both these assertions define to the same degree the cognitive scepticism of both Pascal and Szymborska, leading Pascal to a conception of the emotional nature of knowledge and the presence of mystical intuition; and Szymborska to the cognitive nature of emotions as a game of the intellect, a semantic flirtation whose meaning is primarily epistemological.

It is true, there is no mystery in her poems. At any rate, not in the sense that Pascal understood it: as the presence of mystical intuition. But this does not mean that their cognitive stratum has been reduced, that they are 'ordinary' or 'obvious'. Only the concrete is ordinary, the object in which the poet is mirrored and discovers himself. And it is here that the Cartesianism of her imagination reveals itself — perhaps even of her poetic thinking. From its 'centre' the mind embraces everything: appears to highlight, to foreground and to cover all things. On the canvas of this ordinariness Szymborska builds her extra-ordinariness, her non-ordinariness, her strangeness. She shows from inside, from underneath, from below, from above, from the centre. From the side of nothingness too. It might be said that she realises in the highest sense William Blake's postulate in the opening lines of his 'Auguries of Innocence':

To see a World in a Grain of Sand
And a Heaven in a Wild Flower
Hold Infinity in the Palm of your Hand
And Eternity in an Hour.

There is in Szymborska's poetry something which radiates authentic joy, as does the music of Mozart. A joy which issues from the sensation of a game of intellect and imagination; but above all, from the unaffectedness of her language. I stress: from unaffectedness, not naturalness; like every true artist, Szymborska is not natural. Art is artificial; this banal tautology fully conveys the basic condition of its existence, a condition apparently often overlooked today. The work she performs in the sphere of language is, as with all true masters, almost invisible, unostentatious. This work — this asceticism — has deepened in the last decade; the diction has become prosaic, as if the poet were trying to test whether, under the pressure of the commonplace, joy can pass the test of puzzlement and to what extent. Sometimes (as in 'Pogrzeb' ('Funeral')) in *Ludzie na moście* it seems that she has crossed the boundaries reserved for Miron Białoszewski, where once she steered rather towards the aphorisms of Stanisław Jerzy Lec.

Szymborska is one of the few contemporary poets who writes poems. That is, each of her poems is an autonomous world, a world in itself, and if someone wants to know her 'as a whole', complete, he can acquire such a comprehensive view from just a single poem, while other poets need a whole volume for self-definition. At the other extreme is Białoszewski, whose poems, with the exception of his first collection *Obroty rzeczy* ('The Revolution of Things') seem mutually to complete and explicate each other, as though each poem is only understood fully through others. One could say that Białoszewski is a poet of a single linguistic gesture, which he expands, enriches and deepens; of one key, a key to the world, to reality. Whereas poets like Szymborska and Herbert call up such a key, which is different every time and every time exclusive to the world of the particular poem. In this sense Szymborska is traditional — or better, operates in the spirit of tradition, that is, of completeness, whereas Białoszewski functions in the spirit of modernity, that is, of specialisation and fragmentariness.

Edward Rogerson

Anti-Romanticism: Distance

Anti-Romanticism: distance

A memorial plaque in the atrium of Warsaw University's Institute of Polish Studies commemorates the resistance activities of eight young poets, all students of the Institute during its clandestine wartime existence. Seven failed to survive the War; three in particular — Krzysztof Kamil Baczyński, Tadeusz Gajcy, Leon Zdzisław Stroiński: the poetic stars of their generation — died during the Warsaw Rising.

They are representatives of the first generation to be born into the post-1918 independent Polish state; as young students at the time of the German Occupation, theirs was the generation and the social group which bore the brunt of Nazi attempts to eradicate Poland's fragile national and cultural identity.

Their generation was born into a Polish state which sought between the two World Wars to recreate and uphold the comfortable assumptions of the Polish Romantic tradition. It had seemed natural. When Poland, after a century of Partition, was restored to sovereignty in November 1918, the Romantic ideal of a nation reborn through its spiritual fortitude and purity had been apparently vindicated. With the successful defence of Poland against Soviet invasion in 1920, even the most sceptical Poles were able to overlook how fragile was this new-found independence, and how uncertain the country's prospects.

An obsession with the spirit of the nation gave Poland's social and political élites the intellectual mechanism for a retreat into delusion during the 1930s as Poland became threatened by external and internal dangers. Poland's faction-ridden avant-garde could offer little; their Babel of unedifying concepts, the catastrophism which gripped a younger generation of Polish poets in the years before 1939, found few echoes in Polish society. In the popular imagination, Poland had been restored in 1918; it would be restored again. With military collapse in September 1939, the ideology of Romanticism motivated Polish resistance to Nazi Germany, both within Poland and beyond its borders.

In the event, the Romantic tradition of spiritual purity in the face of oppression was almost powerless to save the nation from twentieth century totalitarianism and the bitter ideological conflicts of a century of total war. The Polish state was destroyed, and the survival of the nation itself was threatened. Even the restoration of a Polish state in 1945 brought little relief: as the six years of Nazi occupation gave way to more than a decade of Soviet-imposed Stalinist terror, the very basis of Poland's hermetically-sealed cultural tradition was viewed by many thoughtful Poles as a dangerous anachronism.

The plaque at Warsaw University commemorates only dead poets, but the entire literary élite was touched by the experience of the Occupation and by the enormity of the crimes perpetrated by the Nazis on Polish soil. The survivors among the contemporaries of Baczyński and his fellow combatants were forced after 1944 to rethink their attitudes to Polish history and society, if they were to survive, both emotionally and in reality, in the post-war world. In the work of leading poets of this generation, most notably Zbigniew Herbert and Tadeusz Różewicz, there is a strong sense of redefinition, of survivors forcing themselves to adapt to new realities.

Such reassessments of cultural traditions are by no means unique to Poland. Poets and writers in the English-speaking world found themselves facing similar problems in the rapidly-changing socio-political patterns of the post-war years. So it is perhaps no coincidence that, when the leading poets of this Polish war generation came to be translated into English, there was an audience for their verse which went far beyond a small circle of Polonophiles. It is no exaggeration to suggest that these poets, and in particular Zbigniew Herbert, were the first to be taken seriously in the West — at any rate since the high-point of Polish Romanticism. Their directness, their abandonment of extravagant metaphor, the universality of their experiences; all this has brought Polish poetry a significant following among a reading public in the West for whom Poland had been, until the turbulent 1980s, an almost completely unknown quantity.

But however direct the message and unmetaphorical the language, the fact remains that this interested readership is largely unfamiliar with the original. The reader is thus completely dependent on the translator for an understanding of the original verse, its style, its flavour. This essay, a study of translated poems from three poets of the war generation (Herbert, Różewicz, Wisława Szymborska), is more of a study of translations, than an exercise in literary criticism. There is, then, a fundamental question under-pinning this analysis: to what extent can one imagine this selection of translations as mirrors of their original Polish texts?

II

Zbigniew Herbert (born 1924 in Lwów — now in the Soviet Ukraine) has achieved a clear pre-eminence among the poets of the war generation. Unpublished until 1956, his continuing rejection of the brutality and (above all) the tawdriness of post-war Poland has made it difficult for him to maintain a comfortable co-existence with the communist authorities. His most recent volume of poetry[1] was until 1989 available in Poland only in unofficial editions.

Herbert is not, fundamentally, a political poet — although the political realities of his native Poland are rarely absent from his mind. His wider concern is to restate the dilemmas which a creative artist faces in a social system which he finds aesthetically distasteful. And this restatement, through a reworking of familiar classical myths and historical archetypes, has a universal appeal which has made it possible for him to transcend the boundaries of Polish language and culture. He is, in fact, the first Polish poet to attract a wide following in the English-speaking world.[2]

Nevertheless, even if his strong moral and aesthetic sense is able to function independently of its Polish cultural context, problems remain. To some extent, the virtuosity of his mythical-historical reinterpretations is sometimes lost by being read out of cultural context. His work imposes its own logic, and its own difficulties.

First: it would be almost impossible, without detailed textual annotation, to catch every nuance, every literary-historical cross-reference, from a poet whose cultural referents are widely sourced. Indeed, such annotation would be counter-productive: a sense of losing the haystack for the sake of the needle. Allusions to the duel of Apollo and Marsyas, or to Arion, are easy enough to identify and interpret; but not everything is so clear. And with an intellect so demanding as that of Herbert, a non-Polish readership depends on the translation to achieve a sense of proportion.

Consider the poem 'The seventh angel'.[3] The seventh angel, Shemkel,

> is black and nervous
> and has been fined many times
> for illegal import of sinners

Herbert's angel order is terrible and majestic: Azrael, the planet-driver, "perfect exponent of theoretical physics"; Raphael, "tuner of choirs"; Azrafael, "interior decorator of the universe". Shemkel is different and inadequate, a human without dignity in a world beyond his understanding. In short, he is not like the others: one can almost hear Herbert murmur 'thank God' under his breath. Herbert doesn't like perfection, doesn't like the grand design. He wants his angel order — and, by implication, his communist social order — to accept frailty, to leave some space for undignified humanity in the utopia it would wish to create.

Herbert's use of angelic imagery is easy enough, but there is a potential problem in translating this imagery from Polish. Shemkel is, as we have seen, not like the others:

> not like the hetman of the hosts
> Michael
> all scales and feathery plumes

The Archangel Michael was commander of the angel host which cast Satan and his angels from heaven (*Revelations*, 12). A military leader, then; but why *hetman*? The answer lies in Polish history. In the independent Polish Commonwealth of the seventeenth century, the *hetman* was the military commander of a province; it was a characteristic of the *husaria*, the heavy cavalry under the personal command of a *hetman*, that they wore as decoration on their body armour a pair of winged plumes. In Polish context, the military image is immediate and vivid; it seems natural that the winged commander of the angel host should be described in the manner of a Polish cavalry officer. By retaining the word *hetman*, Dale Scott shows that Herbert's poetry has a specifically Polish dimension which occasionally resists transference into English.

Inevitably, there are the small details of translation, although with

Herbert the meaning is never so dense as to make translation an impossibility. Again, the issue is one of needles: a word apparently mistranslated; verse structure changed; two lines excluded. As an example: in the poem 'Apollo and Marsyas'[4] I find myself wondering why *stuch absolutny* should be translated as "absolute ear" (Miłosz) or "perfect ear" (Carpenter), when the musical context immediately suggests the phrase "perfect pitch". Or why Miłosz should slightly amend the verse structure. Sometimes such changes are a simple matter of metaphor. For example: the tree to which Marsyas is bound has (according to both translations) turned white — presumably with fright. The Polish text uses the word *siwy*, which is more vague in meaning, depending on the context: either "grey" or "white", or even "old-aged".

But, more interestingly, translation into English leads in two places to the loss of a vital play on words. Thus (in the Carpenter translation):

> only apparently
> is the voice of Marsyas
> monotonous
> and composed of a single vowel
> A
>
> in reality
> Marsyas
> tells
> of the inexhaustible wealth
> of his body

There is here a double sense: the vowel A is also the cry of the tortured mortal, condemned by the jealous god to eternal torment (in fact Miłosz writes "Aaa"). But in the Polish context, the word *a* is a conjunction which can mean either "and" or "but". Thus, in the original text, the apparent monotony of the vowel sound is a means of contrasting the voice of the persecuted Marsyas with the inexhaustible wealth of his body. The same word-play emerges later in the same poem. A simple vowel sound thus becomes the means whereby Marsyas is finally to triumph over Apollo, who leaves the scene of his equivocal victory wondering whether the agony presages the birth-pangs of a new art-form.

But these are problems of textual exegesis. More important is the transference of Herbert's poetic style. Early in his writing career,

Herbert found a distinct voice which exactly suited his intellectual stance, and he shows no desire to deviate from modes of expression which have served him well since the 1950s. This essential unity in his work has led some western critics to express discomfort with Herbert's continuing adherence to the "aridities" of poetic modernism.[5]

Here, I believe, the fault lies largely with the translators. English-speaking critics have frequently been misled by translations which fail to bring out the tensions between the appearance of unpoetic disorder, and a highly ordered Polish text of great elegance and sensitivity. It is significant that, in their introduction to *Report from the Besieged City*, John and Bogdana Carpenter describe the historical and cultural background, talk of Herbert as a public commentator on his own life and times; Herbert the aesthete, seeking poetic experience amidst the brutality and ugliness of contemporary Poland and weighing each word as carefully as did the most elegant wordsmiths of the previous century, is less firmly defined.

This is an important omission. Even in Poland, the quiet voice of this essentially private poet is often overwhelmed by insistent demands for him to adopt a more public role. Thus Herbert's refusal to judge communist society by its material failure is unsettling. 'The Power of Taste',[6] the most powerful poem from *Report*, elaborates Herbert's essentially private stance. The trouble with Marxist society, he claims, is its basic offence against good taste. Thus (in Adam Czerniawski's translation):

> No our refusal dissent and obduracy
> didn't require great character
> we had a pinch of indispensible courage
> but basically it was a matter of taste
> Yes taste
> containing fibres of soul and gristle of conscience

The poem became famous in Poland even before it appeared in officially-sanctioned print.[7] Sadly, it was wilfully misinterpreted by radical oppositional poets who seem to prefer to ignore the evidence of their own ears and eyes. The predominant Herbert voice is quiet, close to the rhythms of normal speech; he contains emotions, stands to one side, observing the world in the manner of a pre-Romantic élitist. But a popular cabaret version of the poem turned the measured tones of Herbert's critique of totalitarianism into a loud diatribe against the rulers of post-Solidarity Poland.

In fact, Herbert is equally critical of the unconditional extremism of communism's opponents. They too have been infected by the debased political and intellectual standards of People's Poland. Herbert wants fulfilment, not bitter polemic. Seeking to be tempted "more cleverly and beautifully", he meets only "coarse-grained rhetoric". Contemporary Poland is brutal and depressing:

> chains of tautologies one or two concepts like flails
> a torturer's dialectic no elegance in argument
> a syntax lacking the charms of the conditional

The tone is one of distaste; the Polish text bristles with short, ugly words: *chrząstki*, translated as "gristle" (Czerniawski) or "cartilage" (Carpenters); *cep* (a flail: but the word also has the colloquial sense of idiot). Czerniawski is more alive to the possibilities, but even he does not capture in English the feeling that one is almost spitting Herbert's dislike of the "home-brew Mephistos" who have debased Polish life. 'Aurora's grandchildren' (the reference is not to Classical mythology, but to the battle-cruiser *Aurora*, which shelled shore positions in Petrograd in support of the Bolshevik insurgents of October 1917) appal him: the unworthy inheritors of the Polish past.

And the contrast with the Polish past is, for Herbert, telling. In the opening line he refers to the Poles' *odmowa niezgoda i upór* (refusal dissent and obduracy): three emotionally-charged words in a culture such as Poland's, where resistance to foreign domination has long been a fact of political life. *Niezgoda* (dissent) as an element in the Polish political tradition pre-dates the decline of the Polish Commonwealth in the eighteenth century. Likewise *upór* (obduracy) is for Herbert a Polish virtue: the word is related morphologically to *opór* (resistance), a word of loaded significance in Poland's most recent history. Herbert, the unashamed élitist, is thus alive to the nation's past in a way which makes People's Poland a distressing place for him. If Poland must be ruled by tyrants, he seems to say, at least let them be enlightened. But from his weary tone of voice, it is clear that he expects to be disappointed.

Many years earlier Herbert elaborated this theme of power and morality in his celebrated poem, 'Elegy of Fortinbras'[8]. The taciturn military commander, Fortinbras, broods with little comprehension on the death of Hamlet and the disarray of the Danish kingdom. Now that the old, legitimate order has passed into history, it is for the survivors to rebuild as best they can:

> now you have peace Hamlet you accomplished what you had to
> and you have peace The rest is not silence but belongs to me
> you chose the easier part an elegant thrust
> but what is heroic death compared with eternal watching

The Hamlet myth has become a powerful contemporary metaphor, and not only in Poland. One thinks instinctively of Tom Stoppard's attendant lords,[9] who go to their deaths with no understanding of their predicament, or of the tragedy around them. Poles, however, seem to identify readily with Hamlet: the cultivated, rightful heir to the Kingdom, condemned to destruction by the inexorable workings of tragedy.

Herbert's Fortinbras speaks eloquently, but tersely. The old order, despite its moral attractions, has proved to be ineffectual and inadequate. Hamlet compared Denmark to a prison; it is the task of the new power to realise his vision. Military images abound; the new Denmark is to be ruled by illegitimate force, a cruel parody of the philosophical vision of its disturbed Prince.

The poem is translated by Czesław Miłosz, and in this instance the interests of the translator coincide with those of the author. Miłosz was an important intellectual mentor to the young Herbert. Despairing after the Nazi Occuation of the traditional Polish image of literature as a means of saving the nation, despairing especially of People's Poland, Miłosz defected to the West in 1951. He restored his faith in literature by recreating his birthplace, a mystical pre-Romantic Lithuania of the spirit. His poetry is out of step with contemporary Poland, though his status as a major poet is readily acknowledged.

Herbert alone shares stylistic and thematic affinities with Miłosz. Both have not surprisingly faced criticism from younger poets of the 1960s New Wave for failing to recognise the use of language as a means of imposing new patterns of social morality from outwith Polish society. Thus, Stanisław Barańczak:

> We were strongly influenced by Herbert and Miłosz . . . .But there was something missing . . . ..They didn't notice the significance of language in the twentieth century.[10]

If anyone is missing the point, it is Barańczak. Miłosz and Herbert have adopted a fundamentally different stance. They recognise the significance of language in the twentieth century, but in their separate ways, this is not their concern. Miłosz has created his own poetic world. Herbert is perhaps more concerned to maintain a moral stance in a contemporary society he finds aesthetically and morally distasteful; he uses his own mythical-poetic vocabulary to comment upon, to re-interpret a society he has done nothing to create. But both writers, aware of the value of the past and of mythological archetypes, have gained a moral distance from tyranny which is more difficult for writers who engage the tyrants on their own political and linguistic ground. Even if translator and author differ in the nature of their response to society, they are agreed that they must respond and challenge, not in the language of the oppressors, but in their own way. 'Elegy of Fortinbras' and its translation belong together, seamlessly, and it is unnecessary to separate them.

III

Tadeusz Różewicz (born 1921) came to prominence in the late 1940s with two volumes of poetry which explored the realities of Poland's wartime experiences and its new social and political order, rather than traditional aesthetic values of poetic beauty.[11] His earliest volumes might be termed 'poetry for survivors': the poetry of a half-strangled voice, its poetic message stripped of emotion. His impartial style has allowed him to write for the present; as the memories of war have faded for the Polish population, so too the severe realist of the early years has become a more intensely personal, serene and reflective poet.

Although Zbigniew Herbert is more celebrated in the West, Różewicz's prolific poetic output has made him a more significant public presence in post-war Poland's literary life. As with Herbert, his poems began to appear in English translation during the 1960s. His close friend Adam Czerniawski first published a selection of his verse in 1969; Czerniawski has now translated over a hundred of Różewicz's poems.[12] There are also three other volumes of translation, and Czesław Miłosz has published an extensive selection in his anthology *Polish Post-war Poetry*.[13]

Despite moving away from the brutal realism of the early verse, Różewicz has not renounced his earlier opinions. In 'Proofs' in 1968 he wrote:

> Death will not correct
> a single line of verse

she is no proof-reader
she is no sympathetic
lady editor

a bad metaphor is immortal

a shoddy poet who has died
is a shoddy dead poet

a bore bores after death
a fool keeps up his foolish chatter
from beyond the grave

(*Trans. A. Czerniawski*)

Fame is an ambiguous blessing; the writer is unable ever to escape the dead weight of his past words and deeds. Nevertheless, unlike several of his Polish contemporaries, Różewicz accepts the price; if death will not correct, then he will not recant. A survivor, living in the present, he does not wish to escape the past. Czerniawski's translation catches the self-deprecating tone, although something is inevitably lost of the almost feminine sensitivity of the first lines because English lacks suitable diminuative forms which would catch the tone of the three feminine noun endings: *ani jednej linijki* ('not one little line'), *korektorka* ('lady proof reader') and *życzliwa pani redaktorka* (which Czerniawski catches nicely with "sympathetic lady editor"). The serious matter of the poem — the immortality of mere words — slips through almost as an after-thought.

And yet: despite the delicacy of touch, this poem offers a clear response to the unresolved question posed in 'The Survivor', one of Różewicz's most celebrated early poems.

I am twenty-four
led to slaughter
I survived

[. . .]

Ideas are mere words:
virtue and crime
truth and lies
beauty and ugliness
courage and cowardice.[14]

This poem, stripped of metaphor and poetic delicacy, shows that Różewicz has nevertheless always been aware of the power and durability of "mere words". Unlike the more aesthetic Herbert, he felt able (even in the years of the Stalinist terror) to write, to offer hostages to the future, in the hope that a teacher would emerge:

> may he restore my sight hearing and speech
> may he once more name ideas and objects
> may he separate darkness from light.

If there is a teacher, it is not Christ, although Różewicz shares with his compatriots an upbringing impregnated with Roman Catholicism. He is acutely aware of Christianity's metaphoric force in Poland's particular situation. But his use of Christian imagery does not betoken recognition of the Catholic Church's moral authority, but rather of its pervasive influence throughout Polish society. This influence is at its strongest in several poems where Różewicz combines his characteristic symbol of trees as a vital and life-giving force, with the crucifixion of Christ and by analogy of twentieth century humanity. Thus the 1955 poem, 'A Tree':

> Happy were
> the poets of old
> the world like a tree
> they like a child
>
> What shall I hang
> upon the branch of a tree
> which is burnt
> and never will sing[15]

The first, third and fifth verses repeat the simple refrain "happy were . . . " set against these images of destruction and crucifixion: the tree has been burned; has suffered "a rain of steel"; in the night, it has been defiled by the weight "of a corpse despised". As if to emphasise humanity's loss of innocence, the poem is in the form of a rondeau, or else a children's dancing rhyme. Krynski and Maguire, whose translation is in parallel to the Polish text, are content simply to translate without any attempt to reproduce rhyme and metre. Czerniawski makes no attempt to recreate a strictly metrical structure, but by keeping his lines terse — never more than two strong stresses — retains much of the rhythmical quality. Compare Krynski and Maguire's:

What would you have me hang
upon the branch of a tree
that burned to the roots
will not burst into song

with Czerniawski's:

What shall I hang
upon the branch of a tree
which is burnt
and never will sing.

Strangely enough Krynski and Maguire have not gained in clarity by abandoning metricality. Czerniawski's translation shows that Różewicz's folkloric rhythmical structure can be reproduced in a format equally direct and easily communicable to an English-speaking reader.

Różewicz's commitment to "mere words" underpins his overwhelming need to redefine, to rebuild a poetic idiom — just as the Poles were forced to reconstruct their national and cultural identity in the aftermath of the Second World War and the Holocaust. Two poems, 'In the midst of life' and 'Draft for a contemporary love poem',[16] attempt to explore the poet's thought-processes as he reconciles the world of his experience with the dictates of his poetic imagination.

'In the midst of life' takes humanity back to the very basis of its existence. After the end of the world, after death, everything must be reconstructed: a table, a knife, bread and, by extension, life:

After the end of the world
after death
I found myself in the midst of life
creating myself
building life
people animals landscapes

There is no room for traditional poetics. Różewicz is reaffirming life, but doggedly and defiantly, as if the mere repetition of key elements of life will restore full vitality to a poisoned society. There is a quality of ritual chant in the repetitions; or, at a more immediate level, a children's reading primer, endlessly repeating the basic elements of grammar and vocabulary:

this is a man
this is a tree this is bread

people eat to live
I repeated to myself

The message is universal:

human life is important
human life is of great import
the value of life
outweighs the value of all things
created by man
and man is a great treasure
I kept repeating stubbornly

'In the midst of life' is direct and unambiguous, and the three translators have hardly varied their approach. If the message is universal, so too is the manner of its expression. The dogged repetitions, the remorseless stresses, do not depend on any linguistic peculiarities: as with the brutalities of the twentieth century (the "things created by man" which Różewicz dismisses), anyone can play. All you need is a jaw firmly set, and a stubborn refusal to lose sight of the essence of life.

Not all of Różewicz's poetry is so sparing of poetic imagery; as Polish society began to emerge from the horrors of the two 'Occupations' (the Nazi tyranny, and the years of Soviet-imposed Stalinist terror), so too Różewicz began to affirm his commitment to life without recourse to the stubborn desperation which characterised his verse in the later 1940s and early 1950s. Written in 1963, 'Draft for a contemporary love poem', despite its affinities with 'In the midst of life', is more sensual. The emotionless repetitions of the earlier poem here give way to traditional poetic imagery: sunsets, flowers, the traditional images of erotic verse. Różewicz has a strong commitment to sensuality which is evident in this poem, even if it ends on a characteristically austere note:

Hunger deprivation
absence
of flesh
is the description of love
the contemporary love poem

Różewicz clearly relishes the tension which is established by the conflict of austerity and sensuality. At its best, it can allow him to deceive his readership with an apparent lightness of touch. For example: his poem, 'Conversation with the Prince'.[17] As with Herbert's 'The Elegy of Fortinbras', the inspiration is the Hamlet myth — the inability of the Danish courtiers to comprehend the extent of the tragedy. Unlike Herbert's taciturn military commander, Różewicz's interlocutor of the silent Prince Hamlet is no man of action, but J Alfred Prufrock, T.S. Eliot's balding, lecherous windbag, "full of high sentence". An attendant lord, certainly, but one firmly in the wings when tragedy overwhelms the Danish kingdom in Eliot's poem:

> Am an attendant lord, one that will do
> to swell a progress, start a scene or two
> Advise the prince; no doubt, an easy tool
> [. . . .]
> Almost, at time, the Fool.

Clearly, T S Eliot is the key to the poem's translation. The author misleads the unwary by claiming in a footnote that "the poem contains quotations from the works of Shakespeare, Eliot and [Gottfried] Benn". There are, in fact, no direct quotations from *Hamlet*; neither is the Polish text self-evidently archaicised, except in the final few lines of the poem. By contrast Różewicz, who neither speaks nor reads English, plunders the Polish translation of Eliot's poems in much the same way that Eliot himself explored in his own poetry the traditions and cadences of Shakespearean and Metaphysical verse. In this context, it is worth noting that Jósef Czechowicz (1909-1939), Eliot's first Polish translator, was an important formative influence on the young Różewicz.

Krynski and Maguire fail to take advantage of an interesting opportunity to recreate something of the English source material in their translation, which therefore stays closer in metrical structure and syntax to the Polish text. They recognise the role of this "jester without king", this "babbler concealed behind the arras", (here I prefer Czerniawski's "kingless fool" and "windbag behind the arras" for being closer in spirit to Eliot's verse), but by avoiding any creative retranslation, they prevent the English reader from appreciating the virtuosity of what might be seen as Różewicz's 'Prufrock'.

Adam Czerniawski makes better use of this opportunity. His attendant lord shuffles among the furniture in dusty rooms, ignoring the greater tragedy in favour of lecherous schemes, as did Eliot's

Prufrock among the coffee-spoons and unspoken lusts of polite society. Różewicz is playing with us, borrowing not only from 'Prufrock', but also from 'The Waste Land', and by extension from elsewhere in Eliot's early verse. Not only that, but subtly undermining the original context. Thus:

he is not free
from reflection
calculates the profit and loss
sweats in terror
thus adding madness
to fear
mixes the taste of desire
with thoughts of rising prices
shuts his eyes sweats and counts

Prufrock never panicked about anything more consequential than his dress-sense and his bald spot as he gossiped and seduced among the teas and marmalade. Does Różewicz mean to imply that he is doing little more than mixing "memory and desire" in some latter-day sybaritic Waste Land? Or are we perhaps in the company of a not yet drowned Phlebas, contemplating the "profit and loss" — a contemporary poet trying to escape the terrors of post-Holocaust 1958 by worrying about inconsequentialities?

Różewicz isn't telling, but this particular "windbag behind the arras" has evidently witnessed much more in his time than a bad case of matricide. The apocalyptic pessimism which prompted Eliot's 'The Waste Land' seems by implication (in the eyes of Różewicz's "contemporary poet" in the year 1958) to be merely one further manifestation of western civilisation's characteristic self-indulgence. Here too, the parallel with Czechowicz is arresting; one of the most influential poetic innovators of the inter-war period, Czechowicz refused to be drawn into the self-deluding pessimism which characterised intellectual life among the fractious Warsaw *avant garde* of the late 1930s. His powerful, emotionally-charged poetry certainly caught a sense of European civilisation's imminent destruction in the years before 1939, but its strength derives from an almost classical restraint, which looks forward to the new generation of poets which was to emerge after 1945.

In 1939 Różewicz and his contemporaries could only watch as their native cities were overthrown. Adam Czerniawski, adapting his translation to the patterns and rhythms of Eliot's poetry, enables an

English-speaking audience to understand how this self effacing poet is able to retain his humanity after witnessing the terrors of the mid-twentieth century.

And, as if to emphasise the point, Różewicz returned to Hamlet some three years later, in his 1963 poem 'Précis'.[18] Here is an ironic summary of the plot of *Hamlet*, intended to help the poet's teenage son to understand the play's relevance for his own time and place. But the essence of the poem is in the last few lines, where Różewicz declines to explain the contemporary relevance of Hamlet's philosophy:

> I pass over in silence
> the question
> which
> the Danish Prince had asked himself
> it's a joke too cruel and vulgar
> for modern man.

Różewicz the poet, the survivor, is on his own. If he has found a teacher, it is within himself. If he has found a philosophy, it is one which must allow him to survive in the present.

IV

Wisława Szymborska (born 1923) is an intensely private poet, one who seeks — through a poetic *persona* which is witty, ironic and entertaining — to maintain a stance of almost galactic indifference to the 'realities' of contemporary Poland. She refuses to speculate openly on Polish mythopaia of the Second World War, and the Poles' equally obsessive fascination with communist totalitarianism. But this is to some extent an intellectual pose; her poems frequently tease the reader with concealed allusions to the Polish predicament. With her lightness of touch and her infectious sense of humour, she has in recent years become one of Poland's most popular poets. Particularly among younger Poles; her slightly arch, teasing mockery has given her something of the status of a mischievous maiden aunt or a favourite grandmother.

Szymborska's verse is less familiar in English translation than that of Herbert or Różewicz. In the 1965 edition of *Polish Post-war Poetry*, Czesław Miłosz included only one of her poems. He expressed misgivings as to her "playing with ideas borrowed from anthroplogy and philosophy, which might [....] make poetry dependent on intellectual fashions and encourage preciosity".[19] A selection of seventy poems, translated by Krynski and Maguire, appeared in 1981,[20] and some recent poems have appeared in anthologies published in 1988.[21] Adam Czerniawski's selection of her verse entitled *People on a Bridge* has just appeared.

To begin with her most recent collection.[22] It was a critical and popular success in Poland, and it is from this volume that several of the translations in Czerniawski's anthology were taken. But there was less uniformity of opinion about individual poems within the collection. There was none of the consensus which usually characterises reactions to collections from Herbert or Różewicz, where preferences clearly emerge for five or six poems within an individual volume. Quite simply: with Szymborska's work, different people prefer different poems.

This might seem to suggest that Szymborska's verse is indeed dependent on mood and fashion (to echo Miłosz's complaint from 1965), on the projection of a certain witty charm which masks her lack of serious purpose. After all, popularity and serious poetic intent do not always interact easily.

But this is unfair, as Miłosz himself later acknowledged. The moral strength, which marks both Herbert and Różewicz, can also be found in Szymborska's work. As with Herbert, she depends on emotional distance and ironic detachment, and she shares his desire to confront contemporary issues on her own terms. But she has her own distinct voice, which frequently involves reversing the obvious logical flow of intellectual argument. 'Children of the age',[23] from *Ludzie na moście*, is an elaborate manifesto for apoliticism in a social system which seeks to politicise its subject population (quotations from the translation by Bassnett and Kuhiwczak):

> We are the children of this age,
> this age is political
>
> All your, his, our
> day and night-time affairs (*dzienne sprawy, nocne sprawy*)
> are political affairs.

The message is clear; to attempt to be apolitical in a politicised society is in itself a political statement — a truth familiar to creative artists across contemporary Eastern Europe. To emphasise her point Szymborska repeats the word "political" twelve times (in a thirty-five line poem), her examples alternately sombre and frivolous:

To be or not to be, that is the question.
What question, tell me, my darling?
The political question.

You need not even be a human being
to acquire political importance.
It is enough just to be oil
fodder or recyclable material.

Here, an Hamletic musing balances uneasily with a delicate, telling reference to Nazism's greatest atrocity (and Szymborska has spent most of her life in Kraków, only a short bus journey from Auschwitz-Birkenau itself). But, as she points out, in a characteristic ironic twist, the political/apolitical balance is rarely so clear:

All this time people have been dying
animals have been starving
houses have been burning
fields have been turning fallow
just as in far off distant
less political ages.

And even in this concluding stanza, she could not resist the thoughtful tease. Not a simple reference to births, marriages and death; but instead burning houses, starving animals and dying people (the Polish text is *ginęli ludzie*, which suggests death by violent means).

A characteristic Szymborska poem, the logic clear despite the twists. Also a poem full of half-references to themes and quotations familiar to her Polish audience: *dzienne sprawy, nocne sprawy* alludes to a popular Polish hymn; the Hamlet quotation is clear enough; and also, in three lines omitted from the translation:

Nawet idąc borem lasem
stawiasz kroki polityczne
na podłożu politycznym.

("Even wandering through forests and woods/ you take political steps/on a political basis.") These lines recall a popular Polish marching song of considerable antiquity. It is odd that the translators should have omitted them; they do not present concepts too difficult to transfer into English. In fact, Bassnett and Kuhiwczak's translation is on the whole very unfriendly, both to the tone of this particular poem, and to its delicate structural balance. Five lines have been omitted, and separate verses telescoped together, so that the nine short stanzas of the original version have become, in translation, two short introductory stanzas followed by three unwieldy ones.

In the introduction to *Ariadne's Thread*, the translators claim the right to abandon literal meaning in favour of what they describe as "creative unfaithfulness". By this they hope to preserve a poem's underlying structures, tone and mood, while abandoning the attempt to reproduce sound and rhyme patterns. They establish an uneasy alternation between textual intelligibility and a process of conscious "defamiliarisation": which seems to be Ms Bassnett's way of persuading the reader that reading and interpreting foreign poetry ought to be made as difficult as possible. Clearly, translation has its inherent dangers, but their methodology is a hindrance in approaching Szymborska — particularly in 'Children of the age'. The poem's verse structure relates less to linguistic patterns than to the development of verse patterns of thought. The unwieldy verse of the English translation obscures the clarity of Szymborska's thought which, although eclectic and apparently disjointed, always maintains its own consistent logical drive.

It is interesting to contrast the almost tortured thought-processes of Bassnett and Kuhiwczak — exponents both of an academic discipline they call "translation studies" — with the other available translations of her verse. In much of Szymborska's work there is a strange tension between the complex, paradox-laden logic of her verse-structure, and a language of deceptive lightness. This is shown to great advantage in the poem 'Theatrical impressions',[24] from her 1976 collection, *Wielka liczba*.

The poem shares thematic affinities with 'Children of the age', questioning the relationship between reality and its stage representations. She contrasts the apparent inconsequentialities of a theatrical tragedy with the wider tragedies of modern life. But the inconsequentiality is relative, since the 'real' world of Szymborska's sixth act is an exercise in fantasy. After the curtain falls on the stage tragedy, victims and murderers alike arise from the battlefield to face the audience:

> Bows individual and collective:
> a white hand on a wounded heart,
> a suicide curtseying,
> a beheaded nodding.

> Bows in pairs:
> fury offering an arm to gentleness,
> the victim gazing blissfully into the torturer's eyes,
> the revolutionary ungrudgingly marching with the tyrant.

Although the play is over, the fantasy drama continues, blocking out the harsh realities of contemporary life. And Szymborska's choice of images is telling: as with her descriptions of life in "less political ages", so too her theatrical world is one where life and fantasy are interwoven. Suicides; victims; revolutionaries; tyrants: a gallery of characters familiar to all the "children of this age", and one with a peculiar — as she would say — "resonance" for the Poles. And the most poignant resonance of all, for a culture scarred by deportations, judicial murder, mass executions: "the miraculous return of those vanished without trace".

Krynski and Maguire's selection from Szymborska's verse is presented in a parallel-text edition, following the precedent of their Różewicz translations in *The Survivor*. They therefore tend towards literalness, no doubt feeling that questions of style can thereby best be unearthed from the Polish text. And, to a certain extent, the principle objective with Szymborska — more so than with Herbert or Różewicz — is to transfer the ideas she explores. Nevertheless, literal translations often don't work: what is colloquial and familiar in Polish cannot be readily transferred literally into English.

Czerniawski's translation is more "creatively unfaithful" to Szymborska's intentions. For example: the opening lines of the poem, which describe the resurrection at the curtain-call of the living and the dead from the drama. Szymborska describes in detail the flurry of activity as the actors readjust their costumes, remove knives from wounds. In these opening lines, the verb forms she uses are in fact verbal nouns, a construction more colloquially comfortable in Polish than in English. Czerniawski avoids the stilted tone this would engender in literal translation by turning Szymborska's gerunds into active verbs:

> [. . .] arise from the stage battlefields,
> adjust their wigs and robes,
> pull out the knife from the breast

But perhaps not so much "creative unfaithfulness" — in any case a portentous description of a problem familiar to most translators — as an attempt to keep faith with both languages. Czerniawski's aim is to ensure complete familiarisation for his foreign readership. Szymborska's impact comes not from the poetic qualities of her language, but from the startling contrast between complicated and often paradoxical ideas, and the deceptive simplicity of the text.

Szymborska matters, above all, because she makes us laugh — a rare gift for a Polish poet in the post-war world. In the midst of her complex anthropological anatomisation of contemporary society, she is capable of the most elegant *jeux d'esprit*, whose only purpose is to play with the absurdities of modern life. As a case in point: 'In praise of my sister', her marvellous parody of the repetitious style which has frequently passed for comic verse in twentieth century Poland:[25]

> My sister cultivates a quite good spoken prose
> and her writing's restricted to holiday postcards,
> the text promising the same each year
> that when she returns
> she'll tell us
> all
> all
> all about it.

V

Herbert, Różewicz and Szymborska are representative of their generation. Born during the 1920s, theirs was the first which was forced to question many of Poland's traditional poetic and cultural assumptions. Polish Romanticism had created an image of Polish culture which it had proved impossible to extend beyond the cultural borders of Polishness: Poland the suffering Christ among nations; a nation apart; a nation of the spirit. The self-delusion which was such a prominent feature of Polish culture during the inter-war years (1918-1939) only served to make the ultimate disillusion the more overwhelming. The fifteen years of Nazi occupation and Stalinist repression destroyed for a whole generation the myths which had sustained the Poles during the Era of Partitions (1795-1918).

But the effect was strangely liberating, and it brought Polish writers closer to the mainstream of Western culture than they had ever been in the nineteenth century. While Poland had always been keen to respond to the influence of Western culture, it had mostly been a one-way process; by contrast, from the mid-1950s, Polish poets were being taken seriously in the West for the first time since the high point of Polish Romanticism. The poets I have discussed — and particularly Zbigniew Herbert — were the first beneficiaries of this interest.

Poland's experiences in a century of total war and totalitarian tyranny reflect the wider European crisis of the twentieth century. When Szymborska speaks of the "common war-booty" it is clear that the War and its depredations belong not just to Poles, but to anyone who chooses to listen. The hermetic Polish culture of the post-Romantic era was a product of Polish self-delusion; with the destruction of that particular Poland came an end to self-delusion, and the opportunity for re-integration into the mainstream European cultural tradition.

But the possibilities of re-integration do not resolve the problems of translation. Each of these three poets is reacting against a cultural tradition which needs to be understood if translation is to be effective. Their Polishness matters, and this needs to be taken into account.

Herbert, Różewicz and Szymborska are intellectual poets — a poetic conception somewhat outside the Polish mainstream, but one which finds familiar echoes in the Anglo-American tradition. Likewise, the irony which underpins the most characteristic verses of Herbert and Szymborska is of a quality which, although alien to popular Polish conceptions of poetics, finds parallels in post-modern Western European poetry.

In Poland, all three have been highly influential, both among their fellow-poets and with the wider, poetry-reading audience. Różewicz and Szymborska have best-seller status; Herbert too, though his frequent publication difficulties have limited public familiarity to those with access to unofficial publications. And yet, the feeling is that their position is one of honour, rather than direct influence. The politicised poets of the 'Generation of 1968' certainly did not share the overwhelming concern of Herbert and Szymborska for ironic detachment. Neither does the spare, unpoetic imagery of their verses square with the predominant Polish popular taste for a florid, neo-baroque excess of sentiment — something which has been a feature of many post-war poets.

If, in the end, translation of Polish poetry has become less of a marginal activity than before 1939, it is not simply because Poland's — and the English-speaking world's — intellectual frontiers have widened. It is an accident of the war, which shaped the horizons of these three poets, that the West plays host to well-educated Polish émigré communities, from which several prominent translators have emerged. I have discussed the work of Miłosz and Czerniawski; many other first or second generation Poles, educated in the West, have helped to bring Polish poetry to a wider foreign audience than has ever historically been the case.

And translation is an accidental business. While there is no doubt of (say) Herbert's overwhelming stature as a major poet, it is none too certain that genius will always find a voice, particularly when that voice is in a language at the margins of European society. A century ago, the great Polish poet Cyprian Kamil Norwid died in Paris, unknown and untranslated. In his day, it simply wasn't important to know about Poland; Poland didn't exist, didn't matter. Only in this century, when Poland has shown considerable headline-grabbing ability, has it become important to know about her history and culture. And even here . . .

Notes

1. *Raport z oblężonego miasta* (Paris, 1983), translated as *Report from the Besieged City* (New York, 1985; Oxford, 1987).
2. *Selected Poems* (London, 1968) trans. Czesław Miłosz and Peter Dale Scott; the volume was reissued by Carcanet, Manchester, 1987. *Selected Poems* (Oxford, 1977) and *Report from the Besieged City* both translated by John and Bogdana Carpenter.
3. Trans. Peter Dale Scott in *Selected Poems* (1968).
4. Trans. Czesław Miłosz in *Selected Poems* (1968) and John and Bogdana Carpenter in *Selected Poems* (1977).
5. For example, see Peter Forbes' review of the translation of *Report from the Besieged City* (*Poetry Review*, Autumn 1987).
6. Trans. Adam Czerniawski in *The Burning Forest* (Newcastle, 1988) and John and Bogdana Carpenter in *Report from the Besieged City* (Oxford, 1987).
7. In Zbigniew Herbert: *Wybór wierszy* (*Selected Verse*) (Warsaw, 1983).
8. Trans. Czesław Miłosz in *Selected Poems* (1968).
9. Tom Stoppard: *Rosencrantz and Guildenstern Are Dead* (London, 1967).
10. In an interview for *The Manhattan Review*. Quoted in *Humps and Wings: Polish Poetry Since 1968* (San Francisco, 1982).
11. *Niepokój* (*Unease*) (Warsaw, 1947) and *Czerwona rękawiczka* (*Red Glove*) (Warsaw, 1948).
12. *Faces of Anxiety* (London, 1969); *Selected Poems* (London, 1976); *Conversation with the Prince* (London, 1982). There is a selection of his translations in his anthology *The Burning Forest*.

13. M J Krynski and R A Maguire: *The Survivor* (Princeton, 1976); Viktor Contoski: *Unease* (Minnesota, 1980); Geoffrey Thurley: *Green Rose* (Darlington, Australia, 1982). Czesław Miłosz (ed): *Polish Post-War Poetry* (California, 1965, 1983).
14. From *Czerwona rękawiczka* (1948). Trans. Krynski and Maguire in *The Survivor*, and Czerniawski in *Conversation with the Prince*. Czerniawski's version is quoted here.
15. Trans. Krynski and Maguire in *The Survivor*, and Czerniawski in *Conversation with the Prince*. Czerniawski's version is quoted here.
16. Translations of both poems appear in Miłosz: *Polish Post-War Poetry*; Czerniawski: *Conversation with the Prince*; Krynski and Maguire: *The Survivor*. Quotations from 'In the Midst of Life' by Krynski and Maguire, and 'Draft for a Contemporary Love Poem' by Czerniawski.
17. The title poem of the volume *Rozmowa z księciem* (Warsaw, 1960). Trans. Krynski and Maguire in *The Survivor* and Czerniawski in *Conversation with the Prince*.
18. Trans. Adam Czerniawski in *Conversation with the Prince*.
19. Quoted in the 1983 edition of *Polish Post-War Poetry*. Miłosz included significantly more of her verse in this second edition.
20. *Sounds, Feelings, Thoughts* (Princeton). A second edition has recently been published in Poland under the title *Poezje-poems* (Kraków).
21. Trans. Adam Czerniawski in *The Burning Forest* and Susan Bassnett and Piotr Kuhiwczak in *Ariadne's Thread* (London, 1988).
22. *Ludzie na moście* (*People on a Bridge*) (Warsaw, 1986, 1988). Both Polish editions had print-runs of 20,000 copies.
23. Trans. Bassnett and Kuhiwczak in *Ariadne's Thread*.
24. Trans. Adam Czerniawski in *The Burning Forest*, and by Krynski and Maguire in *Sounds, Feelings, Thoughts*. Czerniawski's version is quoted here.
25. In *The Burning Forest*. The poem is also translated by Krynski and Maguire in *Sounds, Feelings, Thoughts*.

Adam Czerniawski

Poets and Painters

Poets and Painters

I

Each artistic medium has its strengths and weaknesses. Language enables us to tell a story or set out an argument; but can music narrate, can a picture lead us to a conclusion?

Seeing exciting challenges in these situations artists move towards opposite extremes: some attempt to exploit fully and exclusively the qualities of their chosen medium (painters avoiding all references to the phenomenal world in order to guard the purity of their pigments) or to negate them (poets battling heroically to render language meaningless); others are maximalists, seeking to cross at least one medium boundary: composers force music to narrate, poets aspire to a condition of music, painters claim to reveal religious and philosophical truths.

Perhaps the oldest, and certainly the most persistent, is the ambition of poets to create visual effects. This aspiration is so well entrenched and so generally accepted that it often acts as a criterion of value: a poem is praised for its ability to conjure up images, presumably because they are the product of the imagination, the poetic gift *par excellence*. But if the creation of images is of paramount significance, why do poets insist on using words in preference to brushes, pencils, chisels and cameras? Is it only because they lack the skills and have to fall back on words? That must be so in some cases.

At the same time, a powerful Renaissance doctrine, which also has its roots in antiquity, exhorts painters and sculptors to be conversant with the great secular and sacred writings in order to utilise them as subjects for visual treatment: the portrayal of the phenomenal world is not deemed enough. The painter must choose some crucial incident in a suitably important story: the Crucifixion, the slaying of Hector or the birth of Venus. Here allegory is the extreme case of the conceptual parading as the pictorial, here the most articulate allegory results in the most confused picture. But even these Renaissance works contain as background or incidentals depictions of natural scenery and of artefacts which demonstrate the artists' inevitable desire to present the world in terms of pure phenomena, a desire which shows its first signs of greater fulfilment in Dutch seventeenth century art and the paintings of Chardin, a desire that comes to full satisfaction in the work of the Impressionists.

Of the permutations hinted at here it is the verbal-pictorial that naturally interests us now. The ancient Greek poet Simonides captures this interaction in a neat and celebrated paradox, which states that painting is silent poetry and poetry articulate painting.[1] That this paradoxical truth is discovered so early is surely due to the fact that images and words are our twin elements of cognition: we perceive the world and attempt to give it meaning, we internalise the process in thoughts and mental images. Psychological and philosophical treatises on the nature of human understanding invariably build on this occurrence and interaction of words and images: this duality underlies Plato's concept of Forms, it structures theories of knowledge from Locke, Descartes, Leibniz, Spinoza and Hume to Kant, Mill, Husserl, Wittgenstein and Sartre; it directs psychological research and theorising from the origins of that discipline in the nineteenth century to the present day. Psychologists register the co-relationship between words and images in the human mind, philosophers struggle to understand the cognitive roles of this association and of their twin components.

The poems I intend to discuss are examples of a subtle variant of the word-image bond. It is not that they aim to create images through words, it is rather that they are verbal commentaries or verbal descriptions, or both, of independently existing images, namely paintings.

Creating a verbal image in competition with a painted one may seem Quixotic, even insane. (Curiously, this feeling of incongruity does not haunt us when the movement is in the opposite direction, namely when we encounter pictorial glosses of poems). The enterprise is made to look eccentric by this bland description of it as nothing more than a duplication of the image. True, such poems do exist, but they are usually quite tedious examples of the genre and are not discussed here. A related objection is that the poet, constructing his poem with the assistance of a painter, is having most of his work done for him: he takes over a finished product in which the inchoate flow of sensations has already been painstakingly harnessed into a formally ordered structure by another creative mind.[2] However, the good poet will not be a slavish dependent, he will make the painting work for him as a reference point, a shorthand description or a touchstone of value.

Poets treating of paintings are also challenged in another context: that of 'nature' or 'reality' which highlights the artifice of art. This contrast is invoked to indicate the sterile nature of the aesthetically self-referential painterly poem. But we needn't take seriously Social-Realist and Romantic sentimentalists who regard invocations of 'reality' or 'nature' as solutions to all our problems.

The examples discussed in this essay are intended to demonstrate how varied poets' encounters with painting can be, and how exciting are the results. I shall here consider three poets who in very different ways have made good use of their understanding and appreciation of painted images: Bogdan Czaykowski, Wisława Szymborska and Tadeusz Różewicz. In the poems of Czaykowski and Różewicz such images act principally as reference points and touchstones of value, whereas Szymborska treats them descriptively, but her descriptions are intended as interpretations and are structured accordingly.

II

The concluding stanza of Czaykowski's 'Lake Vaseaux' reads:

> But what I like most
> is the Lake Vaseaux
> art gallery.
> When the waters subside
> your canoe glides over canvases
> by Cézanne or Matisse,
> early Cubists or Japanese masters,
> and your oar
> participates in this unsurpassed art

when the waters
are again composed into a reflection.[3]

We admire the skill and imagination which has brought the artificial to organise the natural. Many strands of perception and cognition mingle in this handful of unpretentious lines. The poet has taken over the visual vocabularies of several painters and applied them to natural phenomena in a way that demonstrates that these very diverse codes, which have not long ago been regarded as shocking examples of barely acceptable semi-private languages of artists bent on perverse distortion of what is 'normally' seen, do correspond to nature. Thus, their employment in this context challenges the assumption that Matisse and Cézanne and the others can at best present us with personal visions of nature which we can admire — or loathe — from a distance but which we could never accept as 'normal' in the way that we accept Hobbema's or Constable's. The modern 'art gallery' is made to serve the poet as he records the restless watery reflections in Lake Vaseaux.

In an earlier poem entitled 'To Adam Czerniawski', composed in the spring of 1981 in the Canadian wilderness, Czaykowski observes:

If I lack anything, it's paintings —
of faces gazing sagaciously, if long dead,
of blue mists in Italian landscapes,
and of forms shattered to shine from within,
for sometimes a form will crack beautifully.[4]

The situation described by the poet implies that we are not likely to get any more poems on the subject of art from him. This is by and large the case, but not entirely, as the more recent 'Lake Vaseaux' (composed in 1988) demonstrates. However, Czaykowski's poetry does draw its main inspiration from nature ('Lake Vaseaux' confirms this contrary thesis too) and this is borne out by the concluding stanza of 'To Adam Czerniawski':

I'm writing this in early spring, which like the fall
is somehow exceedingly poetic.
As yet unfallen leaves are drifting from the trees
and mingling so with drifting blossoms
that you don't know whether this is early snow,
snow falling from almond-trees,
whirling beneath the stars, which shine as sharply
as if dry frost had polished them.

> And then you hear a whistling in the birches.
> Your ever transient bird has come again,
> this bird unseen and barely heard.

Natural beauty is here perceived as consolation for the absence of art, perhaps as a second-best source of inspiration. The student of Czaykowski's poetry need not entirely agree: his achievement over the years is that of a significant nature poet in a tradition that includes both Wordsworth and Leśmian, and the stanza just quoted is a good example of this. Who knows — the proximity of The Louvre might have diminished the intensity of Czaykowski's vision of nature.

Moreover, the art-nature duality is not the only theme of this densely packed, evocative poem which in its discursive flow consciously echoes *Promethidion*, Cyprian Norwid's treatise on Platonist aesthetics, and alludes to virgin Lithuanian forests in Adam Mickiewicz's *Pan Tadeusz*. It is also a poem about the solitary Romantic pilgrim, lost in the expanse of nature, confronting the horror of solipsism: " . . . if I lack anything at all, it's images/of faces listening". It portrays someone "distant from the well-springs of speech", meaning presumably both an exiled Polish poet separated from his native land and a human being who is the lonely language-user and image-maker in a habitat which supports only birds and animals.

Czaykowski's poem makes no reference to any specific works of art. All we can assume from the allusions to portraits and the "blue mists in Italian landscapes" is that he has the European tradition of painting in mind. Somewhat puzzling are the "forms shattered to shine from within". Perhaps the Romantic notion of works deliberately left incomplete or roughly hewn is here intended, and it would thus be a veiled reference to Norwid's claim that (note the presentation of a poetic aesthetic through an art image): "a perfect lyric should be like a plaster cast: those boundaries where forms miss each other and leave cracks ought to be preserved and not smoothed over with a knife."[5]

III

Wisława Szymborska is more specific. She has two poems about identifiable pictures: Breughel's 'Two Monkeys' and Hiroshige Utagawa's 'People on a Bridge'; also one about 'A Mediaeval

Miniature' and one about 'The Women of Rubens'.

Szymborska's treatment of these subjects is one that is most common among poets: a particular image elicits a specific response. Breughel's monkeys make the poet reflect on the relationship between humans and animals; the miniature serves to sketch the mediaeval social and moral world-picture — by implication so very different from the poet's own. The ideological distance is signalled in the poem by the use of a highly stylised, formalised language, mirroring also the — to us — highly stylised depictions in the miniature which the poet engagingly characterises as "super-feudal realism". Significantly, because she feels a kinship with Breughel's (presumed) sympathy for the chained monkeys, the language of this poem is transparent, unobtrusive, shunning all attention-seeking formal graces. By contrast, Szymborska's distaste for the gross mounds of female flesh depicted in Rubens's overblown canvases is again evident in the extravagant language she employs to describe the painter's models as: "fatty amorous dishes", "daughters of the Baroque", "naked like the din of barrels" sprawling beneath "piglet clouds", while "their thin sisters", those "flat ones" for whom "the 17th century had nothing to offer", have to hide on the back of the canvases.

Many of Szymborska's poems are concerned with puzzles arising out of our attempts to distinguish reality from illusion: dreams and the theatre, as well as paintings, provide her with the necessary contrastive domains. But it is in paintings that she finds her richest material. Already in the very early and excruciatingly embarrassing social-realist 'A Painting in the Winter Palace' the poet has to assure a terrified revolutionary zealot, who has burst into a state room in the Palace which contains Czarist-realist paintings bristling with imperial armies, that the perceived threat is imaginary. And in the later 'Landscape', characteristic of her mature work, the onlooker, equally bewitched by painterly illusion, literally escapes from reality into "an Old Master's landscape", where "trees have roots beneath the oil-paint". Once inside the frame, she holds on tightly "so I won't fall out of the picture" and eventually disappears inside the painted house "where unpainted events occur", which she then proceeds to describe.

In 'People on a Bridge', perhaps Szymborska's most ambitious attempt in this genre, we see the poet, using Utagawa's print depicting people running to escape a heavy downpour, to ridicule the artist's (and humanity's) vain efforts to arrest the flow of time. In the previous three poems the poet takes sides: she favours the monkeys, she disapproves of mediaeval social hierarchies and of bloated women, but of course she could, contrariwise, have ridiculed modestly proportioned women, egalitarianism and love of animals.[6] But as regards the inexorable flow of time there is no debate: unlike social injustice, it cannot be stopped. Or rather, in a way, it can, if we have any appreciation of what Hiroshige and many others like him are doing. But that is sophistry or Shopenhauerian aestheticism: desperate attempts to fly in the face of facts.[7] That is why, if he is to sound credible, the speaker in 'People on a Bridge' has to be non-human, "an ideal observer", as philosophers say, unburdened by human anxieties, commenting on human delusions from inter-galactic distance:

> Maybe this was a whim of no significance,
> a freak covering just a pair of galaxies[8]

IV

If Czaykowski represents the extreme of a human exiled into the natural world, deprived of artefacts, Różewicz stands at the other extreme of a man trapped in a cultural hot-house. But this is only part of a complex story: trained as an art historian, and a passionate amateur of the visual arts from Titian, Rembrandt and de Hooch to Nowosielski, Brzozowski, Tchórzewski and the moving cinematic image, he finds himself battling with various modern manifestations of corrupt aestheticism: (i) the plague of mindless hordes of tourists invading museums:

> the guides hurriedly copulate
> with the beauty in the tourists' eyes
> this union brings forth
> bored monsters
> smiling giraffes[9]

(ii) the bane of commercial valuation displacing aesthetic valuation:

> dead alive
> he still begets
> gold

During the silly season
in the tabloids
Pablo Picasso
surfaces next to
the sea-serpent[10]

(iii) the pernicious cult of museums as rarified temples of art:

At this time
the long galleries of the Louvre
are empty

At the same time
Les Halles
bleed in the electric light
the mound of meat
the monstrous cadaver
twitched
[. . . . .]

At this same time
there are no eyes
among the paintings
no one experiences
no one consumes beauty
only the Gioconda
smiles
mysteriously and laboriously[11]

Beneath the surface there are memories of the poet's wartime experiences which caused him to question the value of art, and therefore the poem about Picasso ends with the injunction:

a task
awaits me:
To create poetry after Auschwitz

Given Różewicz's great love of art ("My foreign travels consist partly of sitting in art galleries in front of just one or two paintings"[12]), given the range of situations and experiences which have caused him to wonder about its efficacy and value, it is not surprising that, first, references to art-objects pervade his poetry and that, secondly, these references are often brutal, impatient, as well as at other times clearly laudatory. Many of Różewicz's poems covering several decades illustrate his ambiguous relationship with the medium. Perhaps mainly for this reason his poems with such themes differ markedly from those by Szymborska (or, for that matter, those by Zbigniew Herbert, Miłosz, Baudelaire, Browning, Yeats, Wallace Stevens, Auden, Berryman . . .): there are no set-piece one-to-one confrontations between poet and painting. References to art-works surface unexpectedly in a whole variety of situations. They testify to the strength of Różewicz's commitment to these objects as repositories of value which is matched only by Norwid and Herbert.

(1) In Florence, fresh from a visit to the Uffizi:

> in the long gallery
> a golden
> body
> stretched in sleep
> Venus
> woken by Titian
> floated her hand upon her dark delta
> past the tourists' faces

the poet watches an open-air fashion-show:

> young
> radiant
> women
> appeared under a granite colonnade
> in ballroom gowns
> unearthly creations
>
> a hand
> with almond
> silver
> nails rested against the grey column[13]

(2) Reflecting on the dazzling success at the turn of the century of the poet Kazimierz Przerwa-Tetmajer and his pitiable end in 1940 in a gutter in Nazi-occupied Warsaw, Różewicz focuses on a distinct moment in the poet's youth, where the Böcklin reference acts as a powerful symbol of a vanished age:

München 1899

Kazimierz Przerwa-Tetmajer
looks at Böcklin's
Island of the Dead
in the Neue Pinakotheke
people are sailing away like mists
from the meadow on to the lake They go to rest
another year and it will be the 20th century[14]

(3) Two London youths are observed in the Tate Gallery shop. One who has

the face of a saint
from a sweet Pre-Raphaelite picture
slowly descends to earth[15]

while "another leaves the gents". The poem gradually moves to a conclusion by way of the gruesome distortions of a twentieth century artist:

then they burst out
laughing
and spilled over

two carbuncles
open sores
out of a painting
by Francis Bacon

(4) There are also poems where no artists are named, no pictures identified; poems which, as it were, recreate in words a familiar but unnamed painterly experience to serve the poet's own ends, whether it be a description resembling a de Hooch interior:

A glass of red wine
stands on a table
in a dark room

through the open door
I see a landscape of childhood
a kitchen and a blue kettle
the Sacred Heart
mother's transparent shadow . . . [16]

or a Magritte image of mysterious contradictions:

> The cage stayed shut
> until a bird was hatched inside
>
> the bird remained mute
> until the cage
> rusting in the silence
> opened
>
> silence lasted until
> behind black wires
> we heard laughter[17]

And whereas in the other instances the references had to be identified for the reader to be able to appreciate their role, here are examples where the poet takes over, as it were, a particular painter's iconic vocabulary in order to create a purely verbal self-contained artefact.

(5) The work in which Różewicz tackles the theme of art most ambitiously is 'Et in Arcadia Ego'. It is a long poem of nearly eight hundred lines which records the poet's visit to Venice, Rome and Naples. It contains references to Michelangelo, Titian and Dali, references which play roles similar to those in the shorter poems already discussed. But here they serve as subordinate elements within an overall structure created by the pervasive allusion (enshrined in the title of the poem) to Poussin's (and his predecessors') portrayal of Arcady. The "ego" here has a dual reference: to the artist (the poet) and to death, both present in Arcady (and in Italy, the Mecca of beauty and art). Not surprisingly, Różewicz's poem features both beauty and death — the former in the various tourist attractions, the latter in the shape of an army parade sporting the latest weaponry and a war-time memory of Nazi executions which haunts the poet. The tonality of the poem is further complicated by the poet's reactions to the celebrated beauties. There is sarcasm at the expense of the tourists (already illustrated above). There are doubts regarding the nature of beauty:

> Michaelangelo's Last Judgment
> is being admired
> is it beauty

I don't know how to express
this shock
I had to rest my head on the back of a seat

And there is the concluding unashamed declaration, seemingly purged of the ironies and sarcasms that otherwise pervade the poem:

beauty touched me
I have tried to return to paradise

But those concluding lines are preceded by another reference to death. Różewicz quotes from his own very early poem 'Mask' written in 1946, when his ghastly war-time experiences were still fresh in his mind. The film of a Venetian carnival described in that poem leads to an evocation of victims of German executions in Poland, so the quotation fits neatly after a stanza which begins: "Venice burns/ rain Tintoretto gold":

huge effigies with monstrous heads
laugh noiselessly from ear to ear
and a maid too beautiful for me
an inhabitant of a small town in the North
rides astride an ichthyosaurus
Objects excavated in my country have small black
heads sealed with plaster and horrible grins[18]

* * *

The dialogue with the visual arts conducted by the three poets I have discussed here is also to be heard in the work of many other Polish poets, notably, as already indicated, in the work of Norwid and Herbert, as well as in Staff and Miłosz. But remarkably, it is absent from the poetry of the younger generations born after the war. Perhaps they thought that their insistence on writing simply and directly about tragic contemporary events and states of affairs by definition ruled out any recourse to the mediating role of art. Perhaps there were other reasons.

Notes

1. Reported in Plutarch's *De Gloria Atheniensium*, 3.
2. Cp. "It is hard to write poetry about other poems and only less hard to

write about pictures and statues. In such work there is almost inevitably something second-hand; it seems to have no independent vision and to add nothing new to experience". Maurice Bowra, *The Heritage of Symbolism* (London 1954), p.62. However, Bowra acknowledges that there are exceptions to such failures in, for example, the poems of Rilke.

3. Bogdan Czaykowski: 'Lake Vaseaux', trans. Adam Czerniawski, MSS.
4. Bogdan Czaykowski: 'To Adam Czerniawski', trans. Iain Higgins, (*The Rialto* No.10, Winter 1987/1988) pp.38-39.
5. Cyprian Norwid: Letter to Bronisław Zaleski [November, 1867].
6. These summaries of Szymborska's poems are of course crude: the poems are wittily detached and their bias is indicated deftly and lightly. This is but to draw attention to the fact that good poems are necessarily better than their summaries.
7. I imagine this poem might have found favour with Witold Gombrowicz who in his *Diary* (Vol.II, pp.48-50) condemns the art of painting wholesale because of its fraudulent attempts to freeze time. But what in Szymborska's hands is presented playfully as a metaphysical conundrum, remains in Gombrowicz's case a petulant and simple-minded complaint that paintings are static. Gombrowicz's notorious attacks on poetry are also curiously misguided: in a man who fancied himself possessing both great intelligence and the gift of poetry, these are serious lapses.
8. Wisława Szymborska: 'People on a Bridge', trans. Adam Czerniawski in *The Burning Forest* (Newcastle upon Tyne 1988), p.100.
9. Tadeusz Różewicz: 'Et in Arcadia Ego', Trans. Adam Czerniawski in *Conversation with the Prince* (London 1982), p.110.
10. Tadeusz Różewicz: 'I did espy a marvellous monster', *op.cit.* p.183.
11. Tadeusz Różewicz: 'At the same time', *op.cit.* p.122. Compare, or rather contrast, this sardonic and savage treatment of the Gioconda abandoned by her admirers with the comic night-time antics of the subjects of paintings in a gallery depicted in Szymborska's 'Wrong number', *op.cit.* p.95.
12. 'Tadeusz Różewicz in conversation with Adam Czerniawski', (*The New Review*, Vol.3 No.25, 1976) p.12.
13. Tadeusz Różewicz: 'Butterflies', *op.cit.*, p.136
14. Tadeusz Różewicz: 'Kazimierz Przerwa-Tetmajer', *op.cit.*, p.166.
15. Tadeusz Różewicz: 'Tate Gallery Shop', *op.cit.*, p.195.
16. Tadeusz Różewicz: 'Doors', *op.cit.*, p.129.
17. Tadeusz Różewicz: 'Laughter', *op.cit.*, p.127.
18. Tadeusz Różewicz: 'Et in Arcadia ego', *op.cit.*, pp.98-119.

Krzysztof Karasek

Fish on the Strand

Fish on the Strand

At times a poem is a closure, at times it is an opening. A closure, the last word, or an opening, the first word; a word which covers many perspectives, both past and future, distant and near, the low and the high. The poem as opening reveals the poet's own hierarchy unique to each poet. It decides his destiny and its extensions, it sketches out the territory. Sometimes this poem is outstanding, sometimes not, sometimes it is a masterpiece, sometimes a sketch with tracks, lines and threads running out of it, with the help of which the poem links with reality and the poet's external world. It denotes the emotional territory and the set of cognitive problems, as well as designating the ellipse of revelations. It draws together the historical embodiment and the metaphysical spirituality. But how is one to select such a poem from a poet's output? Each critic is guided by his own hierarchy which both opens and closes. Criticism means a fencing off of the territory and the deepening of the pit, the choice has to be arbitrary and defines both the poet and the critic. The point is that the self-definition of the critic should not mask the poet or the message of his poem. Moreover, he should gently hide behind the poet's word, place himself discreetly behind it as a source of light which illumines the text, so that a poem becomes a window with a large vista onto the landscape rather than onto a grave dug beneath the window. I would like to choose two such poems from the works of two émigré poets of the middle generation, poets who are members of the exclusive vanguard of Polish poetry, poets who co-create, although perhaps in a less spectacular manner than their colleagues in Poland, its topography: Bogdan Czaykowski and Adam Czerniawski. They both belong to the famous literary generation whose start dates back to 1956, the year of great social and political changes in Poland, the year of awakened hopes and lost opportunities. But here it would be proper to say a few words about the differences between these poets and their rivals, about their road to poetry and their personal destinies; about these two poets, who have lived outside Poland since they were infants and, what is more important, in the element of foreign tongues outside the boundaries of their own language; about what enabled them to join contemporary currents of the Polish language so that they have become its co-creators and exponents without complexes and without the favourable terms which are normally applied in Poland to émigré writings.

So we have to start by saying that they both completed their schooling in England and that their poetic beginnings were untypical; that entangled in two cultural spheres, two linguistic spheres, they operated with a stereoscopic vision from the very beginning, following developments both in Poland and in England. To what extent their consciousness of a quotidian existence in the English language influenced or could have influenced their originality, is another issue requiring a separate study. What is more important, however, is what was new and, above all, their own, that they had to offer Polish poetry in the making; what did they contribute to the picture of the new dynamically developing poetry of the late fifties and what role did they play in the revaluation of the poetic landscape of those years and in changing the vision of the world? It seems that a decisive role here was played by personal experiences which were both very dramatic and very painful. Children of war, blown like leaves from one country to another — Czaykowski for eight years through the Soviet Union, Persia and India (it's not surprising that his poetry is so full of the images of the wind — the Hegelian metaphor for history — and of grass which bends under the wind and constantly springs back — the Pascalian metaphor for man), Czerniawski for six years in the Middle East — journeying through languages, landscapes and customs, finally as a teenager finding an anchorage in England, where both poets completed their studies and where — Czerniawski in 1956 and Czaykowski in 1957 — published their first volumes of poetry that were noticed by critics in Poland. The experience of the war, historical and metaphysical at the same time, the experience of space (the Argentinian novelist and essayist Ernesto Sabato, analysing the personalities of Argentinians, concluded that the perception of space, of being lost, of being abandoned, is the chief source of metaphysical feelings) were decisive for the development of both poets. On the other hand, there was British culture already adopted in childhood, which offered not so much formal models as a model of how one should restrain and discipline those experiences: historical and metaphysical, biological and existential, social and purely personal. Restraint at the existential level and restraint at linguistic level.

Thus they experienced a bifurcation, a split, the natural state of the modern poet — the division into a private and a public language. In their case all this acquires an additional, one might say a multi-layered, complication — it is subject to a further division: the alien and the personal. It might be said: many poets have spent varying periods of time beyond the boundaries of their countries, steeped in foreign languages, in exile or as émigrés: Yeats and Pound in Italy, Rilke in Switzerland, amongst Polish poets Mickiewicz and Norwid in Paris. Czaykowski's and Czerniawski's situation was different. They were entering into the element of another language, though perhaps it wasn't foreign (they knew it and spoke it before arriving in England) as poets already moulded, as crystallised personalities; but they were entering it as children, while their linguistic and cultural habits were still being formed. At this crossroad at which they had found themselves they could have become bi-lingual poets, British poets or Polish poets. They remained with the Polish language, knowing that for the rest of their lives they would live outside Poland, outside the sphere of their native tongue, in a situation of bifurcation or rather quad-rification, accepting it and even cultivating it, like Camus's absurdist hero. And yet the word, the poetic word, which had germinated once a long while back in childhood, had not been stifled. It blossomed and even flowered. As for English — the culture and customs embedded in a foreign tongue were becoming an enriching tributary. It worked for the benefit of the seed which they bore within themselves through countries, customs and languages, which they had carried and salvaged. This situation has been exposed most consciously, and certainly most vividly by Czaykowski in his poem 'Argument':

> nowhere nowhere is there
> a place for me
> not here not there

here — freedom
a fish on the strand
there — a cage awaits me
in the horn of plenty

between the audience and the stage
I am the iron curtain
sharing
two underealities[1]

It also expresses the chief dilemma of the other London poets, except that Czaykowski expressed it most directly and nakedly in the almost unpoetic record, 'an argument', a note. This poem appears to have met with his London fellow poets' approval, who identified with his conclusions: "Czaykowski says that he is like a fish on the strand," wrote Zygmunt Ławrynowicz (1925-1988) "we are all this fish. We can return to the sea, we can die on the strand. Naturally, we can also change into a reptile [. . .]. This concerns our attitude to life, the shape of our lives, its creative fruitfulness."[2] While Adam Czerniawski, the editor of an anthology of thirteen young Polish London poets (when the anthology was being compiled their ages ranged from twenty-two to thirty-five) entitled it simply *Ryby na piasku* ('Fish on the Strand').

Czaykowski represented this situation much more vividly and in a much more accomplished manner in another of his poems of exceptional dynamism, immediacy and self-knowledge. This is his 'Bunt wierszem' ('Revolt in Verse'), a poem without which no serious anthology of post-war Polish poetry would be complete:

I was born there.
I did not choose the place.
I'd rather have been born in the grass.
Grass grows everywhere.
Only deserts would reject me.
After all, I could have been born
in a bundle of winds,
as the winds respire.
But I was born there.
They shackled me while I was still a child,
And later released me chained into the world.
Magnetic iron
guiding me constantly to the pole,
you are heavy.

Without you I would be so light
I would shed my weight.

So I carry these chains
and toss them as a lion tosses his mane.
And from over there people cry:
Come back.
Calling out: here, chick, chick.
Millet and weeds scattered on the wind.
In your kennel, dog!
I am a poet (one has to be named).
My tongue is my chain,
Words are my collar.
I was born there
(I'd rather have been born in the grass).[3]

How shall we categorise this poem? Is it a confession or is it a revolt? One might say that the poem attacks reality at its very centre 'from the head'. If we categorise it as a confession, that defines only its personal side, the author's attitude to the object. If we categorise it as a revolt, this defines the direction of the attack and also its dynamism. From this perspective the poem has few equals in the poetry of the '56 generation; it could be compared with the poems of Andrzej Bursa (1932-1975) the total rebel, and, as it happens, Czaykowski's coeval. However, Czaykowski's poem contains something in addition which differentiates it from the poetry of all those in revolt: a certain dialectic which represents a measure of universality. The spear-head of the conflict, with reality, is transferred onto the author. The subject of the poem unmasks himself and demonstrates the target of the attack, the true target which is himself. As Hegel observed in analysing Greek tragedy: tragedy is the situation where everybody is right. In 'Bunt wierszem' both sides of the personality are right and are justified: the side which is here and the side which is there; that which says 'yes' and that which says 'no'; that which is here strains in order to be there, the side which is there — in imagination or reverie — senses its own discomfort, inadequacy and inability to exist. So, to quote Goethe's Faust, that archetype of the modern poet and intellectual, "two souls exist in one body".

But we can also recognise another closer tradition, that of Mickiewicz's *Pan Tadeusz*: "And now carry my longing soul to those wooded hills, those green meadows", the poet writes in the most epic and serene poetic work in Polish. He writes it in Paris. And indeed he returns home, but not physically. In the poem he recreates the life 'there'. In his imagination he returns to a world which had died; it was dying already when he was still living there. To the world of childhood — therefore the world of benign spirits — a world of smells and images and a world of history; what an agreeable theme for writers from 'our' world! And how durable! One of the most interesting themes in modern German as well as modern Polish prose is the theme of the return. Germans return to Gdańsk (Günter Grass), to Mazury (Ernst Wiechert), to Prussia (Siegfried Lenz), while the poet Johannes Bobrowski from East Germany returns to Pomerania and Lithuania in his *Levins Mühle* ('Levin's Mill') and *Litauische Klaviere* ('Lithuanian Clavichords'). Poles return to the Ukraine (Stanisław Vincenz, Leopold Buczkowski, Andrzej Kuśniewicz), to Vilnius (Czesław Miłosz, Tadeusz Konwicki), Lwów (Zbigniew Herbert, Adam Zagajewski) and to Krzemieniec (Włodzimierz Paźniewski). And they are not doing this in a spirit of revenge or revisionism. They are securing the traces of their own spiritual inheritance against the complete disappearance of a world and the fading of memory images. A world which had once existed and is now no more. And this fact is as incomprehensible to the imagination as it is obvious to the eye. They do so in order to secure the traces of a world destroyed by history, moving it hundreds of kilometers to the West or the East; it is not surprising that one of the most beautiful examples of securing one's traces, the short stories of Włodzimierz Odojewski, the chronicler of Polish returns, bears precisely this title: *Zabezpieczanie śladów* ('Securing the traces'). And does not English literature do likewise, so often recalling India, Malaya, Arabia? E.M. Forster, Joseph Conrad and T.E. Lawrence were pioneers in this type of literature before this became an issue for us all. These are forms of spell-casting against history, ocular evidence. Reality is that which is in us, which remains preserved and is carried across landscapes and worlds, wars and events, which is indestructible, even though the real picture, the real town, the real human being, the real land, have ceased to exist. They have departed, vanished, melted into the background. And even the background has melted into non-being and only its reflection remains in us. Reality, even if it is a fragment of the picture — a bird on a branch, a town in a valley — is retained in the corner of the heart, carried across time and history despite history and time.

In Czaykowski's poem the perspective is lyrical rather than epic. This has both its disadvantages and advantages. There is nothing that Czaykowski constructs, he understands lyrical poetry's possibilites.

All he does is recall and invoke. Maybe he would like to reconstruct and this is enough, for can a lyric do more? It can indicate the direction, describe the part of the world, and this is more important than filling the surface with pigments. Prose heals wounds, poetry cultivates them. So here the dramatic and dynamic attitudes constitute a means of conquering time and space — a radical measure. Czaykowski is in revolt, for such is the innate form of the lyric, the poet says 'no', the prose-writer says 'yes', but in fact this relationship is more complex: the poet says 'yes' because he says 'no'. The split in 'Bunt wierszem' is only a form of intervention into an unreal reality, a graft on the bark of the tree of the knowledge of good and evil.

If one were to say: Czaykowski's poem is naked — which is true — this might mean that it is defenceless, that in it the poet reveals himself without in any way covering his nakedness, hiding nothing, not passing over anything in silence, not excluding anything, but this can also mean something else: a naked or a 'poor' form, a form where we would find few new 'rich' words to describe the colouring, shape and nature of the world, with a preponderance of prosaic words which reflect the colloquial flow of speech, a demotic diction. In Czaykowski's poem there is a preponderance of such 'non-poetical' words and expressions (since "Prose names, while poetry pseudonymises", as Tadeusz Peiper says) which are naked because they faultlessly reveal the author's intentions. So let us look more closely at those words which we regard as 'poetic', as describing the colours and shape of the world, the sensuous reality: in what sense do they perform the role of key-words, keys which unlock the mystery and access to the treasury?

They organise the cognitive space of the poem. Let us enumerate them. Grass, deserts, "a bundle of winds"; elsewhere, "millet and weeds scattered on the wind"; air, sea. What might be said at first glance about these words is that they are drawn from the vocabulary of nature, more specifically from the dictionary of her elements. Thinking more deeply about them one may also say that they open the roads of freedom. Another type of words are words which enclose the space ("they shackled me", "chained me"; magnetic iron; the pole; weight), shutting the roads of freedom. And finally, words with a zoological connotation, seemingly filling in the space between those two spheres; words in which we recognise the poet's self-definition: "toss them as a lion tosses his mane", "Into your kennel, dog!"; finally — once more — "millet and weeds scattered on the wind". In the closing lines it transpires that the identification with the lion (who shakes his mane because he is chained) and with the dog (who wears a collar) is entirely justified: the lion's chain turns out to be the tongue, the dog's collar: words, and thus the image of enslavement goes full circle. And it turns out to be an enslavement in a sense other than the one we thought and also other than the one invoked by the poem, for it transpires that what enslaves most vigorously is the tongue and words. More precisely: the Polish tongue and Polish words. The poet suffers on account of words, on account of the fact that he is unable to free himself from them (the chain; the collar), although he is a lion or a dog. The poet suffers on account of the (Polish) tongue, so we may conclude that he suffers on account of Poland, since what is language if not the quintessence of nationhood, its sore centre. He suffers because he is unable to free himself from its imperative (perhaps he might even want to free himself, but that imperative — which he does not comprehend — holds him in its grip) so he suffers, he curses and . . . continues to love ("It isn't the one who understands who loves best", says Miłosz). So one may also say that that poem by Czaykowski is in some sense a patriotic love-lyric in which that which is a curse constitutes an object of love (the poet loves what he curses and hates that over which he casts a spell). Thus, the object of the poem is love-hate, the poet's only true love. For there are two elementary forms of poetry which existed at its origins and will doubtless remain there at its end: cursing and spell-casting. The first is the attribute of the warrior, the second of the priest, and between them — the extremes of cruelty and disinterestedness — a third wedges itself in: it is complaint. It settles contradictions and lightens defeats, it is the most human and most painful. It often eludes the eyes of witnesses, and so it is in the case of Czaykowski's poem, especially when it is hidden in a revolt or a confession, which constitute its perverse masks.

★ ★ ★

So a poem represents an opening of the world, a window through which the countryside may be observed. The critic breaks off the seals, including the seventh, and suddenly finds himself at the other side of the mirror. But the poem opens up a cognitive perspective which is much wider than the room in which the writer found himself, the light which falls through the window reveals unexpected nooks and crannies, brings out objects which are covered in darkness, reaches the poet himself, unveiling his most intimate motifs, his desires and intentions. How is one to reach the poem of a contemporary poet without losing any of its light? Which poem is to be chosen to constitute the opening, since one cannot drink the whole and fill it with the taste of cognition? Which poem is to constitute a break-in into the space and the internal world of the poet? Adam Czerniawski is one of the most self-conscious lyricists in contemporary Polish poetry, conscious of the means and restrictions of the poetic art, of the fact that poetry is an art, a fact so often forgotten today, when poems are condemned to rely on a makeshift palpability, but above all, are reduced in cognitive perspective. The subject of his poems is culture in the widest sense of the word. In his best poems Czerniawski relies on the image. On the whole this isn't an image of nature, but an image filtered through the imagination, most frequently derived from European iconography: from painting, sculpture, literature, from mythology or religion, and its object is the work of art. Thus it was at the start of Czerniawski's poetical road (in such poems as 'Ifigenia' or 'St Sebastian' in *Polowanie na Jednorożca* ('Hunting the Unicorn') of 1956) and so it is in the case of the title poem of *Widok Delft* ('A View of Delft') of 1973.

Poetry of culture assumes that the starting point, the exemplar (which often becomes the poem's subject) is known to all, or at least to most of the readers. The essence of its paradigm is convention and a reference to that exemplar (which can also be a mythological trope) is the movement within the realm of the same symbolism or group of symbols. It is a mode of wordless communication, since it assumes the presence of some common image in the mind of the reader. It refers to the image's presence in the reader, and in adulating or destroying this image the poet confirms its iconographic and therefore its semi-aesthetic and semi-religious character. In that sense the poetry of culture is both a challenge and a task.

St Sebastian was one of the most revered saints of the Renaissance but it was only in the third quarter of the fifteenth century that his iconographic expression acquired a definite form. The 'St Sebastian' of Antonio Pollaiuolo (dated 1475) in London's National Gallery, the 'St Sebastian' of Antonello da Messina (dated 1476) and the 'St Sebastian' of Lorenzo Costa (dated 1485-1490) in the Dresden Gallery, the two St Sebastians of Andrea Mantegna, the one at the Louvre (dated 1475-1480) and at the Venetian Cà d'Oro (dated 1490) are all so different, and yet are all thematic variants which stem from a common trunk. And, over and above, St Sebastian happens to be the saint who offers relief from pestilence.

The influence of the pestilence of 1348 on European history is still not well known, and yet this great leveller which had devastated half of Europe (in some regions the toll was up to two-thirds of the population) had contributed more than anything else to the creation of a new consciousness and a new form which was later to be called the Renaissance. That in whose shadow the Middle Ages had lived, which constituted an ever-present image, suddenly became an every-day occurrence. The Apocalypse was fulfilling itself in everybody's eyes and, paradoxically, the more common death became, the more it awakened in men a desire for life and for an escape from asceticism. A delight in even tiny manifestations of existence accompanied the progress of the disease, as if in those fleeting moments which life was offering a full and true dimension of salvation was opening up.

Italian artists were the first to capture this phenomenon. In his writings, whose framework, encompassing the plenitude of joy, of brimming life, is constituted by the plague, Boccaccio has captured the whole richness and the whole misery, the whole beauty and the whole ugliness of existence, and although he did not permit one to forget the wickedness of the flesh, he wasn't agreeing to wholesale wickedness either. This was sensed by artists of other epochs also: Pushkin in his 'Banquet during the Plague' and Camus in 'The Plague'. Each work was concerned to present an alternative vision, one which would not allow death to triumph, but the principle was in each case the same: death, the invasion by death, awakens life, a desire to overcome death, and the overcoming meant being enchanted with the minutest manifestations of existence, even the smallest form of life that is bodily and transient. This is the crucial caesura between the consciousness of Mediaeval people and that of the new consciousness of the Renaissance, and not just in an artistic sense. Artists were perhaps able to formulate it more quickly than others but it was accepted by all, it was the spirit of the time and a defence against annihilation, against a spell.

In the Louvre Mantegna's St Sebastian stands tied to the column of a ruined triumphal arch. At his feet are scattered fragments of antique sculpture. He looks like Samson, reminiscent more of a classical figure than a human being. The nude is classical both in the Graeco-Roman (with emphasis on the Roman) and the Judaic sense: a suffering noble head (it was copied by Michaelangelo for his David), a face full of pain and a certain melancholy; the body speaking with its every muscle. This body is blemished, it is dying pierced with arrows. In its expression, however, it negates death. The bodiliness which is thus presented in this painting is challenging. This new consciousness, the measure of the classical harmony of nature and externalised tragedy, was perhaps nowhere else expressed as fully as here. And perhaps nowhere else is the birth of new form so manifest: a turn towards the ancient world, to classical exemplars, permits a turn towards nature in all its 'pagan' shamelessness.

In a painting executed ten years later, the one at the Cà d'Oro, St Sebastian appears to negate his previous embodiment. Here Mantegna has placed the main accent on expression, and if we were to define its character even approximately, we would have to say that it is full of provocative ardour, pride and even revolt. All the classical stage-setting of the Louvre painting with its dominant Stoicism has disappeared and nothing remains apart from just the flesh. The expression and the form are totally different. St Sebastian fills out the whole surface of the picture; the background is dark, or rather there isn't any background there at all. The body is torn by convulsive fits, the face does not disguise despair in an expression which is almost 'expressionistic', as in Mantegna's famous 'Deposition from the Cross'; it represents opposition and revolt against both the classical 'imprisonment' and against Stoicism, the acceptance of fate.

This St Sebastian is someone who is not afraid and moreover does not acquiesce in his fate. This is not only a freeing from the fetters of classicism, which Mantegna had acquired from his father-in-law Jacopo Bellini, a classicism which was a way of portraying the past; this is a vision of a personal, unbridled imagination and consciousness answering to no-one, of a man who himself decides upon the forms of his vision and his thought. Also of one who experiences: in this painting St Sebastian is both Christ and Marsyas, his revolt has been concentrated in the bodiliness which hurts and cries and which is a form of his mind. Death here becomes a cry, an act *contra naturam*, the painting evokes a protest from the spectator's eyes. Looking at him we realise that the artist did respond to the challenge which he had presented to himself alone.

Suffused with light and in Renaissance harmony, Antonello da Messina's St Sebastian stands out by his lightness, despite having a body which is just as beautiful, or even perhaps more beautiful than that in the Mantegna, because less muscular (the measure of harmony is designated by the small, barely sufficient, one might say, number of arrows) with a background completely in the style of Venetian painting. St Sebastian is tied to a tree, at his feet is a fragment of a broken column, in the background there are arches from a Venetian building and the statutory bit-players (dignitaries? city fathers? citizens?) sitting on balconies, and some tramp or soldier seemingly oblivious to the scene of torture.

I examine the reproductions, ordering them into a certain rhythmical sequence. The iconography of each painting departs from its exemplar (which is in a sense canonical) only in small detail; the symbolism, the expression and form, or rather the variants of this form, draw a subtle narrative of deviations and reconstructions, both aesthetic and ethical, of the rebellions. Is it not the same with music employing the variation form? Here, as in a mirror, we can observe the feeding principle of art: the immutability of the exemplar, the differences in internal fulfilments and a positively religious necessity. The whole depth of the symbolism of the world and of the people living in it has here been preserved: in the expression of the face, the attitude of the head, the number of arrows piercing the body, in the form of the body itself. While in the background, which may or not be there behind him, the drama of consciousness is played out. It reveals itself like the pages of a book: the torture of the world and the torture of light, the salvation of the body and despair, beauty and anger, revolt and suffering. Also revealed is the terror of existence which this sequence of icons has to express through the light scattering on the body of Antonello da Messina's St Sebastian, in the fury and anger of Mantegna's revolted Sebastian, in the serenity of the spirit in Lorenzo Costa's Sebastian and the saint's acquiescence in Pollaiuolo's painting.

Czerniawski's poem appears to refer to this tradition, but the image which the poet invokes is 'impure' in relation to the paintings, it appears to be smudged. The exemplar flickers and vanishes from our eyes. All we recognise is a part of it, while that other — the one from our world — appears to be in shadow; the image-object of this poem only apparently belongs to the sphere of culture, in reality the exemplar is saturated with a new contemporary or, more accurately, a sensuously experienced content. In it the permanent and the old (the icon, the symbol and myth) struggle and contend with the fluid, the changeable, but equally present, and therefore with the real, with history. The two spheres overlap, they either talk to each other or are in conflict, in any event they influence each other; but the poet does not employ the picture mechanically, that is, he does not make it an object of adoration, but rather refers to some part of it, while questioning or ignoring others; he is looking for analogies or similarities. Under the influence of this treatment the painting undergoes deformation or transformation in order finally to take shape. The author betrays the icon in order to remain faithful to himself. We can therefore say that it is not the painting — as in classicism — that is using the poet but rather that the poet consciously and deliberately is using it for his own ends, exploiting it for his own needs to express himself (the painting makes it possible). Perhaps it is thanks to the painting that he is able to express himself at all; perhaps this is precisely the character of his imagination and talent.

Thus the use made of the icon, the attachment to the icon, the magical, religious and aesthetic tie with it does not therefore kill in Czerniawski's poetry the living bonds which link words with reality (both spheres are complementary in it). At most the icon constitutes a link and an 'objective correlative', bonding each true poetic word with the world. What then is that other real aspect of the icon, what saturates it?

In the St Sebastian poem there is superimposed on the actual image from Christian iconography, from the iconography of Renaissance painting — and therefore half-sacred, half-aesthetic — the image of a Warsaw freedom-fighter, a sixteen-year-old youth shot in the street someone, we may suppose, close to the poet. Stretched in this way as though on a cross, the poem is placed in two orders, it is both traditional and real (had Wróblewski hit on this idea we would have had one of his most successful 'Executions').[4]

The attempted reconstruction of an event of some years ago (the execution, the grieving mother) achieved through the iconographical model (St Sebastian) turns into a descent into darkness (childhood, the war and the occupation); it seems that only against this background can one understand the author's longing for aestheticism and beauty, that is, for infinity (in this Czerniawski is close to Zbigniew Herbert). As the true space of his own poetry he sees the space of culture but — we must add — a culture in whose background his biography is discreetly placed:

SAINT SEBASTIAN

In memory of Jacek Świtalski (1928-1944)

I

Today, beneath the wall,
He stands blindfolded:
Held at bay beset by an invisible blind circle,
He closes his eyes for the last time

II

Late at night
When Irena gave the signal,
The women departed for the way
Of thorny stones

An owl's shriek

Hardened naked flesh decayed
Torn by arrows

III

From the cold walls of a stone chamber
Mosaic eyes stalked
An old man in the robes
— Plundered in the East —
Of a magus-king.
(Stifled with gold myrrh
The dazed marble god
Ruled the world from the altar.)
He was like a child,
Smashing the toy-life of someone
Who also, when the old world was dying,
Laid his hand across his eyes, seeking a star in the eastern sky.

IV

Frightened eyes
A white delicate
Hand on
Scorched flesh
Whispers
Tears
And the howl of dogs in the dark.

V

But at that time
He saw them before him
Flexing their muscles and bows in the sun.

VI

While after death Lazarus
Led a quiet life,

At table he and Martha
Served the deathbound Lord.[5]

But to return to the iconography. How many traps are set here! During the poet's recent stay in Poland I asked him which of the Sebastians I had invoked represented the poem's paradigm. None! It was the 'St Sebastian mourned by St Irena and her companions' in the Berlin Staadtische Museum by Georges de la Tour, the French painter of the first half of the seventeenth century. When I compare it with the poem, I see how Czerniawski's version, although its essence is to report the death of Jacek Świtalski, adheres strictly to the de la Tour version. The scene — the torture is now over — is more reminiscent of Christ's deposition from the cross than the traditional Renaissance canonic posture. St Sebastian's body fills the whole bottom half of the picture, it is placed horizontally, an arrowhead sticks out of his breast (and it looks more like a spear than an arrow); with one leg drawn up the body displays a relaxed but yet a theatrical posture. Above the body three women seem to be concluding some sort of a ritual. The first one is holding a candle with a very long flame which creates a strong chiaroscuro, the second is spreading her arms in a gesture of helplessness, the third is praying and the fourth is wiping away tears. The recumbent body is lit from above, the women's outlines from in front. As in all of de la Tour's paintings, the strong contrast between the lighted and the dark sections dramatises the situation. The paint is placed flatly: red, a flaming pink and black. The light outlines the plasticity and concreteness of the event. All in all, the whole scene is very theatrical.

An art historian has observed that in many respects this picture invites comparison with fifteenth century paintings. Nothing can be further from the truth. Apart from the name of St Sebastian, nothing links it with the fifteenth century, not even the iconography. De la Tour, who began painting under the influence of Caravaggio (as in the case of many others, Caravaggio had opened his eyes to the affairs of this world) was interested mainly in the problem of light. He was particularly drawn to night light. He was called the painter of candlelight. It enabled him to represent both the internal drama and the pathos of the situation. In the motionless figure of the saint de la Tour appears to express not only the martyr's virtues, but also sublime beauty and heroism in the spirit of Corneille and Racine. De la Tour's art, characterised by a certain immobility, represents an arrest, an enclosure in time, and not, as in the Renaissance, the opening up of time. This is underlined by the simplified, one might almost say the poster-like drawing of the figures.

* * *

The metaphor of the world which emerges from a drive to truth and beauty often stops at the threshold of mystery in order to offer a tribute to the unknown which flows within us. If a contemporary poet is charmed and opened up by a particular kind of imaginings and a particular kind of consciousness, the secret of the imperative which steers him towards one rather than another world must be respected. A watch taken apart ceases to show the time, a watch which keeps the time does not need to be taken apart.

Two poems, two independent worlds. Two autonomous spirits, one violent, direct, self-wounding — defencelessly naked; the other apparently calm, balanced, cool — like a cube of ice which nevertheless scalds; the autonomy, as Hans Magnus Enzenzberger calls it, of the knife-poem, the autonomous poem, in which all contradictions have been included. Two poems, two worlds poised over experience and memory. What ruses, what quibbles must a critic use in order to come close to the substance, which he is touching with his eyes only, so as to create his own metaphor (since everything he says will merely be like brushing against, like coming close — a metaphor)?

Everyone has to fill the cognitive space with himself and each one, the poet and the critic, is alone on his path, led by his own language, like a dog on a lead, and we have little chance to escape from this situation. And yet, surely, in both versions: the pre-legislative (the poet's) and the legislative (the critic's) language is the shape of images of people living 'somewhere else', and in a sense the shape of consciousness of place and time. The critic merely deepens the pit wrenched from the earth by the poet's meteorite.

Notes

1. Bogdan Czaykowski: 'Argument' (1956), trans. Iain Higgins.
2. Quoted as an epigraph in *Ryby na piasku* ed. Adam Czerniawski, (London 1965).

3. Bogdan Czaykowski: 'Bunt wierszem' ('Revolt in Verse') (1955-56), trans. Iain Higgins.
4. The Polish painter Andrzej Wróblewski (1927-1957) completed a series of 'Executions' during 1948-49.
5. Adam Czerniawski: 'Saint Sebastian' (1953), trans. Iain Higgins.

Jacek Łukasiewicz

The Poet as Torturer

The Poet As Torturer

Rafał Wojaczek (1945-1970) was born in Mikołów in Silesia. Very briefly he attended courses in Polish studies at the Jagiellonian University in Kraków; when he was nineteen he arrived in Wrocław, where for six months he worked as co-ordinator in the city's cleansing department, and thereafter had no fixed employment. He drank a lot. He committed suicide in Wrocław at the age of twenty-five.

Wojaczek's first poems were published in the Warsaw monthly *Poezja* in 1965 with an introduction by Tymoteusz Karpowicz. He published two volumes of poetry: *Sezon* ('Season') in 1969 and *Inna bajka* ('Another Fairy Tale') in 1970; posthumously two further collections prepared by the author were published: *Ten którego nie było* ('He who wasn't') in 1972 and *Niedokończona krucjata* ('The Unfinished Crusade') in 1973. His collected poems edited by Bogusław Kierc with an introduction by Karpowicz were published in 1976. In addition to the poems in the previously published volumes this collection includes selections from manuscripts, *Dziennik* ('Dairy') from the psychiatric clinic where Wojaczek stayed during 1965, the novel *Sanatorium*, a handful of short stories and comic verses and the only review Wojaczek ever wrote.

He bore the Archangel's name Rafael. If however the Archangel dwelt in him, he was imprisoned in a burdensome body and a sensitive psyche. Wojaczek tried to liberate him by constructing another open "I" next to "I - the prison", to which he was condemned, in order to become free. How and from what did he construct his second self? At first he didn't know. Perhaps he didn't even fully understand that this is what he was after: to create an *alter ego* ironically named in the title left for the posthumous collection: *He Who wasn't*. A sense of unreality is embodied in the early poems. There is no reason to doubt their authenticity:

> There's a bannister
> but no stairs
> There's I
> but there's
> no me[1]

he wrote in the title poem of *Sezon* (Season). He didn't know which "I" is the more important — the one in the nominative or the one in the accusative ("me"). The accusative appears the more appropriate, expressing as it does a side-long look at oneself. But he too will quickly be replaced by an impersonal form:

> There is no to sleep
> There is no to breathe
> There is no to live[2]

and the ending of this poem clearly takes us outside, into an objective world which one can accept joyfully without a painful uncertainty: "Only trees sway / uncommon trees". It's they that: "give birth to a black cat / which runs along every path".[3]

Kierc comments that "the black cat" is the converse of the lyrical "I". Perhaps these types of allegories, embodiments or disguises, although they did appear in Wojaczek's poetry (for instance the black man) were not, in the poetry as a whole, the basis for self-creation.

His second, comprehensive "I" was to have the same biography as the first, but as an objectified theme remaining independent of the accidental, a consciously chosen form.

Wojaczek the craftsman paid a great deal of attention to his material. When a sculptor picks up a stone and wonders what shape to give it, the stone doesn't undergo change during that period, it remains the same. Words (even archaic ones) are different at each moment. One takes them as they are at a particular moment and builds poems out of them.

Wojaczek had met Karpowicz. That was his luck, for Karpowicz discovered in him the compulsion to create poetry, and a powerful talent. He turned out to be a very independent student; he worked in areas which Karpowicz either rejected or had subjected to destruction: in regular syllabic verses, in tonic verses, in old tropes and rhetorical figures, in poeticisms treated seriously, and took the full consequences.

When was he seized with the idea of constructing a second "I"? It's impossible to say precisely. In any event, this was linked with the realisation that one does not acquire purifications and liberations through the expression in full sincerity of the first "I". Contrary to appearances, contrary to those who saw his poetry as a display of exhibitionism, Wojaczek rejected the Romantic gauge of "sincerity".

He wrote ostentatiously about his physiology and psychology as if consciously selecting material for a lazy psychoanalyst: "mother sausage — my edible mother"). The symbols appeared on the surface, there were no direct confessions, no complex associations, the images appeared ready for the interpreter's scalpel.

The relativity of the first "I" is also demonstrated in the numerous poems uttered in the first person singular by a woman.[4] He was undoubtedly fascinated by androgyny but above all by the fact that an archangel could embody itself in a woman as well as in Wojaczek the man. This seemed like the stirring in himself of the archangel before his liberation.

At times Wojaczek would record incidents in his life exactly and directly both in prose and in some of the poems. But at the same time he would demonstrate their conventionality, their unimportance and crushing ordinariness. His first "I" was created by circumstance, just as his own body, his physiology, was pure circumstance.

Already in *Sezon* he was aware that what he was creating was "bodily", close to eroticism, but not eroticism itself, since it was not real bodiliness, but the art of words: "a drop of blood / flows from the lips / and where is your tongue / which would soothe the pain / caused by the bitten / word love"[5].

The new body was to be praiseworthy, the kind of body one has after a resurrection. At the time when he was writing the *Sezon* poems he would send his friends copies of a photograph which is now well-known, of himself as a boy in sweater with the initials INRI scored in pen on his forehead. This "Christification" was ironic: it could apply only to the already created second "I". The first was to be presented in the hero of the novel *Sanatorium* through the crushing banality of his day, his eating, defecation, masturbation, encounters and conversations.

But can such a praiseworthy body arise in a poem? Isn't a poetry which pretends this a mere deception? To what extent, if at all, did Wojaczek possess a consciousness of the non-seriousness of art, and therefore also of the dishonesty in the business of the artist who takes himself too seriously?

His saving grace was good craftsmanship. One may say, good old-fashioned craftsmanship. The first banal thematised "I" was subjected to criticism and negation through description. But this was not always so (particularly in the erotic though not in the auto-erotic). Such terms as "body", "dream", "reality", "spirit" interacted and fused in such poems as 'Imię i ciało' ('The name and the body') and 'Która zmęczona śpi' ('She who's tired sleeps'). Here we have a sensuous metaphor and an equally sensuous supporting alliteration: "and only the name/ pulsating/ in dried dugs". There is here the wonder of a boy: " what is it/ that I am not distinct from her body", or in that same poem:"what is it/ that I can't remove my dream/ from her dream".

The closed verse exalts the image of the subject, while being ironic about it at the same time. Here we have a courtly poet. (Both Andrzej Bursa in his poem sequence *Luiza* and Stanisław Grochowiak in the poems in the collection *Rozbieranie do snu* (Undressing for Bed) have similarly, though each in his own way, exalted their poetic heroes):

> I speak to you so softly as though I were alight
> And stars shine in the meadow of my blood
> The star of your blood stands in my eyes
> I speak so softly that my shade is white[6]

The exalting images of oneself, those "stars in the meadow of my blood" can be justified only through the quality of poetic technique which is here linked with a life passion, with a drive to a fulfilment and transfiguration so intensive that it is equivalent to a self-destruction. The form is testable, the poetic technique clearly visible, while the poet's craftsmanship remains the only practical activity which objectifies itself in the product without thereby losing its links with physiology (the rhythm of blood, and so on).

Poetry thus understood is an activity which is both goal-directed and experimental. One doesn't know the outcome: whether the next poem will succeed or not (in art there never are such guarantees) or what will be the outcome of the poetic activity as a whole. Will this result in the liberation of "myself-archangel" or will it give rise to a homunculus? Here is the embryo of the second "I":

> I'm afraid of you, blind poem
> I'm afraid of the white dream
> I write you thus: white poem
> and every letter is a cypher of fear
>
> That's the taste of her absent
> flesh, a mile of dream away,
> the hoar of sleep on the lips
> and a rough palate
> like the rough skin of a star[7]

"Blind poem", "white dream" have been blended into a "white poem". Both parturition and birth (experienced subjectively) of the second "I" is accompanied by fear. And it is also linked with eroticism that is both exalted and poeticised, and at the same time physiologically specific.

This poetry submits the subject's bodiliness to irony. In the poem 'Ballada bezbożna' ('Godless Ballad') the cosmic "I" appears as a bodily and ironic creation. The gigantic body does not reach anything: neither God, nor another human being, nor itself. It is clearly alienated. From its perspective the motherland-home and the practical "I" (the first "I") appear to be perceived during a heavy pessimistic hangover:

> Where I glance with my left eye, there I see:
> Poland, and a bishop seated backward on a pig enters the church
> Where I look with my right eye my miserable life
> Habitually goes street-walking at dusk[8]

Both perceiving oneself as prostituted and oneself as a Titan stumbling over a spiritual emptiness are presented within playful quotation marks.

The "body" of the second "I" has to emerge slowly. In 'Ballada o prawdziwej krwi' ('Ballad about true blood') blood in both the literal senses and in metaphorical clichés:

> neither blue nor plebeian
> neither Aryan nor Jewish
> neither innocent nor Christlike[9]

is rejected as false. The *true* blood (in the body of the second "I"): "feeding on the pine-needles of stars/ it widens its realm".[10]

Of course this is a metaphor. The "second body", the body of the poem, is created and enlivened with rhythm, which is cunningly modified, by, for instance, the blurring of the caesura, the introduction of an additional accent in a verse, and so on. An important role is played by rhyme. Few contemporary Polish poets have given such weight to rhyme. For Wojaczek it wasn't a sign of tradition, a relic, nor an indicator of songfulness, it was rather something his very own and "bodily" like blood of harmony flowing through the verses and binding their endings. A sentence imposes itself over the outline of the poem: it is natural, transparent, often parallel, embracing the whole work.

We also find here old genres, for instance the sonnet 'Ta rzeka' ('That River') irregularly rhymed. The rigour of the sonnet has been preserved to the extent that it is contained in a natural form, as though in the physiology of a real second "I", rather than being taken as a stylisation or a cluster of stylisations.

The regular metre becomes an asylum. A similar asylum in these poems is constituted by The Virgin Mary, the home (which in Polish has the masculine gender) and mother-land about which he writes: "And you are as ironic as the one who writes this poem"[11]. It is also death. In the sonnet 'Mimikra' ('Mimicry'), dedicated to the well-known dancer Barbara Bittnerówna, the theme of death is subjected to elaborate versificatory treatment.

For the "body" of the second "I" to arise the destruction of the first "I" has to come about. In one of the most frequently cited poems by Wojaczek, 'Piosenka z najwyższej wieży' ('A Song from the Highest Tower') such a destruction is demonstrated: methodical, precise, transferred on to a woman and shown in an exemplary manner:

He searches on Groping he's discovered
The tail-bone and chopped it off
He's trimmed the vulva with a pair of scissors
And gouged the eyes

He pushes through the mincer
Both buttocks and smears
Blood on glass we know why
And splits each of her hairs in four[12]

Such analytical procedures: laboratory (blood on a slide) and scholastic (a hair split in four) lead to the discovery of the first principle, the principle of life, the principle of construction:

> For he still believes he's bound to find
> Who but a poet could be
> Such a patient torturer
>
> I know him he's called Rafał Wojaczek[13]

But the rigour of these verses is already a part of the second "I" emerging from the artful composition of the particular poems and the no less careful composition of each volume. There remains Wojaczek, "who wasn't", whose blood by metamorphosis has changed into a shining star.

The Wojaczek legend alive amongst poets and readers proclaimed that he both lived and died thus in order to match up to the self-image in his poetry, that he longed for a complete consonance between his life and his art. This is not true, because the image of the "practical" Wojaczek in the poems represents a wretched man — specifically and consciously wretched. Against this image is set "that other" which is neither a faithful nor an unfaithful recreation of the practical "I" but an honest and independent (though tied with that life in various ways) creation, and therefore a fiction. (This last assertion is probably contradicted by the faith which animates Rafał Wojaczek's poetry.)

He has been accused of exhibitionist undressing in his poetry. The word "undressing" is inaccurate, for it is rather the case of wading in bodiliness, in saliva, sperm, sweat and secretions. In his prose this leads to a degradation of physiology and also to various forms of eroticism; in poetry the metamorphosis is linked to an exaltation which is often ironic:

> So when I could no longer make out the trail
> of rats' paws on the path; when November
> was dripping from my hair; when the sticky star
> that grew from my unzipped trousers
> fell in the mire,
> then I was you.[14]

The "I was you" is however only another name for a terrifying and banal loneliness. One should not succumb to it.

In 1968 Wojaczek wrote the poem 'Piosenka o poecie' ('A Song about a Poet'). I don't like it much. Its argument is presented in the first verse:

> Because he's constantly beaten like a child,
> The poet, totally ignorant of art,
> Clenches the poem's fist and strikes[15]

He strikes a woman:

> He beats his wife for being a woman
> And his mother for the same reason
> And beats his father for not being her.
> He spits at authority in swift syllables.[16]

But he not only beats people and breaks windows, his poetic activity also takes the form of a similar aggression:

> And he breaks windows with rhymes and with an accent's
> Kick he so knocks the embryo's head
> In the womb that its mother will recognise her son
>
> By the dumbness when he's born.
> The poet does other things as well
> But then he is no longer a poet.[17]

This poetry, revealing its own compensatory functions, rises above them. The poem displays a curious mixture of life and art: of striking the foetus and striking an accent. This from an author of elaborately rhythmical poetry; in it the breaks in rhythm are always excellently calculated in order to preserve the authenticity of the primary material, in order to avoid that "blemish of harmony" of which Miłosz had accused the Skamander poets.

This poem, along with others by Wojaczek, may be read against the background of the debates of the late sixties. It was a time when the norms of intimacy were being violently broken down. A revolt against social forms and its culture would simultaneously become a choice — or choices — of a new life-style. This was the ironic "fierce revolt, the best yet" (from 'Mój szerokostopy mózg' ['My wide-footed brain'].)

The 1968 revolt in Poland took a different course, it wasn't directed either against God or the prevalent culture in general but against the ruling party and its leaders. It was precisely in that year in 1968 that a section of them readily opposed this revolt with a narrow and false nationalism. But Rafał Wojaczek was interested in something other than current politics or in a struggle with an ideology enslaved by language. He simply remained untouched by that language.

The split into a practical "I" and a poetic "I", into a mortal body and a praiseworthy body could not last much longer, was becoming insufferable. The annihilation of the practical "I" signified the end of the creation of the poetic "I" and the end of the poetic task. At the beginning of 1970 many poems like the following were appearing:

> The writing gets tangled art disappoints
> the hand drops the pen seeks a knife[18]

or earlier:

> Someone's smashing the window-pane, burns rags
> Someone's recorded the judgment, pocketed his pen,
> removed the paper
> Someone's reading aloud, gulps the syllables, but me
> I'm gone[19]

And:

> Was it on a sunny day or maybe in a snowstorm
> Rafał Wojaczek
> Aged twenty-plus also a confirmed alcoholic
> The son of Edward and Elżbieta née Sobocka
> Hanged himself on his own belt
> Fastened to something suitable was it a boiler pipe[20]

Also:

> Triumphing hair: they guessed
> there was no brain since — rats ate it![21]

And finally:

> When the moon's dog pants like a running dog
> When the moon's dog bites your brain like a mad dog
>
> Even though your hands embrace your head —
> Then Saggitarius — myself appears and writes fullstop.[22]

"You" and "I" in this poem are characteristic. The end of the work and the end of life come at the same moment, with the distinction that they have different meanings.

Wojaczek was well aware that it is improper to place life and inadequate poetry on the same level. However, placing life and outstanding (enduring) works of art on the same level by no means such a nonsense. So he desired to create enduring works. There is much evidence that poetry was the crucial aim of his life. The rest was miserable, offered momentary ecstasies, brought about terrors, was difficult to control, lead to conflicts with society and problems:

> What is it you're embroidering that saves so much blood,
> Which rose will the yarn suffice for?[23]

and further:

> So forget the page, sleep.
> Then death will write Nobody.[24]

In post-war Polish poetry there were one or two poets who in different ways were in revolt and in different ways had died tragically early: Andrzej Bursa, Ryszard Milczewski-Bruno and Edward Stachura. None of them however produced a poetry which was so rigorous and so peculiarly comprehensive as Wojaczek did. Its life equivalent was for him a "naive harmony", as he wrote in one of his poems. But he knew that it was possible to transfer this harmony into art so that it ceased to be naive. He needed tripartite experiences: the experience of his own painful psyche, the experience of the external world, of other people — and finally the experience of an artist, the experience of the work. The first had to be overcome, thematised and exploited through negation. The second, used as themes, could (but did not have to) become the brighter side of the world presented in poetry. The third category of experiences, the poetic, emerged as the most important. They were turning into form, into a second "I" leading not to illusions but — he doubtless believed — towards a gradually fulfilled hope.

Notes

All references are to: Rafał Wojaczek, *Utwory zebrane* ('Collected Works') Wrocław 1976.

1. 'Sezom' ('Season') p. 93.
2. *Op. cit.*
3. *Op. cit.*
4. Verbs in Polish are gender-specific. [Ed.].
5. 'Dla ciebie piszę miłość' ('I write love for you') p. 100.
6. 'Mówie do ciebie cicho' ('I speak to you softly') p. 104.
7. 'Boję się ciebie, ślepy wierszu ('I'm afraid of you, blind poem') p. 106.
8. 'Ballada bezbożna' ('godless Ballad') p. 127.
9. 'Ballada o prawdziwej krwi' ('Ballad about true blood') p. 128.
10. *Op. cit.*
11. 'Gwiazda' ('Star') p. 109.
12. 'Piosenka z majwyższej wieży, ('A song from the Highest Tower') p.157.
13. *Op. cit.*
14. 'Wspomnienie' ('Recollection') p. 113.
15. 'Piosenka o poecie' ('A song about a poet') p. 146.
16. *Op. cit.*
17. *Op. cit.*
18. 'Rymy na przednówku' ('Pre-harvest rhymes') p. 193. March 1970.
19. 'Fuga' ('Fugue') p. 193. 1969.
20. 'Koniec świata' ('The end of the World') p. 194. 1970.
21. 'Pięć zdań o włosach' ('Five sentences about hair') p. 152. 18th Feb. 1970.
22. 'Gdy pies księżyca' ('When the moon's dog') p. 151. 25th Jan. 1970
23. 'Rękopis' ('Manuscript') p. 153.
24. *Op. cit.*

Zbigniew Bieńkowski

The New Wave: A Non-Objective View

The New Wave: A Non-Objective View

The New Wave, a poetic movement which sprang up in Poland in the early seventies, was neither an artistic school nor an historical event. We can't therefore compare this tendency or literary movement either with the Avant-garde, which had flourished in the twenties, or with the group centred on the Warsaw bi-weekly *Współczesność* which was the cultural consequence of the Polish 'October' of 1956. The Avant-garde, and particularly the Kraków Avant-garde, grouped poets and artists around a very clearly formulated artistic programme by the poet and theoretician Tadeusz Peiper (1891-1961) who imposed on the poets a rigid formal discipline. Peiper's programme of 3xM ("*Miasto — masa — maszyna*" = "The city — the masses — the machine"), the social and cultural programme of the New Art, was intended to express the new situation immediately after World War I, when the world, using Peiper's words, "changed its skin". The Avant-garde poets bandied together to realise the model of poetry as the "Metaphor of Contemporaneity" whose assumption was a cultural and social optimism. Avant-garde poets did not twitter like their contemporaries in the conservative Skamander group, who rejoiced noisily at the recovered "rubbish heap" (this was the Avant-garde deflational language to describe the newly recovered Polish independence and freedom). They intended rather to co-create a new reality, to bring about through the poetic word what workers were realising in metal and mortar. The Kraków Avant-garde equated freedom with modernity. The programme of the Kraków Avant-garde imposed sharp formal rigours, parsimonious, elliptic expression, concise imagery and compressed conclusions, all of which provided the poems with dynamism. One could speak about Avant-garde form and the model of the Avant-garde which was instantly recognisable. The New Wave did not programme either the form or the content of its poetic message.

Nor, as we said, was The New Wave an historical event like *Współczesność*, by which we mean the group of poets, highly differentiated in terms of age and artistic genealogy, who had together burst into print after October 1956. The easing of repression, which in the realm of culture meant the demise of Social Realism, had opened up for poets closed and forbidden areas of the imagination and thought. Such poets as Zbigniew Herbert, Miron Białoszewski and Tymoteusz Karpowicz were able to emerge from a forced silence, while younger ones like Ernest Bryll, Jerzy Harasymowicz and Stanisław Grochowiak, who were just then reaching maturity, were able to speak with their own unconstrained voice, returning to it its forbidden spontaneity.

But there was no spectacle accompanying the start of The New Wave, no manifesto, no scandal preceded it. The Avant-garde did not avoid self-advertisement, it sought and provoked scandal; and while *Współczesność* knew how to take advantage of its 'historicity', The New Wave was not enriched by either scandal or history. The New Wave did not emerge immediately as a fully-fledged phenomenon. It gained attention slowly, gradually, in student periodicals, at the peripheries of official literary life. It seemed a marginal product of the disintegration of values, of the rotting of the regime which governed Poland in the sixties and seventies: in the declining years of Gomułka and the "joyous creativity" of Gierek. Regrettably, writing about purely artistic phenomena in Eastern and Central Europe it is impossible to avoid political intrusions. Through various 'deals' which are fixed, art is linked with the big contest and small political skirmishes. *Współczesność* which 'exploded' after the Polish October (the death of Stalin and Beria and Khrushchev's coming to power made possible a regeneration of national strength in Poland and the return to power of Gomułka) was the artistic expression of a general euphoria and awakened hopes in social and political changes. The euphoria subsided very quickly. Gomułka's rule became more and more rigid year by year, he initiated a struggle with the Party revisionists, extending it to the whole area of culture. A vacuum and stagnation were created by the removal from the Party of the philosophers Leszek Kołakowski and Krzysztof Pomian, the closure of *Po Prostu* (the organ of young intelligentsia) and the departure from the Party of such writer-intellectuals as Jan Kott, Adam Ważyk and Jerzy Andrzejewski. All literature, including poetry, fell victim of censorship. A whole decade of an artificial cultural life had begun. By pouncing on even allusive traces of criticism the censors forced poets to escape into allegory, stylisation and away from anything to do with current reality. Some of the poets, not necessarily the least talented, had discovered for themselves a *modus vivendi* in affirmation and a more or less clear acquiescence in the order of things. This gave rise to a courtly poetry which avoided all reference to concrete particulars, which expressed emotional generalities, which described an inauthentic world, a world which did not really exist, an imagined paper-thin world. This gave rise to neo-classical and Baroque mannerism, to pure aestheticism, to 'turpism', a reversed aestheticism which exalted ugliness as the beauty of everyday — these are the variants of the artificial poetry written by such poets as Jarosław Marek Rymkiewicz, Bryll and Grochowiak. This was the cultural compost-heap, the natural breeding ground for The New Wave.

The first available form of protest against this courtly, compliant, artificial artistic reality, tolerated by the censor, was so-called 'linguism'. Here poetry had found a means of protest in its rejection of clichés, of the conventions of newspeak which was an instrument for enslaving thought and imagination. Poetry's immemorial and constant role is to stimulate a dynamic attitude to speech. Poetry has formed its principle of action out of its protest against clichés, out of its rejection of emotional, philosophical and journalistic slogans. Poetry begins by breaking through the inertia of language. This is its zero point. In the specific cultural and political situation in Poland in the late sixties and early seventies the protest against clichés and slogans had a value, a resonance, which was more than aesthetic. In those years there was a linguistic battle over citizens' rights. Linguistic poetry, cleansing the expression of feelings from clichés and slogans, acquired a political significance. Poetry became an instrument in a struggle for openness, for a right to represent a reality without pretence, without make-up. 'Linguistic' poetry as such, the manipulation of language, the experiments by Białoszewski, Karpowicz and even Edward Balcerzan and Witold Wirpsza were, if not an introduction, then at least an encouragement to the appearance of the phenomenon to be called The New Wave.

The first New Wave voices and attempts at the formulation of a theoretical basis for a lingustic protest came from Poznań. In his collection of essays called *Nieufni i zadufani* ('The Distrustful and the Arrogant') Stanisław Barańczak ascribes to poetic language the role of a goad, a stimulator of a process of non-compliance. According to Barańczak it is enough to experiment, to play games with language in order to upset the equilibriums and to shake the arrangements of an artificial reality. This is why this sparkling critic doesn't in his reflections move away from purely aesthetic positions and treats language purely instrumentally. Both in his own poetry and in his theoretical pragmatism he treats language as a place for showing-off and going over the top. He is inclined to discover incitements to revolution in linguistic humour. Barańczak's effective and showy theory has been modified, supplemented and enriched by Ryszard Krynicki, who has added a philosophical perspective to linguistic experimentation. Krynicki had drawn attention to the antinomy residing in the relationship between language and the reality expressed through language. Krynicki sees in language the living being of culture which is subject to the same pressures and manipulations as human society. Language is not an aesthetic value. In his poems and critical postulates of the period Krynicki sensitises the imagination of poets to the mythopoeic, rigidifying role of language in relation to reality. He is concerned to reverse the process of expression: reality is to be demystified and made trustworthy through words. Poetry is to catch language *in flagrante delicto*, since language degrades reality through myth, symbol and cliché, and to reverse the dependence on myth, which threatens facts, and on symbols which threatens objects. As understood — not narrowly, aesthetically, but broadly, philosophically — linguistic poetry is capable of performing the function of demystifying and renewing the picture of the world.

Barańczak and Krynicki have introduced a linguistic ferment into the picture of the real world stabilised in a convention of inauthenticity. The picture began to vibrate, the world began to shake in its foundations. The linguistic ferment had accomplished an important role, a role of encouraging people to other and more direct and spontaneous forms of protest. Kraków and later Warsaw had a more vigorous and spontaneous part in the formation of The New Wave front. And here it was no longer 'linguism' and the attitude to language but an immediacy in the reaction to reality which became the main accent mobilising young poets to express their emotions and convictions. Speaking plainly, presenting reality in its immediacy, expressing feelings and experiences in all their simplicity and rawness

— these were the slogans proclaimed in the Kraków periodical *Student*. As I have already indicated, The New Wave was not a poetic school, it wasn't an historical event, nor did it bind a group in any particular literary circle. Kraków, Warsaw and Poznań were all independent centres and each one had its own character. The Kraków group called 'Teraz' ['Now'] had at its disposal excellent radical and critical pens. The Warsaw poets centred on the 'Orientacja' group, oscillated between Poznań linguism and a post-avant-garde constructivism. Kraków reached back to the tradition of avant-garde theory. Its varied artistic genealogy endowed The New Wave with an openness and a seemingly programmatic avoidance of rules, which continues to affect the development of The New Wave poetry to this day. Right from the start (though there is no particular moment one can specifically point to) all these poets: Adam Zagajewski, Ryszard Krynicki, Julian Kornhauser, Stanisław Barańczak, Krzysztof Karasek, Jarosław Markiewicz, Ewa Lipska, Stanisław Stabro and Wit Jaworski, were all unlike each other and seemingly divided by the very material of the world they represented.

And yet they were bound together if not by a programme then at least by a postulate. This was a negative postulate. They shared a hostility towards acquiescence and passivity which they equated with facelessness; and a distrust of conventions and set rules with their stylistic consequences. In his *Nieufni i zadufani* Barańczak defined the lyrical protagonist, the subject of the poetry which is coming to be and as yet not classified as New Wave, as an active personality participating in the creation of facts and values in the world. The subject of poetry cannot be *homo fugiens*, an artist devoid of personality. Barańczak has prepared a catalogue of attitudes which he negates:

> *Homo definiens*: a flight into a conviction that the world has a single meaning. *Homo omnipotens*: a flight into the conviction about one's own poetical omnipotence.*Homo grandiloquus* a flight into a stylistic convention which encompasses the world in the categories of Sublimity, Decorativeness and Harmony.*Homo sentimentalis*: a flight into an easy one-sided way of reacting to reality.*Homo simplificans*: a flight into simplification and authority of others [. . .]. These models of behaviour which I have characterised are variants of an overarching model: of flight. The motif of flight, of a search for a hiding place or asylum, a secure shelter from the conflicts which tear the world apart is the genesis of peace, harmony and the Arcadian gardens of bliss . . .

Barańczak's negative postulates have been developed and extended by the Kraków co-creators of The New Wave: Zagajewski and Kornhauser in the much discussed and excellently composed book *Świat nieprzedstawiony* ('The Unrepresented World') which has come to be regarded as the programme and chief theoretical justification of The New Wave. Was it merely so regarded? At any rate, no other programme which might have replaced *Świat nieprzedstawiony* has ever been formulated.

While the theoreticians of The New Wave had no clear vision of literature, nor could define it unambiguously, they did clearly and unambiguously define the objects of their attack. They knew exactly what they did not want. They defined themselves through negation. As far as the authors of *Świat nieprzedstawiony* are concerned, mannerism, stylisation and allegory are forms of indirectness in contrast with the directness in the expression of attitudes to the world, a directness which they postulate. The struggle between directness in the presentation and expression of the world and indirectness is not new. This conflict surfaces in almost every generation. In the generation immediately preceding The New Wave it had only a purely aesthetic character: neo-classicism on the one side, 'linguism' and 'turpism' on the other. Barańczak's *Nieufni i zadufani* was a reflection of this conflict. Kornhauser and Zagajewski offered an independent look at the totality of the phenomenon by cutting through boundaries and divisions. Their pamphleteering manifesto placed Stanisław Lem, Tadeusz Nowak, Andrzej Kuśniewicz, Harasymowicz, Rymkiewicz, Grochowiak and the 'Hybrydy' group on the same plane — the purveyors of prettiness and the purveyors of ugliness, neo-classicists and mannerists, futurology and allegory. Not all these attacks have reached their target, not all the charges are convincing. The function of a pamphlet is not a considered judgment; its purpose is to pull down, or at least to verify the trustworthiness of myths which arrest the development of art. The pamphleteering mode of the attack, the lack of precision, were beneficial to the development of The New Wave poetry, since nothing — apart from the obligation to present the world (quite an obligation, in fact!) — restricted the range and extent of the imagination. Only the presence of the concrete had been programmed in, and as for the material and the dynamic of the concrete, that could be materialist, spiritualist, metaphysical or sensualist. And this is precisely what happened. The laudable imprecision of the programme made it possible to locate within this movement such mutually divergent positions as those of

Zagajewski and Karasek, Barańczak and Markiewicz, Lipska and Krynicki, to name only those pairs which were the most antagonistic.

Writing about The New Wave today from a distance of fifteen years one mustn't overlook its roots. The New Wave did not spring from nowhere. It too has its tradition, a tradition consisting of an eagerness to unmask and express the truth about the real world. Krynicki in his poems in *Akt urodzenia* ('The Act of Birth') and Kornhauser and Zagajewski in their theoretical diagnosis refer to the already mentioned Tadeusz Peiper, the first poet and theoretician of modernity in Poland. It is from this creator of the Kraków Avant-garde that The New Wave poets have taken over his uncompromising stand and his thirst for novelty. Using his words they cry: 'The skin of the world has changed!'. They reject Peiper's principles and formal canons (his theory of pseudonymity and of the 'Blossoming Poem') but they worship his attitude. In one respect Peiper's significance is unquestionable. In the most modern Polish literature he is the first on a list of writers who have approached the world with the conviction that it is a totally new world, that the old walls have fallen, that one has to start anew, to begin by asking oneself the most important questions and to place the first letter on the blank sheet of literature. This list includes Tadeusz Borowski, Tadeusz Różewicz as the author of the volume *Anxiety* and Marek Hłasko. Some of The New Wave poets add Andrzej Bursa to this list, others (for instance Karasek) add Rafał Wojaczek, that tragic suicidal victim of his own nonconformism.

There were conquerors and conquered in the battle initiated by The New Wave almost fifteen years ago. The conquered, that is the precious mannerists, have departed the field but not all of them have retreated to the margin: some, like Grochowiak, have become part of the history of literature, others like Bryll or Rymkiewicz have re-educated themselves: some, like Bryll, have changed their poetics or, like Rymkiewicz, are doing well in effectively cultivating another field of *pastiche*. And the conquerors? They have dispersed into various areas of the world of the imagination and into various areas of the real world. But is it proper and sensible to create this division into the conquered and conquerors? In some sense, they were all conquered and they were all conquerors. What is decisive here is the point of view, the personal point of view of the fighters: what were they fighting for, what did they wish to save? The poets of The New Wave placed one demand on themselves: that their art should be in agreement with their human condition, speaking directly, spontaneously, without costumes, without a stage, without an auditorium. They did not promise each other mutual loyalty, or agreement as regards form and value. Each one of them spoke from a position where he had found himself historically, psychologically or situationally: outside a beer-booth, at the turn of fate, in recollection, in the lust for life, a desire for fame or love:

Let's look truth in the eyes: in the absent
eyes of an accidentally jostled
pedestrian with an upturned collar; in the intense
eyes turned up towards the departure times
of long-distance trains; in the short-sighted
eyes peering closely at the newspaper small print;
in the morning eyes hurriedly bathed free
of disobedient sleep, during the day
hurriedly wiped free of disobedient tears,
hurriedly covered with coins, for death also
is disobedient, runs too hastily into the blind alley
of the eye-sockets; so let's give everything
over to these looks, let's face up
to the eyes, like a slogan chalked on the wall, let's dare
to look truth in these grey eyes which she never takes off us,
that are everywhere, hammered to the pavement underfoot,
glued to the poster and fixed in the clouds;
and even if our legs never give way beneath us,
this alone will be able to throw us
on our knees.[1]

*

Tongues are the wild flesh that grows in a wound,
the open wound of the mouth, which feeds on false truth,
tongues are the bared heart, beating outside, a naked blade
that's a defenceless weapon, the gag that stifles
suppressed uprisings of words, the beast growing used
to human teeth, the inhuman that grows in us
and outgrows us, the beast fed on the body's poisoned meat,
the red flag that we swallow and spit out with blood,
the forked thing that encircles us, the true lie that deludes
the child who, learning the truth, truly lies.[2]

*

We wear second-hand words, sublimity and despair
consumed in another's mouth,

we walk over the trap-doors of another's terror,
we discover old age in encyclopaedias,
in the evening we pretend a war has broken out,
we talk to Baczyński,[3]
we pack in a hurry,
we recall poets from the olden days,
we go to the station, condemn fascism,
and then triumphantly,
in a first-class compartment,
in the first person plural,
we display our powers of penetration,
as if we were not blessed
with perfect pitch of silence.[4]

*

A language failure has occurred nationwide.
Since the small hours language engineers
have tried to hold back floods of words.
Drowned meanings have sunk to the bottom.
Words have got out of order.
[. . . . .]
Coiffured speech
vanished in cascading streams.
There have been rumours of phoneme revaluation.
[. . . . .]
Megaphones have been hung from trees.
Armoured cars drove in
with word-jugglers.
But language weakened. At the end of its tether.
An aphasia epidemic spread.
Sense wandered off
amidst the first blossoms
of suspicions and strawberries.
Manipulators worked four shifts.
The thread was lost.
Nothing but black suits of type
now hung in newspapers.
Shapelessness emerged from the mouth.
Whispers and confessions perished.
Somebody still tried to rise to an answer
but it was drowned in dazzling flood-lights.
Earth moved.
The first pelargonium fell.
Torrential rain washed out discarded allusions
scraps of dictionaries and maps.

Several weeks later
a survivor
interviews himself:
One must start anew now
it's best to begin by mimicking birds
he says
painfully dragging the grinding sound
of meaning from his mouth.
[. . . .][5]

★

What constitutes an internal change?
At first we speak the same tongue
as those demanding change, a change
of tongue and central heating, a change
of warm clothing and collars, we
speak the same tongue of honesty
and demagoguery, the tongue which has grown
into our penetrating silence, let's then
change the tongue, the tongue of change and the state,
a singular tongue and passionate for the plural
number, very plural, for time future,
we then all say: let's change the one
in the relay race, let's lengthen the distance,
make it, let me state, long enough to make the state
a profitable finishing-post, let's use the same
inexpensive, cultural tongue of the tribune,
of life, the life of a periodical and periodically
the social periodical, of society changing
its tongue, changing it for the tongue, for a megaphone
and this, citizens, grounds the internal change,
the change in internal affairs.[6]

★

I was falling chaotically into night's darkness
I wake at peace with myself.
My conscience rises clear
like the sun.
And yet when I was falling
through night's darkness
from the unheard tower
of old and new humanity,
someone, who had no wish

to fight me, was saying:
Don't accept yourself:
in agreement with yourself
you'll agree to everything,
the blindingly clear conscience
won't let you notice
fresh stains of spit
on Słowacki's collar.[7]
I wake with a corpse in my mouth.[8]

★

What am I doing here, among these people,
amid this clamour, in a mousy hat,
with a moulting skull
and soft skin on my palms, able
only to touch, to shake hands,
what am I doing here?
Among these books, in this room,
roused suddenly by collapsing buildings,
this perspective of falling and constantly re-born bore-shafts
bury me deeper and deeper,
what am I doing here?
With an edition of my latest diary,
with an umbrella, squashed shoes,
frayed trouser-legs,
consumed with passion for the dark,
what am I doing here?
In this cage, on this island?
And won't I repeat myself,
won't I see myself suddenly in the half-turned mirror,
amid this furniture, this clamour,
and won't I repeat myself?
[.........................]
won't I melt
into a cloud, won't I disappear?
[.........................]
And where will I be if I am not here
and I am not there? If I wade
waist-high in the saliva of words, while my dog
sneaks stealthily towards a temptation of snares.[9]

While The New Wave programme (assuming it to be a programme) was striking in its lack of precision, its deliberate ambiguity which allowed it to incorporate both Romantic and Classical stances, both a coolness and a warmth of emotions (so long as they did not avoid confrontation, so long as they measured up directly to reality, to the concreteness of life in a concrete world) the poetry itself has a striking richness and variety of colours and voices in the words which the poets threw directly at reality. In these words we have both truth and the fear of truth, both certainty and wavering, both the arrogance of consciousness and the arrogance of ignorance. Each of the voices which I have quoted was to develop a contrapunctally orchestrated sound with its own fullness. Each one deserves a separate analytical study. Writing about the phenomenon of The New Wave as a certain outstanding and clearly defined whole, I am drawing attention not so much to the contributions by the poets, but rather to the various ways in which they measure up to their common enemy: illusion, although these variants and methods cannot be separated from the poetic individualities.

Right at the beginning a differentiation had appeared which had only deepend with time. A concern for objectivity, for an unemotional picture of the world, compels Zagajewski to avoid the first person: he says "we" in order not to say "I". Does he need this distance in order to hit the harder or in order to insure himself against the possibility of defeat? In saying "Don't accept yourself", Markiewicz sees the threat from the inside and in struggling against illusion he will struggle with his own vision of himself. Will he conquer it or will it conquer him? It is out of helplessness and lack of understanding, out of his being lost in various corners of the world and meanings of existence, that Karasek has formulated the great question which has become the emblem of the whole generation. Is this problem soluble? Will Barańczak come to know the truth and will he be able to sustain its stare? Does language function more effectively as gibberish (according to Kornhauser) or as an instrument of pain (according to Krynicki)? Ewa Lipska is the only one who doesn't pose questions which have no unambiguous answers. She at the very start has a picture of the whole in which pain, joy, hope, love and death co-exist with similar rights of equality.

All the poets of The New Wave have proceeded into a world of broad and big opportunities from a position where they first expressed their fear and courage and certainty. It is too early to ascertain whether they have achieved the goals which they have set themselves since, after all, they are still active. Kornhauser has been arrested by concreteness in which he has found a home. Similarly, Barańczak has settled in a comfortable postion. I do not have in mind the successful career he has achieved through his university work and talent as a translator. I have in mind the cosiness of the nest of his poetry secured from the storms and uncertainties of passion. A benign peace reigns in Barańczak's poetry and this is surprising given how dynamic, stormy and combative it was at the height of its youth in *Bez tchu* and *Dziennik poranny* ('Breathless' and 'Morning News'). *Atlantyda* ('Atlantis') and especially *Widokówka z tego świata* ('A Postcard from this World') represent a pretty and interesting description of the poet's surroundings, the description of both the natural a psychological landscape of New England. This landscape is not shaken by any seismic movement of the poet's internal life. An accomplished technique, an empty metaphysic: this pretty picturing of an internal void is enticing.

However, Krynicki's smithy is still blazing. Krynicki had traversed a greater range of artistic landscapes than the other poets of The New Wave. Amongst his contemporaries he is perhaps the most sensitive to form. He began as a practitioner with Peiper, passed through a stage of Julian Przyboś's Constructivism, has attained a refined mastery in sketching internal landscapes (his love-poems are masterpieces), in order finally to find a home in the poster, the golden thought — this poetic equivalent of Pop Art. Krynicki was never satisfied with a programme of mirroring, expressing and demystifying reality. This poet has the violent ambition to intervene, to change, to repair and cleanse the world in order to make it a habitation for free and law-abiding people. Through his poetry he kneels in prayer, weeping and calling on the Saviour. There is an incompatibility between the aspirations of saintliness and the aspirations of beauty. Krynicki's poetry attempts to perform an apostolic mission, it moves us by its anachronism. His eyes fixed on Pan Cogito, Krynicki stutters out his wisdom. Krynicki is The New Wave's possessed.

Three variants of The New Wave: the poetry of Zagajewski, Markiewicz and Karasek designate the directions and evolutional stages of contemporary imagination. These are incompatible and irreconcilable. The poetry of Zagajewski and Karasek are the two extremes of the same desire. Through thought, memory, philosophy and history Karasek's poetry longs to embrace the cosmos which as an indivisible whole is the poet's dwelling place. Zagajewski's poetry, on the contrary, springs from limitation, from the poet's ability to adjust the world to his ability and possibility of experiencing it. Both in the youthful *Komunikat* ('The Communiqué') and the mature *Jechać do Lwowa* ('Travel to Lwów') the poet's "I" is on the defensive, does not impinge, it is neither a call nor a challenge. This most discreet and most modest "I" in contemporary poetry makes itself manifest in Zagajewski's poems through an identifiction with everything that creates a poet, and recollection, collective memory, the accidental, a choice of feelings and their absence. The "I" of this poetry is still unfinished, unstable, it is still becoming, it is growing and swelling, it is the future, the future which saves him from opportunism. The "I" of this poetry is constantly open, rich in possibilities which the present lived moment, the time of participation in the coming-to-be of the world, gives it. Through its talent for mimcry, and adaptive ability, and above all through its rejection of Hamletic pride, the "I" of Zagajewski's poetry has a sense of its plenitude, a plenitude in co-existence with the world of people and objects. For that very reason the "I" of this poetry doesn't need to embody itself in the first person singular in order to impose its presence.

As for Karasek's poetry there is a splendid and miraculously achieved absence of distance both in relation to himself and to the world. Both the external and internal distances are on the same plane. Objective phenomena and subjective experiences overlap and become closely knit to form a single knot and stream of consciousness and conditioning. The external landscape, the city streets, the phenomena of the world, the events in life, those dreamt and those in waking life, mesh with experiences, premonitions and obsessions, forming an existential thicket, entangled and compressed, where the material and the mental are mutually contaminated. Karasek's poems are lyrical, expansive long poems where despite the expansiveness, tautness of the imagination competes with the lightness of expression. An ideal absence of distance: not a shade of irony, sarcasm or pose. The poet burns bridges behind him, strips himself down to helplessness. In the contaminated subjective-objective reality nothing follows from anything. The anti-Arcadian dream in Karasek's poetry appears in an ideal state: chaos, the natural state of existence. All experiences, feelings and sensations melt into a single magma-lava of consciousness. Moments experienced once, in history, in myth, in dream; moments of immediate presence and moments only about to emerge from the future grow together into a single time of a single life. And there is no life apart from individuality. And this intimate private time of a single life is precisely the time of an epoch. The private does not miniaturise, rather it expands the experiences of an individual onto a cosmic scale. The "I" in Karasek's poetry is the immodest evidence of the existence of the world.

If it were to make sense to speak of synthesis in art, then the synthesis of The New Wave would be Markiewicz's poetry. It has placed its money on metaphysics, it alone in its battles for the truth of reality wishes to reach the ultimate boundaries and the ultimate meanings of existence. Critics searching for a concept which would define the essence of this poetry have coined the notion of "fighting metaphysics". Let me quote the critically penetrating voice of Adrianna Szymańska, a poet with a metaphysical imagination:

> Markiewicz is not subject to either national or political restraints, his poetry has universalist aims which he does realise. In the melting pot of his poetic sensibility there are themes being stirred which include the mythical and the historical, the religious and the psychological, the social, the ecological and demographical. All essential myths and ideas of the present fill his lyrics and longer poems like a hot lava which are cognitively constantly on the boil (. . .). One might submit the object of this poetry to the evaluating diagnosis of the author himself: 'Each object says about itself so much that it is impossible to say anything more'. The supremacy of basic concepts — truth, necessity, existence, God — contrasted and complemented with concepts of illusion, accident and non-being make up a suggestive totality of the poet's experience. It is precisely the human need for dignity, wholeness and harmony, the need to extricate them from multiplicity, partiality and chaos of existence, that compel the poet to break up the world into atoms of questions and doubts and to put it together in a new space of transcendence. The metaphysical yearning for an ultimate reconciliation with that which is incomprehensible in the space and time of life becomes satisfied in an act of creation.

The New Wave continues to be an active phenomenon, stirring the emotional life of the present. It radiates and is reflected in new poetical facts, for example in the poetry of the late Konstanty Puzyna and the poetry of the young Waldemar Żelazny.

Notes

1. Stanisław Barańczak, 'Spójrzmy prawdzie w oczy' ['Let's look truth in the eyes'] trans. Barbara Plebanek.
2. Ryszard Krynicki, 'Język, to dzikie mięso ['Tongues are the wild flesh'] trans. Barbara Plebanek.

3. A reference to Krzysztof Kamil Baczyński (1921-1944), one of the young poets killed in the Warsaw Uprising against the Germans. [Ed.]
4. Adam Zagajewski, 'Nosimy używame słowa' ['We wear second-hand words'] trans. Barbara Plebanek.
5. Ewa Lipska, 'W kraju nastąniła awaria języka'.
6. Julian Kornhauser, 'Na czym polega zmiama wewmętrzna?' ['What constitutes an internal change?'] trans. Adam Czerniawski.
7. A reference to Juliusz Słowacki (1809-1849), the great Romantic poet and dramatist who died in Paris of tuberculosis. [Ed.]
8. Jarosław Markiewicz, 'Bezładmie spadałem' ['I was falling chaotically'] trans. Adam Czerniawski.
9. Krzysztof Karasek, 'Co ja to robię' ['What am I doing here'] trans. Adam Czerniawski.

Aleksander Fiut

Traps of History, Traps of Literature

Traps of History, Traps of Literature

The abundant and varied poetry which was written in Poland after the declaration of Martial Law on December 13th, 1981 though artistically uneven, deserves to be read for at least two reasons. First, being an immediate record of events of historic consequence, it is a unique chronicle of history in the making. Secondly, it testifies to the formation of a new national mythology, looking back — with or without approval — to the inventory of traditional symbols and stereotypes. These two spheres of meaning interplay and enrich each other in many poems: contemporary political realities find an echo in the mythical past or, conversely, hieratic scenes from Polish history suddenly come alive in the light of current events.

The very fact that at times of acute tension in Poland tens or even hundreds of writers take up their pens — albeit not always with an expert hand — in order to put the collective experience into verse — which is something of a unique phenomenon in Europe — can surely be explained as a traditional Polish reaction. There is no doubt, of course, that the desire to record days full of drama stems from the urge to provide testimony for future generations. But external circumstances alone — it being easier to write, store and distribute poems at times of repression because of their compact form — are not enough to explain why this should be done in verse. It must be remembered that in Poland the writing of patriotic verse has been practised for centuries — ever since the May 3rd Constitution of 1791: during the nineteenth-century uprisings against Russia and up to the Nazi occupation. During the period of Martial Law many authors, some of them anonymous, consciously revived this tradition, especially in prison folklore which travestied a rich repertoire of patriotic and folk songs. In the collective consciousness poetry still enjoys the privileged status which it had throughout the nineteenth century, probably because it is poetry which has preserved and imposed the archetypes of national calamity on the collective imagination. These archetypes spring to life almost spontaneously when danger is imminent, helpfully providing ready models both of attitudes and the means of recording them, and are all the more convincing because they belong to the canon of Polish literature.

The titles of poems and collections of poems confirm the quasi-documentary character of some of them: *An Internment Diary, Report from a City under Siege, The 'White Meadow Prison' Diary, The Fire, Notes from 1982-83*. A poem is born — a record of reality: dry, devoid of emotion, terse, shunning pathos, occasionally tinged with irony or sarcasm. This was the style used to record scenes of imprisonment, life in prison or internment camps, searches of peoples' homes, interrogations or hiding from the secret police. The poet participated in and witnessed events that were experienced by people from various social strata; a number of poets were themselves also direct victims of persecution. No wonder, then, that forms, which usually encourage outpouring of feelings and the subjective evaluation, display a marked lack of personal comment. Moreover, individual and collective experiences imperceptibly overlap. 'With all Respect', a poem by Wiktor Woroszylski, depicts a scene from an internment camp:

> You are not prisoners says the warden
> this is something completely different
> don't feel yourselves prisoners gentlemen
> We are coming out shouts the guard on duty
> quick line up gentlemen
> A woman in uniform with long eye-lashes
> adjusting the revolver on her shapely hip
> is warning us I'm sure you realize gentlemen
> that an attempt at escape is sudden death[1]

A protest against political violence, against the persecution of people because of their convictions, here takes the form of an ironic revelation of the gulf that exists between well-known facts and the propaganda, between appearances and the brutal truth. Also present is a strong and widespread sense of the grotesque nature of a reality in which natural divisions have been abolished, in which roles have been reversed and the law has come to offend common sense.

The spontaneous identification of the poetic *I* with the social *we* has consequences which are both positive and negative. On the one hand, in accordance with the expectations of the public, poetry stands up for values traditionally associated with the ethos of the nobility whose rightful heir Solidarity considers itself to be. The cult of freedom and democracy, respect for individual rights, love of God and one's country have acquired special intensity after World War II, when they were put in jeopardy by the existence of a totalitarian Communist régime. The idealization of the gentry's Republic — a peculiar political entity which lasted from the fifteenth to the eighteenth century only to collapse under the repeated assaults of its powerful neighbours — is quite understandable in view of the fact that Poles have been fighting for their independence for the last two hundred years. Moreover, in the mind of the average Pole this reference back to native democratic tradition and stress on ties which link Polish culture with that of the Mediterranean, rooted in classical antiquity and Christianity, both manifest his membership of Western Europe, and act as an antidote to the Byzantine authoritarianism of Russia. One frequently recurring *motif* in Martial Law poetry is therefore that of finding oneself still at the crossroads between Asia and Europe.

On the other hand, listening to voices in the street and faithfully reflecting the stream of collective emotion, Martial Law poetry often reproduces an oversimplified and at times false picture of reality. Thus, the declaration of Martial Law is presented as a war waged by a ruthless régime against the entire nation "the war between Poland and Jaruzelski", by schematic divisions into *us* versus *them*, innocent victims versus inexorable oppressors, society versus an alien régime, and by comparing the Martial Law period with that of the Nazi occupation. One of the most frequently employed symbols was the crow — a name for the authorities coined acronymically from the Polish name of the Military Council for National Salvation — *W*ojskowa *R*ada *O*calenia *N*arodowego, hence *wrona*: crow — evoking an immediate association with the derogatory term for the Nazi eagle, the emblem of the Third Reich.

A simplified picture of moral opposites not infrequently leads to literary schematicism, depicting reality in black-and-white terms. Let 'Visitation', a poem by Tomasz Jastrun, serve as an example:

> Four of them
> In the middle of the night
> One in uniform
> One with crowbar
> Two with smiles
> [.................]
> Four angels of communism
> In their mouths black tidings from on high[2]

The policemen coming to arrest the poet — "they" — are almost alien creatures who have arrived from a distant planet or from a totally different sphere of reality. This is just one of the national myths echoed in Martial Law poetry, namely that the source of evil lies outside one's immediate environment, the symbol of which is the home. A genuine, frequently recurring image of the secret police breaking down doors is particularly significant. It represents not only a brutal infringement of civil rights or an intrusion into privacy but first and foremost constitutes a violation of those values which found shelter from the control of the omnipresent State in the family circle.

Another symbol, the snow — the December of 1981 was exceptionally cold and snowy — operates on the basis of a similar antinomy. According to Daniel Bourne, "Sometimes the snow is seen in a positive way, an innocence which is violated. But more frequently snow, and by extension Nature, is seen as a collaborator with the authorities. In Bienkowski's poem 'The Snow — A.F.' snow has indeed become associated with hypocrisy, the white, supposedly festive gloss concealing the dirty underlying reality":[3]

> On that night there was snow.
> Its whiteness bleached the dirty and the grey.
> Its fluffiness smothered
> the cry of pain and despair.
> The stars wrapped
> the poor and tattered
> in festive robes.
> But nothing could be done
> to hide the crime.

In the morning people walked out on the streets
and in spite of everything swept the snow away.
They uncovered what had been dirty.
They listened as long as the cry would last.
With their poverty they shuffled
to the future which did not come.
And they did not forgive
what was still a crime.[4]

Thinking in terms of historical analogies does, of course, have important advantages: it helps to preserve the national sense of identity, gives comfort when the country's very existence is under threat and keeps the nation's collective memory alive. But at the same time it can be deceptive and dangerous. Inert collective visions, half-conscious convictions as well as plain delusions make it well-nigh impossible to adopt an attitude which is free of stereotypes, especially those of Romantic origin, thus preventing the poet from seeing Polish facts in their proper perspective. This applies in particular to Jarosław Marek Rymkiewicz and Ernest Bryll, who try to resurrect the nineteenth century myth of an innocent, forsaken nation fighting a losing battle against overwhelming odds and shedding its blood while an indifferent world stands idly by.

However, despite all the possible similarities, the Poland of the Partitions is not to be equated with the recently demised Polish People's Republic — nor did Tsarist Russia bear much resemblance to the Soviet Union. Furthermore, Polish society in the nineteenth century was fundamentally different from the nation which emerged after World War II — if only because it was multinational, multidenominational and still dominated by the nobility. Equally deceptive are references to the symbols and models of the wartime resistance movement — an impulse, which is quite understandable in a society in which memories of the war are still fresh, but which leads to the falsification of historical truth when transferred to literature. One cannot possibly compare Martial Law to the German occupation, since it was not a foreign force which introduced the terror and moreover, the enemy as an outsider is, in a way, tantamount to casting spells on evil. It is conducive to easy self-acquittal and self-justification. The division into *us* and *them* leads to double falsification. *They* are excluded from society, which is just one remove from insinuating that *they* are acting on behalf of a foreign power. Conversely, *we* is supposed to be synonymous with a united society which is resisting the authority of an alien government.

The true state of affairs was, however, more complicated: there are many people in Poland who were happy with the Communist régime and who had a stake in its survival. Moreover, the spectrum of attitudes towards the State is not confined to the simple *patriot-traitor* opposition. Poetry has not delved deep enough to expose the tragic and disgraceful fact that the declaration of Martial Law was not a consequence of a foreign invasion but was a step taken by Poles — that in order to subdue a mass movement there was no need to use force, it was enough merely to make a show of it. It just will not do to lay the whole blame on General Jaruzelski or to show soldiers being forced to play an ambiguous role, as is the case in 'A Scene by the Fire', by Ernest Bryll:

> My city frozen into silence. The tanks
> stand in the shadows like chunks of coal.
> Soldiers so uncertain of what is what
> they bend their heads down close to the flame.
> [. . . . .]
> A small fire and smoke. A man on duty
> puts his head in his hands. Do his eyes hurt?
> Has he scorched himself? Is he crying?
>
> We don't know. They are standing too far away.[5]

One would, however, like to know what these soldiers thought, what their moral dilemmas were, what reasons guided the decisions of their commanders. The wall that divided society ran not between the nation and the authorities but cut through social classes, families and the minds of individuals. Only a few poets, such as Jan Polkowski, noted that Martial Law was a national lesson in humiliation, a denial of greatness in suffering and sacrifice. Nobody took up the theme of the end of the myth of the Polish Army which, as everyone had believed, would never turn against fellow Poles. It is this accusation which may be levelled against the poetry of Martial Law: while giving an accurate account of facts and people's feelings it stopped short of attempting to give a critical appraisal of either, failing to provide gut reactions with an objective commentary. In the words of Stanisław Barańczak, "it confused collective experience with collective myth",[6] it created a beautiful legend which concealed the less edifying aspects of reality.

Before attempting to explain why this was so, it ought to be observed that this reluctance to come to terms with the unpleasant truth gave rise not only to poetic reportage and Romantic martyrology but also to poems of universal appeal. The most prominent and artistically interesting achievements of Martial Law poetry give a timeless quality to current political events in a striking variety of poetic styles, using various methods of presentation and representing various ideologies — anything from Romantic stylization, as in the case of Jarosław Marek Rymkiewicz to the defenceless nudity of language as in the case of Ryszard Krynicki. In poems written by Anna Kamieńska, Bronisław Maj or Jan Pokowski temporality is given a certain eternal dimension, the Christian symbols of suffering and sacrifice having been written in a novel and unique way into the political here and now. In 'Tortures' a poem by Wisława Szymborska, the Polish experience transcends geographical and political boundaries:

> Nothing has changed.
> The body is susceptible to pain,
> it must eat and breathe air and sleep,
> it has thin skin and blood right underneath,
> an adequate stock of teeth and nails,
> its bones are breakable, its joints are stretchable.
> In tortures all this is taken into account.
>
> Nothing has changed.
> The body shudders as it shuddered
> before the founding of Rome and after,
> in the twentieth century before and after Christ.
> Tortures are as they were, it's just the earth that's grown smaller,
> and whatever happens seems right on the other side of the wall.[7]

The beating, acts of persecution and torture which took place under Martial Law become part of the timeless spectacle of suffering, a variant of the *before and after Christ* pattern. A philosophical meditation on the limits of Man's ability to endure pain — pain which is always the same regardless of the greater sophistication of the instruments of torture — or a moral protest in defence of a humiliated and wrongly punished individual, may be used to depict a situation in Poland or in any other place where human rights are trampled on. Here again, the experience of living under Martial Law loses its particular quality of uniqueness.

How are we to explain the existence of such a forbidden area, studiously avoided by poets, who nevertheless approach it from various directions? The reasons are complex and involved, but three of them would appear to be most significant.

The first is the extraordinary situation in which the writer of Martial Law poetry finds himself. Andrzej Zawrat (Leszek Szaruga) claims that this poetry has overcome the traditional antinomy of what is individual versus what is national. "In the Romantic model the poet was placed above people, above society: the lyrical hero — the poet — suffered *for* millions, whereas the contemporary Polish poet *evokes the suffering of millions*. He speaks therefore not *in the name* of society, but rather his is the genuine voice of the society to which he belongs."[8] It must be added that as well as being the source of the poet's strength, this is also his weak point. The situation in which he finds himself confirms his sense of moral righteousness, it makes him feel that he is taking a fully active part in the national tragedy, eventually it makes him feel less isolated from his readers. As never before, the poet suffers persecution along with others; he is admired and universally respected. His voice is listened to with attention and his poems reach an audience that he could never have dreamt of. However, the price that has to be paid for feeling good — too good perhaps — is the suspension of one's own critical judgement, the avoidance of thorny issues and subservience to public opinion. Equating the poetic *I* with *we* makes the poet a slave of compensatory myths.

The second reason for the emergence of a forbidden thematic area is probably the lack of a language which could cope with the immense complexity and obscurity of life under Martial Law. At first sight every kind of poetic idiom would appear to be suited to express the experiences of Martial Law. One of the striking features of this poetry is the ease with which it copes with a complex array of facts and the concomitant variety of reactions which they evoke. This ease is illusory, given that the poems in question fail to capture the essence of an experience that is unique and without precedent in the history of Poland or any other country. Romantic visions sneak in to fill the remaining void, partly because — for various reasons — post-war Polish poetry has not yet fully fathomed the essence of life under Communism, nor has it made a thorough-going reappraisal of traditional symbols and stereotypes. Serving defensive functions, it has considerably developed both its ability to pander to escapism and its skill in exposing lies and evil. It has, however, always been on the side of justice, which to a great extent has considerably limited its scope.

A third, and perhaps even more significant reason may be mentioned, namely a tendency to think in terms of simplified analogies on the one hand, and, on the other hand, conveniently to see reality as a collection of isolated facts. This is symptomatic of a crisis in the way we think about history — a crisis which has long afflicted Polish literature and which has come to a head at a time of political turmoil. Hence the paradox: the pressures of history are overwhelming and all-embracing and there is no escaping them, especially in this part of Europe; yet the vicious circle of national misfortunes raises the question not only of their moral justification, but also of the sense, direction and purpose of the history of mankind. For the latter, however, there is no longer any standard explanation to hand. What we are witnessing is the final demise, in literature at least, of two nineteenth-century intellectual systems which see the mechanism of history either as a mysterious manifestation of Divine Providence, the secret of which will be revealed at the end of the world, or as a manifestation of immutable economic laws which, were they to be mastered, would — we are told — in all certainty change the world into a paradise. In other words, both Christian eschatology in its Romantic version and its profane Marxist counterpart have failed. This failure has been a particularly painful experience for Polish literature which cannot fully come to terms with it, since it dashes all the hopes of a captive nation for a better future.

Polish Romanticism gave sense to history at the cost of usurpation and blasphemy. To see Poles as a chosen nation was a usurpation. To equate their suffering with that of Christ was a blasphemy. But by committing the ordeal of the Polish nation to God's justice, the Romantics made moral sense present in a hidden dimension of history as a whole. It is hard to believe nowadays that a bright future awaits mankind as a result of the doings of a chosen nation or a chosen social class. Nor is it easy to believe in the presence of God in history. To be sure, traces of such convictions are to be found here and there in Martial Law poetry in the shape of attempts to resurrect messianic models or to revive faith in the ultimate victory of the people. These are, however, both few in number and circumspect to the point of timidity.

This brings us to the question of the attitude of the poetry of Martial Law to a comprehensive view of history. It cannot, after all, forever seek refuge in the museum of national relics. We may find the answer in one of the most remarkable artistic achievements of the period: Zbigniew Herbert's 'Report from the Besieged City'. In this poem one can find almost all the over-simplifications and patterns characteristic of Martial Law poetry; they are, however, concealed more cleverly or expressed with greater subtlety. Thus, we find the familiar opposition of *us* versus *them*; the poet assumes the role of an anonymous eye-witness of dramatic historical events; he studiously avoids forbidden subjects and instead revives the martyrological syndrome.

The narrator and protagonist of the poem is a chronicler who records "who knows for whom — the history of the siege". "City" has three clearly distinct meanings which overlap: Poland under Martial Law, Polish statehood since its beginnings and a respectable classical *topos* evoking the heroic defence of, for instance, Troy, Jerusalem or Carthage. These three meanings introduce qualities of time and space which are forever present, the eternal *now*, in which a contemporary political allusion may imperceptibly merge into a description of a situation which existed centuries ago or may acquire the significance of a timeless generalization:

> monday: empty storehouses rats are the unit of currency
> tuesday: the mayor murdered by unknown assailants
> wednesday: negotiations for a cease-fire the enemy has imprisoned
> our delegates
> we don't know where they are held that is tortured

In the process Herbert mythologizes Poland's past:

> the siege has lasted a long time the enemies must take turns
> nothing unites them except the desire for our extermination
> Goths Tartars Swedes troops of the Emperor regiments of the
> Transfiguration
> who can count them

It is true that — down the ages — Poland has frequently been invaded. But it is also true that in the fourteenth century Poland herself expanded eastwards and that in the sixteenth century she was one of the European superpowers powerful enough not to have to fear aggression.

The image of Poland as an eternally besieged fortress is enhanced by the irony with which the poet presents the West's attitude to her during World War II and the period of Martial Law:

and so in the evening released from facts I can think
about distant ancient matters for example our
allies beyond the sea I know they sincerely sympathise
they send us flour lard sacks of comfort and good advice
they don't even know their fathers betrayed us
our former allies at the time of the second Apocalypse

Endowing the poem with a classical lineage certainly enhances the dignity of the Romantic martyrological model which, in this modernized disguise, becomes almost invisible. The skillful manipulation of symbolic accessories and the transition from national to universal mythology are sustained by a subtle interchange of narrative perspectives — from *I* through *we* to *he*. A feeling of distance is ensured by the introduction of a *persona* partly identified with the author himself:

cemeteries grow larger the number of defenders dwindles
yet the defence continues it will continue to the end
and if the City falls but a single man escapes
he will carry the City within himself on the roads of exile
he will be the City[9]

Lofty and beautiful as these lines may appear, they cannot conceal the fact that a poet who confers the dignity of myth on current events by that same token loses the uniqueness of a keenly felt historic moment. He has not overcome the national mythology, but merely dressed it up in a more dignified costume. Those values which are absent from the eternal order of the world and which have been excluded from history are to be found in an individual who is ready to defend them at any price, against all odds, though he is aware that failure is inevitable. This gesture — as the protagonist is fully aware — is as helpless as it is heroic. History, like Nature, is bound up with its own rituals and remains indifferent to human problems. It is no accident that the colours of the banners of successive aggressors "change like forests on the horizon". Yet can this fact be accepted without reservation by writers who view the history of the world in the light of the history of the nation, and who are continually obsessed with the idea of belonging to a nation which has been chosen to suffer for other nations or to lead others? Perhaps they must content themselves — to quote Czesław Miłosz — with "decency — alas".[10]

We can therefore say that Martial Law poetry clearly identifies some basic dilemmas, and surely not only Polish dilemmas. How can one salvage the nation's sense of identity if the images which constitute its very essence have been overladen with obsolete meanings? How can one defend fundamental cultural values which habitually take on the appearance of ancient myths and stale symbols? How can one arouse the collective imagination from its historical inertia in such a way as to free it from fossilized mythology, while not severing its ties with that part of tradition which is still worth preserving? And finally: how — without divorcing oneself from history — can one find a way of looking at things which could give meaning to and explain not only the experiences of individuals but also those of whole nations?

Notes

1. Wiktor Woroszylski, 'With All Respect' (trans. Richard Lourie), *Green River Review*, Vol. XV, No. 1/2, p.23.
2. Tomasz Jastrun, 'Visitation' (trans. Daniel Bourne), *Partisan Review*, Spring 1987.
3. Daniel Bourne, *Artful Dodge*, Fall 1985, No. 12/13, p.67.
4. Zbigniew Bieńkowski, 'The Snow' (trans. Daniel Bourne), *Artful Dodge*, Fall 1985, No. 12/13, p.74.
5. Ernest Bryll, 'A Scene by the Fire' (trans. Daniel Bourne), *Artful Dodge*, Fall 1985, No. 12/13, p.73.
6. Stanisław Barańczak, 'Przed i po', *Aneks*, London 1988, p.121.
7. Wisława Szymborska, (trans. M.L. Krynski and R.A. Maguire), *Triquarterly*, 1983, Vol. 57, No. 1, p.25.
8. Introduction to: *Poezja stanu wojennego. Antologia*, (London 1982) p.9.
9. Zbigniew Herbert, *Report from the Besieged City and Other Poems*, (trans. John and Bogdana Carpenter), (Oxford 1987) pp.76-78 [with slight modifications — Ed.].
10. Czesław Miłosz, 'Szlachetność, niestety', *Kultura*, (Paris 1984) No. 9.

Bibliographies of Books and Articles in English

(*Compiled by Bogdan Czaykowski and the editor*)

I. Anthologies devoted wholly or in part to Polish poetry

Susan Bassnett & Piotr Kuhiwczak, *Ariadne's Thread, Polish Women Poets*, London 1988.

Andrzej Busza & Bogdan Czaykowski, *Gathering Time: Five Modern Polish Elegies*, Mission Canada, 1983.

Robert Conquest, *Back to Life: Poems from behind the Iron Curtain* London 1958.

Victor Contoski, *Four Contemporary Polish Poets*, Madison 1974.

Bogdan Czaykowski, *Modern Poetry in Translation: Poland*, London 1975.

Adam Czerniawski, *The Burning Forest: Modern Polish Poetry*, Newcastle upon Tyne 1988.

Adam Gillon & Ludwik Krzyżanowski, *Introduction to Modern Polish Literature*, New York 1982.

Antony Graham, *Witness out of Silence: Polish Poets Fighting for Freedom*, London 1980.

M. Holton & P. Vangelisti, *The New Polish Poetry*, Pittsburgh 1978.

Wacław Iwaniuk & Florian Śmieja, *Seven Polish Canadian Poets*, Toronto 1984.

Michael March, *Child of Europe, A New Anthology of East European Poetry*, London 1990.

Czesław Miłosz, *Post-War Polish Poetry*, 3rd enlarged edn, Berkeley 1983.

Jerzy Peterkiewicz & Burns Singer, *Five Centuries of Polish Poetry*, London 1960.

Bogusław Rostworowski, *Humps and Wings, Polish Poetry since '68*, San Francisco & Los Angeles 1982.

Leopold Tyrmand, *Explorations in Freedom*, New York 1970.

Daniel Weissbort, *The Poetry of Survival*, London, 1991.
Celina Wieniewska, *Polish Writing Today*, Harmondsworth 1967.

II. Individual Volumes

Miron Białoszewski (trans. A. Busza & B. Czaykowski), *The Revolution of Things*, Washington 1974.
Andrzej Busza (trans. Jagna Boraks & Michael Bullock), *Astrologer in the Underground*, Athens USA 1970.
Jerzy Ficowski (trans. Keith Bosley & Krystyna Wandycz), *A Reading of Ashes*, London 1981.
Jerzy Harasymowicz (trans. Catherine Leach & Seymour Mayne), *Genealogy of Instruments*, Ottawa 1974.
Jerzy Harasymowicz (trans. Victor Contoski), *Planting Beeches*, New York 1975.
Zbigniew Herbert (trans. Czesław Miłosz & Peter Dale Scott), *Selected Poems*, Harmondsworth 1968.
Zbigniew Herbert (trans. Bogdana & John Carpenter), *Selected Poems*, Oxford 1977.
Zbigniew Herbert (trans. Bogdana & John Carpenter), *Report from the Besieged City and Other Poems*, Oxford 1987.
Ewa Lipska (trans. John Colombo & Wacław Iwaniuk), *Such Times*, Toronto 1979.
Wacław Iwaniuk (trans. Jagna Boraks & others), *Dark Times*, Toronto 1981.
Ryszard Krynicki (trans. R.A. Davies & J.M. Gogol), *Citizen R.K. does not live*, Forest Grove USA 1985.
Czesław Miłosz (trans. the author & others), *The Collected Poems (1931-1987)*, Harmondsworth 1988.
Cyprian Kamil Norwid (trans. Adam Czerniawski), *Poezje/Poems*, Kraków 1986.
Tadeusz Różewicz (trans. Adam Czerniawski), *Faces of Anxiety*, London & Chicago 1969.
Tadeusz Różewicz (trans. M.J. Krynski & R.A. Maguire), *The Survivor and Other Poems*, Princeton 1976.
Tadeusz Różewicz (trans. Adam Czerniawski), *Selected Poems*, Harmondsworth 1976.
Tadeusz Różewicz (trans. Victor Contoski), *Unease*, St Paul USA, 1980.
Tadeusz Różewicz (trans. Adam Czerniawski), *Conversation with the Prince and Other Poems*, London 1982.
Tadeusz Różewicz (trans. Geoffrey Thurley), *Green Rose*, Darlington Australia 1982.
Leopold Staff (trans. Adam Czerniawski), *An Empty Room*, Newcastle upon Tyne, 1983.
Leon Zdzisław Stroiński (trans. Adam Czerniawski), *Window*, London 1979.

Wisława Szymborska (trans. M.J. Krynski & R.A. Maguire), *Sounds, Feelings, Thoughts: Seventy Poems*, Princeton 1981.
Wisława Szymborska (trans. Adam Czerniawski), *People on a Bridge*, London 1990.
Florian Śmieja (trans. Reuel Wilson and the author) *Not a Tourist*, London (Ontario) 1986.
Anna Świr [szczyńska] (trans. Czesław Miłosz and Leonard Nathan), *Happy as a dog's tail* New York, 1985
Anna Świr [szczyńska] (trans. Grażyma Baran and Margaret Marshment), *Fat like the Sun*, London, 1986
Aleksander Wat (trans. Czesław Miłosz), *Mediterranean Poems*, Ann Arbor 1977.
Aleksander Wat (trans. Czesław Miłosz and Leonard Nathan), *With the Skin*, New York 1989.
Kazimierz Wierzyński (trans. Clark Mills & Ludwik Krzyżanowski), *Selected Poems*, New York 1969.
Karol Wojtyła (trans. Jerzy Peterkiewicz) *Collected Poems*, London 1982.
Adam Zagajewski (trans. Renata Gorczyńska), *Tremor*, New York 1986.

III. Critical Studies

Jonathan Aaron, ' "In the Absence of Witness": The Poetry of Wisława Szymborska', *Parnassus* (1983-84:2).
A. Alvarez, *Under Pressure, The Writer in Society: Eastern Europe and the USA*, (Harmondsworth, 1965).
A. Alvarez, *Beyond All This Fiddle*, (London, 1968).
Stanisław Barańczak, 'My Part is Agony', *Parnassus* (1981:2).
Stanisław Barańczak, 'Polish Poetry of the "State of War" ', *Cross Currènts* (1983).
Stanisław Barańczak, 'Miłosz's Poetic Language: A Reconnaissance', *Language and Style* (1985:4).
Stanisław Barańczak, *A Fugitive from Utopia: The Poetry of Zbigniew Herbert* (Cambridge, Mass., 1987).
Stanisław Barańczak, ' "Countles Shades of the Colour Gray": The Recent Poetry of Wisława Szymborska' *Cross Currents* (1988:7).
Stanisław Barańczak, 'Skamander after Skamander: The Post-War Path of the Pre-War Polish Pleiade', *Cross Currents* (1990:9).
John Bayley, *Selected Essays* (Cambridge, 1984).
John Bayley, *The Order of Battle at Trafalgar* (London, 1987).
Calvin Bedient, 'Czesław Miłosz: Examining the Witness', *Salmagundi* (1985-86:68-69).
Stanisław Bereś, 'Czesław Miłosz's Apocalypse' in Edward Możejko, ed., *Between Anxiety and Hope: The Poetry and Writing of Czesław Miłosz* (Edmonton, 1988).

E.D. Blodgett, 'Miłosz as Witness', in Edward Możejko, *Between Anxiety and Hope*, *op. cit.*

Jan Błonski, 'Poetry and Knowledge', *World Literature Today* (1978:3).

Joseph Brodsky, 'Presentation of Czesław Miłosz to the Jury', *World Literature Today* (1978:3).

Andrzej Busza, 'Cultural Dislocation and Poetry' *Canadian Literature* (1987:1).

Bogdana Carpenter, *The Poetic Avant-garde in Poland, 1918-1939* (Seattle, 1983).

Bogdana Carpenter, 'The Barbarian and the Garden: Zbigniew Herbert's Re-evaluations', *World Literature Today* (1983:3).

Bogdana Carpenter, 'The Prose Poetry of Zbigniew Herbert: Forging a New Genre', *Slavic and East European Journal* (1984:1).

Bogdana Carpenter, 'Zbigniew Herbert's Attack Against Myth', *Cross Currents* (1984:3).

Bogdana Carpenter, 'Zbigniew Herbert: The Poet as Witness', *The Polish Review* (1987:1).

Bogdana Carpenter & John Carpenter, 'Zbigniew Herbert and the Imperfect Poem', *The Malahat Review* (April 1980).

Bogdana Carpenter & John Carpenter, 'Zbigniew Herbert: The Poet as Conscience', *Slavic and East European Journal* (1980:3).

Bogdana Carpenter and John Carpenter, 'The Ordinary Material Object: Its Extraordinary Fate', *World Literature Today (1980:3)*.

Marisha Chamberlain, 'The Voice of the Orphan: Czesław Miłosz's Warsaw Poems', *Ironwood* (1981:18).

Christopher Clausen, 'Czesław Miłosz: The Exile as Californian', *Literary Review* (Spring 1983).

Paul Coates, *Words after Speech* (London, 1986).

Paul Coates 'Irony and Choice: Miłosz in the Late Forties and Early Fifties', in Edward Możejko, ed., *Between Anxiety and Hope*, *op. cit.*

Viktor Contoski, 'Czesław Miłosz and the Quest for Critical Perspective', *Books Abroad* (1973:1).

Bogdan Czaykowski, 'The Unloquacious Craftsman: The Poetry of Leopold Staff', *Oficyna Poetów* (1971:2).

Bogdan Czaykowski, 'The Fly and the Flywheel: Some Reflections on the Poetry of Czesław Miłosz', *Oficyna Poetów* (1972:3).

Bogdan Czaykowski, 'The Poetry of Brutality', in Richard Freeborn et al, eds., *Russian and Slavic Literature* (Cambridge, Mass., 1976).

Bogdan Czaykowski, 'Post-War Polish Poets' in WJ.Stankiewicz, ed., *The Tradition of Polish Ideals* (London, 1981).

Bogdan Czaykowski, 'Harmony Restored: Mickiewicz's *Pan Tadeusz* Reconsidered on the 150th Anniversary of Its Publication', *Cross Currents* (1984:3).

Bogdan Czaykowski, 'The Idea of Reality in the Poetry of Czesław Miłosz', in Edward Możejko, ed., *Between Anxiety and Hope*, op. cit.

Bogdan Czaykowski, *Polish Writing in Canada* (Ottawa, 1988).

Adam Czerniawski, 'A "Flawed" Master', *Oficyna Poetów* (1973:2).
Adam Czerniawski, 'The Polish Poet as Custodian of the Nation's Conscience', *The Polish Review* (1979:4).
Adam Czerniawski, 'The Power of Taste', *Poetry Wales* (1984:2).
Adam Czerniawski, 'Polish Poetry and the Polish Predicament', *Bête Noire* (1988:5).
Adam Czerniawski, 'Between Virtue and Pleasure: Modern Polish Poets', *Encounter* (1988:5).
Adam Czerniawski, 'Are Poets Necessary?', *Poetry Review* (1987:3).
Adam Czerniawski, 'Poetry as Celebration', *The Irish Review* (1988:5).
Adam Czerniawski, 'Tadeusz Różewicz', *Poetry Review* (1989:3).
Adam Czerniawski, 'Wisława Szymborska', *World Authors 1980-85* (New York, 1990).
Donald Davie, 'Miłosz: The Wartime Poems', *PN Review* (1983:2).
Donald Davie, *Czesław Miłosz and the Insufficiency of Lyric* (Knoxville, 1986).
Donald Davie, 'Ironies Out of Poland: Zbigniew Herbert', *Poetry Durham* (1987:17).
Helene J.F. De Aguilar, 'A Prince Out of Thy Star: The Place of Czesław Miłosz', *Parnassus* (1983-84:2).
Terence Des Pres, 'Czesław Miłosz: The Poetry of Aftermath', *Nation* (December 30, 1978).
Krzysztof Dybciak, 'Holy is Our Being . . . and Holy the Day', *World Literature Today* (1978:3).
D.J.Enright, *The Alluring Problem* (Oxford, 1986).
D.J.Enright, 'At the Feast of Brief Hopes', *Times Literary Supplement* (1988:2-8, 9).
Aleksander Fiut, 'Facing the End of the World', *World Literature Today* (1978:3).
Aleksander Fiut, 'Czesław Miłosz's Search for "Humanness" ', *Slavic and East European Journal* (1987:1).
Aleksander Fiut, *The Eternal Moment: The Poetry of Czesław Miłosz* (Berkeley, 1990).
Zbigniew Folejewski, 'Czesław Miłosz: A Poet's Road to Ithaca Between Worlds, Wars and Poetics', *Books Abroad* (1969:1).
Władysław Folkierski et al, eds., *Juliusz Słowacki, 1809-1849* (London, 1951).
John Freedman, 'The Possibilities and Limitations of Poetry: Wisława Szymborska's *Wielka liczba*', *Polish Review* (1986:2-3).
Henry Gifford, *Poetry in a Divided World* (Cambridge, 1986).
George Gömöri, *Polish and Hungarian Poetry* (Oxford, 1966).
George Gömöri, *Cyprian Norwid* (New York, 1974).
George Gömöri, ' "Truth" and "Beauty" in Miłosz's Poetry', *World Literature Today* (1978:3).
Michael Hamburger, *The Truth of Poetry* (London, 1969).
Robert Hass, *Twentieth Century Pleasures: Prose on Poetry* (New York, 1984).
Seamus Heaney, *The Government of the Tongue* (London, 1988).

Richard Howard, 'An Heroic Apostate', *Parnassus* (1979:2).
George Hyde, 'Poetry from Poland and Czechoslovakia', *The Rialto* (1987-88:10).
Louis Iribane, 'The Naming of Hell', *Times Literary Supplement* (25 August 1978).
Louis Iribane, 'The Human Thing: A View of Czesław Miłosz', *Canadian Forum* (Dec. 1980).
Ivar Ivask, 'The Endless Column', *World Literature Today* (1978:3).
Hans Robert Jauss, 'Norwid and Baudelaire as Contemporaries: A Notable Case of Overdue Concretisation', in P. Steiner et al., *The Structure of Literary Process* (Amsterdam, 1982).
Andrew Kahn, ' "Idiots Live More Safely": Seeing Through Zbigniew Herbert's "The Divine Claudius" ', *The Polish Review* (1987:1).
Andrzej Kaliszewski, *Herbert* (Warsaw, 1989)
Nina Kolesnikoff, *Bruno Jasieński: His Evolution from Futurism to Socialist Realism* (Waterloo,1982).
Manfred Kridl, *The Lyric Poems of Julius Slowacki* (The Hague, 1958).
Piotr Kuhiwczak, 'Before and After the *Burning Forest*: Modern Polish Poetry in Britain', *The Polish Review* (1989:1).
Frank Kujawiński, 'Leśmian and Edgar Allan Poe', *The Polish Review* (1988:1).
Catherine Leach, 'Remarks on the Poetry of Tadeusz Różewicz', *The Polish Review* (1967:2).
Madeline C. Levine, *Contemporary Polish Poetry, 1925-1975* (Boston, 1981).
Wojciech Ligęza, 'Commonplaces: Polish Émigré Poetry 1945-1980', *The Polish Review* (1989:1).
Richard Lourie, 'A Context for Tadeusz Różewicz', *The Polish Review* (1967:2).
B.Mazur & G.Gömöri, eds., *Norwid: Poet — Thinker — Craftsman* (London, 1989).
Vasa D. Mihailovich, Zbigniew Herebrt, Bogdan Czaykowski et al, eds., *Modern Slavic Literatures: A Library of Literary Criticism* vol. II (New York, 1976).
Czesław Miłosz, *The History of Polish Literature* (London, 1969).
Czesław Miłosz, *The Witness of Poetry* (Cambridge, Mass., 1983).
Edwin Morgan, *East European Poets* (Milton Keynes, 1976).
Edward Możejko, 'Between the Universals of Moral Sensibility and Historical Consciousness', in Edward Możejko, ed., *Between Anxiety and Hope, op.cit.*
Leonard Nathan, 'The Composing Voice: Reading "Ars Poetica?" ', *Ironwood* (1981:18).
Olga Nedeljkovič, 'Cyprian Norwid: A Nineteenth Century Poet of Christian Humanism', *The Polish Review* (1986:1).
Tom Paulin, *Ireland and the English Crisis* (Newcastle upon Tyne, 1984).
John Peck, 'Last Things', *Ironwood* (1981:18)
Jerzy Peterkiewicz, 'Cyprian Norwid's *Vade-mecum*: An Experiment in Didactic Verse', *Slavonic and East European Review* (1966:102).

Jerzy Peterkiewicz, *The Other Side of Silence* (London, 1970).
Jerzy Peterkiewicz, 'The Idyll: A Constant Companion of Polish Poets', *Slavonic and East European Review* (1955:82).
Jerzy Peterkiewicz, 'Leśmian and Czechowicz: Two Uncomitted Poets', *Slavonic and East European Review* (1959:89).
Jerzy Peterkiewicz, 'Introducing Norwid', *Slavonic and East European Review* (1948:11).
Jerzy Peterkiewicz, 'The Four Horizons' *Botteghe Oscure* (1958:3).
John Pilling, *An Introduction to Fifty Modern European Poets* (London, 1982).
Jonathan Raban, *The Society of the Poem* (London, 1971).
P.J.M. Robertson, 'Czesław Miłosz: The Poetics of Value', *Queen's Quarterly* (1983:4).
Mark Rudman, 'On Miłosz: No Longer in Continuous Time', *Ironwood* (1981:18).
Samuel Sandler, 'Versions of Leśmian', *The Polish Review* (1988:1).
Aleksander Schenker, 'Introduction' to Czesław Miłosz, *Utwory poetyckie/ Poems* (Ann Arbor, 1976).
Harold B.Segel, 'Czesław Miłosz and the Landscapes of Exile', *Cross Currents* (1982).
Irena Sławińska, 'The Image of the Poet and His Estate', *World Literature Today* (1978:3).
Judy Stone, 'Czesław Miłosz: Child and Man', *New York Times Book Review* (28 June, 1981).
Rochelle Stone, *Bolesław Leśmian* (Berkeley, 1976).
Jacek Trznadel, 'The European Significance of Jan Kochanowski from the Renaissance to the Romantics', *Cross Currents* (1984:3).
Tadeusz Ulewicz, 'The European Significance of Jan Kochanowski from the Renaissance to the Romantics', *Cross Currents* (1984:3).
Lillian Vallee, 'What is "The World" (A Naive Essay)', *Ironwood* (1981:18).
Thomas Venclova, 'Poetry as Atonement', *The Polish Review* (1986:4).
Helen Vendler, *The Music of What Happens: Poems, Poets, Critics* (Cambridge, Mass., 1988).
John Wakeman, 'Tadeusz Różewicz', *World Authors 1970-1975* (New York, 1980).
Reuel Wilson, 'Rafał Wojaczek: Genius of Despair', *Slavic and East European Journal* (1987:2).
Wiktor Weintraub, *The Poetry of Adam Mickiewicz* (The Hague, 1954).
Hallie Anne White, 'Irony and Poetic Point of View in Norwid's "Ironia" ', *Slavic and East European Journal* (1988:4).
Tadeusz Witkowski, 'The Poets of the New Wave in Exile', *The Polish Review* (1989:2).
Baron Wormser, 'Grave Combats', *Parnassus* (1989:2).
Wiktor Woroszylski, 'Miłosz in Polish Eyes', *New Republic* (23 May, 1981).
Marek Zaleski, 'The Place of Miłosz in Polish Poetry', *Ironwood* (1981:18).

Index

Ł

M

Ś

T

Z

Ż

Notes on Contributors

Neal Ascherson is the author of a history of Poland, and a leading newspaper columnist who has written for *The Observer* and, currently, *The Independent on Sunday*.

Bogdan Czaykowski Born in Poland, 1932, educated at University College Dublin and the University of London. Now Professor of Polish Literature and History at the University of British Columbia in Vancouver. Author of history books and literary studies of Mickiewicz, Norwid, Miłosz and others, and translator of Polish poetry into English. His own *Collected Poems 1953-1988* appeared in 1990.

Donald P.A. Pirie is a lecturer in the Department of Slavonic Studies at the University of Glasgow, specialising in all areas of East European literature.

A. Alvarez is a poet, author and former Advisory Editor of Penguin Modern European Poets in Translation.

Paul Coates. Educated at Cambridge, Sussex and Warsaw, now Assistant Professor of English at McGill University, Montreal. He has published books of literary theory, Polish cinema and identity and ideology.

Krzysztof Karasek Born 1937 in Warsaw where he studied philosophy. He is a poet and the author of numerous essays on modern literature, and is currently compiling an anthology of Polish poetry since 1956.

Edward Rogerson is a writer and translator specialising in Central European culture and history. He is currently preparing a study of the reconstruction of Poland in the early post-war years.

Jacek Łukasiewicz Born 1934 in Lwów. A poet and author of several books on modern Polish poetry, he lectures in Polish Literature at the University of Wrocław.

Zbigniew Bieńkowski Born 1913 in Warsaw, he studied French literature in Warsaw and Paris. A poet himself, he translates modern French poetry and has published several critical works.

Aleksander Fiut is Associate Professor of Polish at Jagiellonian University in Kraków and has taught at Lille, Berkeley, Illinois and Vienna. He is particularly interested in the borders between literature, sociology, philosophy and politics. His books *The Eternal Moment: The Poetry of Czesław Miłosz* and (with Ewa Czarnecka) *Conversations with Czesław Miłosz* have been widely acclaimed.

George Hyde. Born in Scotland in 1941 and educated at Cambridge and Essex. Now a lecturer in English and Comparative Literatures at the University of East Anglia. He has published books on Nabokov and on Lawrence and has translated Mayakovsky and Kantor.

John Bayley is Professor of English at St Catherine's College, Oxford, and the husband of novelist Iris Murdoch. He has published many books, including works on Tolstoy and Pushkin, and is presently working on a study of A.E. Housman's poetry.

Edwin Morgan Born Glasgow, 1920. Professor of English at the Universities of Glasgow and Strathclyde, but now retired. Poet, translator and critic, his *Collected Poems* appeared in 1990.

John Osborne is currently Lecturer in American Studies at the University of Hull. He is the editor of the arts magazine *Bête Noire* and a widely published critic.

John Lucas is Professor of English at Loughborough University. He is the author of many books, most recently *Imagining England* a discussion of nationhood in English poetry. His volume of poems, *Studying Grosz on the Bus* appeared in 1990.

John Pilling is Reader in English at the University of Reading. He has published widely on Samuel Beckett and is the author of *An Introduction to Fifty Modern European Poets.*

Tom Paulin is a well known poet and editor, and a leturer in English at the University of Nottingham. His most recent publication is *The Faber Book of Vernacular Verse.*

The Editor: Adam Czerniawski was born in 1934, in Warsaw. He left Poland in 1941 and settled eventually in London, where he studied Literature and Philosophy, succeeding to Sussex and Oxford. A poet, his *Selected Poems 1953-1978* appeared in Poland in 1982. He is perhaps better known as a translator of Polish poets such as Norwid, Staff and Różewicz. His book *The Burning Forest* (1988) is a selection of his translations of seventeen Polish poets, and a new book of translations of Szymborska, *People on the Bridge* appears in 1991.